The Inside Track to
Careers in
Real Estate

Stan Ross

**Urban Land
Institute**

ULI—THE URBAN LAND INSTITUTE is a nonprofit education and research institute that is supported by its members. Its mission is to provide responsible leadership in the use of land in order to enhance the total environment.

ULI sponsors education programs and forums to encourage an open international exchange of ideas and sharing of experiences; initiates research that anticipates emerging land use trends and issues and proposes creative solutions based on that research; provides advisory services; and publishes a wide variety of materials to disseminate information on land use and development. Established in 1936, the Institute today has more than 29,000 members from over 80 countries, representing the entire spectrum of the land use and development disciplines. The Institute is recognized throughout the world as one of America's most respected and widely quoted sources of objective information on urban planning, growth, and development.

PROJECT STAFF

Rachelle L. Levitt
Executive Vice President, Policy and Practice
Publisher

Gayle Berens
Vice President, Real Estate Development Practice

David Mulvihill
Managing Director, Professional Development
Project Director

Nancy H. Stewart
Director, Book Program
Managing Editor

Lori Hatcher
Director, Publications Marketing

Libby Howland
Manuscript Editor

Betsy VanBuskirk
Art Director

Anne Morgan
Graphic Artist
Book Design

Byron Holly
Senior Graphic Designer
Cover

Susan S. Teachey/ON-Q Design, Inc.
Book Layout

Craig Chapman
Director, Publishing Operations

COPYRIGHT © 2006 BY ULI—THE URBAN LAND INSTITUTE

ULI–the Urban Land Institute
1025 Thomas Jefferson Street, N.W.
Washington, D.C. 20007-5201

LIBRARY OF CONGRESS CATALOGING-IN-PUBLICATION DATA

Ross, Stan, 1936–
    The Inside Track to Careers in Real Estate / Stan Ross, with James Carberry.
        p. cm.
        Includes bibliographical references.
        ISBN-13: 978-0-87420-954-9 (alk. paper)
        1. Real estate business—Vocational guidance—United States.
I. Carberry, James, 1940– . II. Title.
HD1375.R598 2006
333.33023'73—dc22

10 9 8 7 6 5 4 3 2 1
PRINTED IN THE UNITED STATES OF AMERICA.

PREFACE

Author's Note

My career really started in 1961. I had graduated from Baruch College in 1956, had served in the U.S. Army for two years, and was working as an accountant for a small firm in New York. Feeling that I should find more interesting and challenging work, I decided to answer a help wanted ad placed by Kenneth Leventhal & Company, a small Los Angeles–based accounting firm specializing in real estate. I met with Kenneth Leventhal, the founder of the firm, and he persuaded me to move to Los Angeles to join his organization.

We provided traditional accounting services to clients, but we differentiated ourselves from other accounting firms by customizing our services to the needs of developers, builders, and other real estate businesses and by helping our clients solve business problems—such as how to finance multimillion dollar development projects. Initially, these clients were mostly small enterprises owned by individuals, families, or a few business partners. Over the years, many of them grew into large organizations with a number of managers and many employees. Some became public companies and some expanded beyond southern California into regional, national, and even global markets. As our clients grew, we grew with them. By the time the Leventhal firm merged with Ernst & Young in the mid-1990s, it was the largest U.S. accounting firm specializing in real estate and I had succeeded Kenneth Leventhal as managing partner. As a real estate consultant, I had been exposed to every sector of the industry.

Today there are many more job and career opportunities in real estate than when I started out. You can start a real estate career at a small, privately held company or at a large, publicly held organization. You can work for a developer, a builder, a property owner and manager, a real estate lender or investor, a broker, a consultant, or a firm in any number of other businesses. You can work for a company that operates in a small local market or worldwide. You can choose your sector—office, retail, industrial, hotel, residential—and market niche, such as low-income housing or historic preservation. You can start your own business.

And there will be even more career opportunities in the future. Tomorrow's demand for real estate professionals will come from traditional real estate businesses—development, ownership, property management, and real estate services—as well as from rebuilding efforts following natural or other disasters and from initiatives to promote sustainable forms of development that improve the quality of life and preserve natural resources. Opportunities for investment and development will also open up in emerging markets, such as China and India. As a real estate professional just starting out, you will be a problem solver, like we were at Leventhal, for example, helping to persuade the local government and a project's neighbors that higher-density housing is in the community's best interest or helping to overcome the challenges of cleaning up a well-located but contaminated property for development.

I am often asked—by high-school and college students and people who have attended my lectures—about career opportunities in real estate. Many of the people with whom I have spoken have no real sense of the many opportunities and the different career paths that real estate offers. In researching books on real estate careers, I found that some cover particular segments of the industry or particular careers, such as brokerage, but that none offers a comprehensive perspective of career opportunities. And so the idea for this book was born.

This book is intended to help you decide whether you want to pursue a career in real estate, and, if so, to help you plan your career. With proper planning, you can have a career that is exciting, challenging, fulfilling, and financially rewarding. If you are a junior or senior in high school, now is the time to start thinking about what college you might want to attend to prepare for a real estate career. If you are a college undergraduate, now is the time to consider what courses and degree program will give you the educational foundation to begin a career in real estate. If you already are a young real estate professional, now is the time to be considering your next move up the career ladder; or whether you should seek a graduate degree. If you are thinking of a mid-career change into real estate, you now need to assess your skills and experience and perhaps take courses or enroll in a degree program in real estate or a related area to sharpen your skills.

My final word of career advice is this: As you advance in your career, use your talents, skills, and experience to give back to the community. Tutor high-school students, for example. Mentor a real estate professional just starting her career. Help a nonprofit organization open and operate a shelter for the homeless. Provide financial support to a low-income college student. When you look back on your career years from now, you will have a sense of professional accomplishment as well as the satisfaction of having helped others.

Stan Ross
Chairman of the Board, USC Lusk Center for Real Estate
Vice Chairman (retired), Real Estate Industry Services, Ernst & Young

Publisher's Note

ULI has had a long history of working with universities to encourage interdisciplinary education for young people interested in pursuing real estate careers. In the early 1980s at the behest of its members, it provided seed money to several universities for the development of interdisciplinary curricula. Since then, the Institute has developed many different programs and activities that support real estate education. ULI offers a number of graduate student scholarships each year; encourages students to become members with special student membership rates; and provides special programming at its annual spring and fall meetings aimed at students interested in pursuing a career in real estate. In addition, the Institute encourages young people to take advantage of what ULI has to offer through a reduced membership fee for people under 35 (the fee is less than half the fee for regular members) and discounts on most ULI events. In as many ways as possible, ULI exposes young people to a variety of leaders and opportunities in the field of real estate, and feeds them practical information on development trends in North America and abroad.

Stan Ross, a life trustee and governor of ULI, has continued this tradition with this book, which provides insightful, thoughtful career advice that is based on his years of experience in the real estate industry. It meets a longstanding need for a publication that offers a comprehensive look at career opportunities across real estate. Both students and professionals will find it of great practical use.

Rick Rosan
President
Urban Land Institute

Principal Author

Stan Ross is chairman of the board of the USC Lusk Center for Real Estate and senior fellow at the Lusk Center. He previously was vice chairman in charge of real estate industry services for Ernst & Young LLP, and a member of E&Y's management committee, which set policy and strategy for the firm. Prior to that, he was managing partner of Kenneth Leventhal & Company, an accounting firm specializing in real estate, where he was responsible for its overall business planning, strategy, direction, and operations. Ross continues his diverse activities in the real estate industry as a consultant and serves on several boards of directors, including those of the Irvine Company, Forest City Enterprises, and the University of Judaism.

With expertise in mergers and acquisitions, reorganizations, and the development of creative financial structures, Ross is widely recognized for his experience in strategic planning for real estate companies. He was involved in the initial organization of the Resolution Trust Corporation (RTC) and was a member of the auditing standards board of the American Institute of Certified Public Accountants (AICPA), which sets the auditing rules for the accounting profession. Ross is a frequent lecturer at universities, accounting symposiums, and real estate conferences and he has written numerous articles on real estate and accounting matters. He is a life trustee and governor of the Urban Land Institute and a trustee of Baruch College, from which he graduated in 1956 and which awarded him an honorary doctor of laws degree in 1999.

Contributing Author

James Carberry is the principal of Carberry Communications, a San Francisco–based business writing and editing service. During his career, he has been a corporate writer and editor, a business writer based in Singapore, and, for ten years, a reporter for the *Wall Street Journal*. He is a graduate of the University of Missouri School of Journalism.

Acknowledgments

This book would not have been possible without the help of many people, and all contributors are listed starting on page viii.

I want to give special mention to the many USC undergraduate and graduate students, most of whom are now working in real estate, who made time in their busy schedules to meet regularly with me to discuss the development of the book, to interview more than 150 real estate professionals and other students for the book, and to provide feedback on the drafts of the chapters, charts, diagrams, and other content. These former students are:

Ryan Aeh	Yeghig Keshishian
Daniel Almquist	Crystal Kirst
Stephen Anderson	Kenny Lim
Ryan Barker	Craig Oram
Heidi Brandl	Joshua Peters
Justin Capen	Brian Pianca
Caroline Choe	Leanne Quon
Eric Clapp	Stephen Roberts
Marcus Cook	Kenneth Rock
Ryan Davis	Shlomi Ronen
Nicole Ennix	Tyson Skillings
Mark Evans	Adam Smith
James Furey	Matt Stuart
Timothy Grizzell	Brian Thomasch
Andrew Gunion	Gail Tubbs
Jill Hamers	Allyson Watkins
Tara Hayden	Robb Wehmueller
Yvette Hwee	Wen Yeh
George Kelly	

Special thanks go to members of the USC Lusk Center for Real Estate for their guidance and support, especially to Stuart A. Gabriel, director and Lusk chair in real estate; Raphael Bostic, associate professor in USC's School of Policy, Planning, and Development and director of the Lusk Center's Master of Real Estate Development (MRED) program; and Nicole McAllister, executive director for development and external affairs.

Sonia Savoulian, director of alumni and student services at the Lusk Center, played a critical liaison role with the USC student teams by organizing the meetings with the students and helping to lead the discussions. She also assisted in developing the concept and structure for the book, and offered insightful comments on the drafts of the manuscript.

A special thanks also to Jim Carberry, my collaborator in writing this book. Jim applied his journalistic skills in converting my many technical memos and drafts into understandable language. We had many discussions about the content, resolved many differences, and made numerous revisions. Undoubtedly this book would not have been completed without his contribution.

I want to thank the interviewees—the industry leaders, young professionals, human resources directors, recruiters, faculty and alumni of other schools, and others—whose words and advice are presented in the Q&As and Career Profiles throughout this book. Their direct observations and words of wisdom are what make this book unique. (Please note that the job titles provided in the book's Q&As and Career Profiles are for the job that the interviewee held at the time of the interview. Some of these people may have since moved on to another position, job, or company—which, in some cases, is reflected in the list of contributors starting on page viii.

I particularly thank the following people for taking time out of their busy schedules to be interviewed: Donald Bren, chairman of the Irvine Company; John Bucksbaum, CEO of General Growth Properties; Veronica Hackett, managing partner of the Clarett Group; Bruce Karatz, CEO of KB Home; Raymond Mikulich, managing partner of Lehman Brothers; Albert Ratner, cochairman of Forest City Enterprises; Dale Anne Reiss, director of real estate, hospitality, gaming, and construction at Ernst & Young; Isadore (Issy) Sharp, chairman and CEO of Four Seasons Hotels; John Shea, chairman of J.F. Shea Co.; Donald Trump; and Sam Zell, chairman of Equity Office Properties Trust.

Kenneth Leventhal, founder of the accounting firm of Kenneth Leventhal & Company, is especially acknowledged, not only for his comments on the book, but also and more significantly for being my mentor, partner, and friend—for giving me the opportunity, direction, and support to build a successful career in both accounting and real estate.

Thanks to Chris Lee, president and CEO of CEL & Associates; Bruce Endsley, senior vice president of human resources at the Irvine Company; and John Wasley, partner at Heidrick & Struggles, for meeting with the USC student teams to discuss careers in real estate.

I would not have been able to complete a project of this magnitude without the able support of my longtime associates Connie Lockhart and Karen Correa. A special thanks to Karen for her countless hours of help in organizing and managing this project, contacting people to arrange interviews and review quotes, tracking numerous changes and updates to the manuscript, and otherwise keeping this project from flying apart.

Many thanks to the Urban Land Institute for agreeing to publish this book and for managing the process from the editing of the manuscript to the design, layout, production, and marketing of the book. As a first-time book author, I especially appreciate the guidance and support provided by

Rachelle Levitt, Gayle Berens, David Mulvihill, and Lori Hatcher. Libby Howland, former editor of *Urban Land* magazine, applied her editing skills in turning our manuscript into an easy-to-read book. Thanks also to Francie Murphy of Francie Murphy Associates for reviewing the manuscript and assisting with plans to market the book.

Finally, my heartfelt thanks to Marilyn, my wife of 49 years, who has been my enthusiastic supporter throughout my career and especially in my pursuit of this book project. I also want to thank my daughters Ellen, Alison, and Michelle for their support. I am blessed with 12 grandchildren—Mark, Jamie, Joey, Destin, Lauren, Maya, Amy, Adam, Daniel, Michael, Semantha, and Brian. I hope that some of them will read this book someday and elect a real estate career.

Stan Ross
Chairman of the Board, USC Lusk Center for Real Estate

Vice Chairman (retired), Real Estate Industry Services, Ernst & Young

Contributors

(and, for quoted interviewees, page numbers on which their Q&A, profile, or observations appear)

Karen Addison
Property Manager
DTC Meridian
Denver, Colorado

Ryan Aeh (70)
Director of Acquisitions
The Olson Company
Seal Beach, California

Stephen Anderson (71)
Associate
Tishman Speyer Properties
San Francisco, California

Eric Michael Anton (109)
Senior Managing Director
Eastern Consolidated Properties
New York, New York

Pamela Arms (118)
Director of Finance
University of Pennsylvania
Philadelphia, Pennsylvania

Joseph Azrack (13)
Former Chairman
AEW Capital Management
Boston, Massachusetts

Stephen Barker (66)
President
Boeing Realty
Irvine, California

Ray Bayat (61)
Principal
Netco Investments
Santa Monica, California

Stephen Benson
Development Manager
Playa Vista
Los Angeles, California

Raphael Bostic (96)
Associate Professor
USC Lusk Center for Real Estate
Los Angeles, California

Heidi Brandl (150)
VP
IHP Capital Partners
Irvine, California

Kelley Brasfield (119)
Associate Director
Metropolitan Life
Newark, New Jersey

Donald Bren (4)
Chairman of the Board
The Irvine Company
Irvine, California

Robert Bridges (99)
Adjunct Professor
USC Marshall School of Business
Los Angeles, California

Amanda Britt
Portfolio Manager
Bank of America
Charlotte, North Carolina

Mark Bromley (61)
CEO and Chairman (retired)
Gables Residential
Atlanta, Georgia

Darryl Brown (3)
Director
West Angeles CDC
Los Angeles, California

Michael Buckley (106)
Director
Columbia University MSRED
Program
New York, New York

John Bucksbaum (42)
CEO
General Growth Properties
Chicago, Illinois

Wade Cable (3)
President and CEO
William Lyon Homes
Newport Beach, California

Darryl Carter
Cochair and CIO
Capri Capital
Irvine, California

Alan Casden (30)
Chairman and CEO
Casden Properties
Beverly Hills, California

Don Casto
Partner
Don M. Casto Organization
Columbus, Ohio

James Chaffin (2)
President
Chaffin/Light Associates
Hilton Head, South Carolina

Brian Clarke (69)
Director of Financial Analysis/Land
   Development
The Irvine Company
Newport Beach, California

Alice M. Connell
Group Managing Director
TIAA/CREF
New York, New York

George Connell
President
Progressive Housing Foundation
Atlanta, Georgia

Marion Cunningham (113)
Managing Director
MIT Center for Real Estate
Cambridge, Massachusetts

David Dale-Johnson (100)
Director (retired)
Program in Real Estate, USC
Los Angeles, California

Joseph Davis (14, 131)
President and CEO
Irvine Community Development
   Company
Newport Beach, California

John Dawson (64)
VP, Worldwide Development
McDonald's Corporation
Oak Brook, Illinois

Richard DeBeikes (2)
President
DeBeikes Investment Company
Irvine, California

Clare DeBriere
VP
Ratkovich Company
Los Angeles, California

Vanessa Delgado (89)
Director of Entitlements
Primestor Development Inc.
Pico Rivera, California

Larry Ebert (67)
Director of Corporate Real Estate
Capital One
McLean, Virginia

Robert Edelstein (114)
Real Estate Program Director
UC Berkeley
Berkeley, California

Bruce Endsley (131)
Senior VP, HR
The Irvine Company
Irvine, California

Brian Falls
Financial Analyst
Playa Vista
Los Angeles, California

William Ferguson
Chairman and CEO
Ferguson Partners
Chicago, Illinois

Stuart Gabriel (96, 100)
Director
USC Lusk Center for Real Estate
Los Angeles, California

David Geltner
Director
MIT Center for Real Estate
Cambridge, Massachusetts

Richard Gentilucci
Senior VP, Real Estate
Shamrock Holdings of California
Burbank, California

Greg George
Real Estate Manager
Home Depot
Orange, California

John Goering (104)
Professor and Director of BS in Real
   Estate Program
Baruch College
New York, New York

David Gold
Principal
William E. Simons & Sons Realty
Los Angeles, California

Jona Goldrich (5)
CEO
Goldrich & Kest
Culver City, California

Gabriel Guerrero (100)
President
Southern California Commercial
   Real Estate
Los Angeles, California

Veronica Hackett (90)
Managing Partner
The Clarett Group
New York, New York

Peter Hall
Partner, Real Estate Practice
Heidrick & Struggles
San Francisco, California

Jon Hammer (88)
CEO
Hammer Ventures
San Diego, California

Chris Harahan
Assistant VP
Lowe Enterprises
Los Angeles, California

Judy Herbst (124)
Senior VP of Human Capital
General Growth Properties
Chicago, Illinois

Mary Beth Heydt
General Counsel
Thrifty Oil
Santa Fe Springs, California

John Hoeller
Senior VP, Property
Glimcher Realty Trust
Columbus, Ohio

Irene Hosford (120)
Managing Partner
Hosford & Creasey
Dallas, Texas

Eddie Hsieh
CFO
Nevis Homes
Arcadia, California

Susan Hudson-Wilson (79)
CEO
Property & Portfolio Research
Boston, Massachusetts

Sean G. Hyatt (79)
Development Manager
Related Companies
Irvine, California

Clyde Jackson
President and CEO
Wynne/Jackson
Dallas, Texas

Shubra Jha (74)
Associate Director
CB Richard Ellis Investors
Los Angeles, California

Gary Jones
VP
Standard Pacific Homes
Irvine, California

John Jones
Financial Analyst
Playa Vista
Los Angeles, California

Alex Kalamaros
Leasing Specialist
City of Los Angeles
Marina del Rey, California

Bruce Karatz (39)
CEO and Chairman
KB Home
Los Angeles, California

Dan Kassel
CEO
Granite Homes
Irvine, California

Clint Kelson
Partner, RCK Investments
Century 21/RCK Investments
Heber City, Utah

Patrick Kennedy
Principal
Panoramic Interests
Berkeley, California

Bentley Kerr
Project Partner
Bluestone Communities
Newport Beach, California

Joseph Kim (61)
Associate
Secured Capital
Los Angeles, California

James Klingbeil (59)
CEO
Klingbeil Company
San Francisco, California

Gene Kohn (64)
Principal and Cofounder
Kohn Pedersen Fox Associates
New York, New York

Bill Kuhnert (70)
Development Controller
DDC Stowe LLC
Stowe, Vermont

Sandra Kuli
Principal
Kuli Consulting
Malibu, California

M. Leanne Lachman
President
Lachman Associates LLC
New York, New York

Stephen Lanni (73)
Acquisitions Manager
SARES-REGIS Group
Irvine, California

Robert Larson (12, 54)
Former CEO
Taubman Company
New York, New York

Anne DeVoe Lawler (120)
Partner
Jameson Babbitt Stites & Lombard
Seattle, Washington

Christopher Lee
Principal
CEL & Associates
Los Angeles, California

Jenny Lee (96)
Student, MBA Program
University of Chicago
Chicago, Illinois

Ming Lee (54, 55)
Principal
Strategic Partners LLP
Los Angeles, California

Kenneth Leventhal (10, 15)
Chairman (retired)
Kenneth Leventhal & Co.
Los Angeles, California

David Levrier (145)
Senior VP and Chief Administrative
   Officer
Hines
Houston, Texas

Kenny Lim
Land Acquisition Manager
Corman Leigh Communities
Temecula, California

Peter Linneman (116, 119, 112)
Albert Sussman Professor of Real
   Estate
The Wharton School
Philadelphia, Pennsylvania

John Loper (14)
VP
Fritz Duda Company
Los Angeles, California

Anthony Malk (71)
VP
Eastdil Realty Company
Los Angeles, California

Nicole McAllister (102)
Executive Director of Development
and External Affairs
USC Lusk Center for Real Estate
Los Angeles, California

Renée McDonnell (14)
Senior VP
IHP Capital Partners
San Francisco, California

Michael McKee (19)
Vice Chairman and COO
The Irvine Company
Irvine, California

Doug McKinnon
VP, Denver Office
Hines
Denver, Colorado

William McMorrow
Chairman and CEO
Kennedy Wilson
Los Angeles, California

Alan Merson (3)
VP
Morley Builders
Los Angeles, California

Jeffrey Mezger (60)
COO
KB Home
Los Angeles, California

Jim Middlemas
Manager
Lyon Property Management
Newport Beach, California

Raymond Mikulich (9)
Managing Director
Lehman Brothers
New York, New York

Steven Mongeau (70)
Project Manager and Planner
Cimm's/L&R Construction
Glendale, California

Andrea Mullens
Human Resources Manager
Shea Homes
Walnut, California

Bret Nielson (5)
VP, Leasing and Acquisitions
Caruso Affiliated
Santa Monica, California

Jim Osterling (102)
Principal
Bridge Residential Advisors
Pasadena, California

Henry Paparazzo
CEO
Heritage Development Group
Southbury, Connecticut

Ashley Parker
Office Leasing and Acquisitions
    Adviser
Richard Bowers & Company
Atlanta, Georgia

Richard Peiser (110, 112)
Michael D. Spear Professor of Real
    Estate Development
Harvard Graduate School of Design
Cambridge, Massachusetts

Donald Perry
President
Capri Capital
Norcross, Georgia

Daniel Pfeffer (32)
CFO
Midtown Equities
New York, New York

Brendan Pierce
Development Executive
Clark Real Estate Advisors
Centerville, Virginia

Bob Pratt (64)
Director of Design and Construction
Tishman Speyer Properties
New York, New York

Brian Prinn (57)
Vice Chairman
Lowe Enterprises
Los Angeles, California

Jared Prushansky (122)
VP
Lubert-Adler
Philadelphia, Pennsylvania

Colleen Rainford (105)
Loan Officer
CapitalSource Mortgage
New York, New York

Albert Ratner (22)
Cochairman of the Board
Forest City Enterprises
Cleveland, Ohio

Dale Anne Reiss (6)
Director of Real Estate, Hospitality,
    Gaming, and Construction
Ernst & Young
New York, New York

Julie Richland
President
Contract Recruiting Inc.
Palos Verdes, California

B. Robin Rieke
VP, Business Development
The Shoptaw Group
Atlanta, Georgia

Marinel Robinson (76)
Principal
DeComa Structural Industries
Torrance, California

Ken Rock (75)
Senior Cost Manager
Tishman Speyer Properties
New York, New York

Jack Rodman (64)
Managing Director
Ernst & Young
Beijing, China

Shlomi Ronen
Associate
George Smith Partners
Los Angeles, California

Richard Rosan
President
Urban Land Institute
Washington, D.C.

Jeff Rouze (92)
Principal
Hollywood Hillview Apartments
Hollywood, California

Ki Y. Ryu (56)
Project Manager
TMG Partners
Santa Monica, California

Lynne Sagalyn
Professor
The Wharton School
Philadelphia, Pennsylvania

Jane Salter
Partner
Ernst & Young
Tampa, Florida

Sonia Savoulian (99)
Director of Alumni and Student
    Services
USC Lusk Center for Real Estate
Los Angeles, California

Robert Schuur (68)
Manager of Finance and Planning
Southern California Edison
Los Angeles, California

Lynn Sedway (61)
Founder and Executive Managing
  Director
Sedway Group
San Francisco, California

Tarek Shaer
Manager of Urban Development
Lennar Communities
Mission Viejo, California

Robert Shames
Assistant Professor of Accounting
University of Southern California
Los Angeles, California

Carl Shannon
Managing Director
Tishman Speyer Properties
Mountain View, California

Isadore (Issy) Sharp (79, 85)
Chairman and CEO
Four Seasons Hotels
Toronto, Canada

John F. Shea (34)
Chairman of the Board
J. F. Shea Company
Walnut, California

Stuart Shiff (115)
Co-CEO and Cofounder
Divco West Properties
Palo Alto, California

Bill Shoptaw (7)
CEO
The Shoptaw Group
Atlanta, Georgia

Renata Simril (77)
VP
Forest City Enterprises
Los Angeles, California

Adam Smith (127)
Land Acquistion Manager
John Laing Homes
Newport Beach, California

Kenya Smith (108)
Project Manager
The Athena Group
New York, New York

Francine Starks (87)
CEO
Terra Nova Consulting
Los Angeles, California

Joshua Steiger (6)
Asset Manager
National Partnership Investment
  Corporation
Beverly Hills, California

Monica Stevens
VP for MBA Recruiting
Wells Fargo
San Francisco, California

Tyler Stonebreaker
Development Associate
Snyder Langston Operon Group
Newport Beach, California

Jim Talton (128)
Executive VP of Human Resources
Forest City Enterprises
Cleveland, Ohio

Marilyn Taylor
Partner
Skidmore Owings & Merrill
New York, New York

Gary Tenzer (14)
Executive VP
George Smith Partners
Los Angeles, California

J. Ronald Terwilliger (58)
Chairman and CEO
Trammell Crow Residential
Atlanta, Georgia

Ronald Tong (74)
Sales/Leasing Agent
Colliers International
Pleasanton, California

Donald J. Trump (3)
CEO
Trump Organization
New York, New York

Gail Tubbs (74)
Relationship Manager
Wells Fargo
Los Angeles, California

Greg Tylka
Corporate Real Estate Manager
California National Bank
Los Angeles, California

Zachary Vaughan (71)
Director of Acquisitions
IPC US REIT
Toronto, Canada

Jacob Walters
Project Manager
Crescent Real Estate Equities
Dallas, Texas

Bing Wang (112)
Managing Partner
HyperBina
Boston, Massachusetts

John Wasley
Partner
Heidrick & Struggles
Los Angeles, California

Allyson Watkins (157)
VP
The Shoptaw Group
Atlanta, Georgia

Ray Watt (21)
CEO
Watt Enterprises
Santa Monica, California

Larry Webb (2)
CEO
John Laing Homes
Newport Beach, California

Blake Williams
Project Manager
Hines
Houston, Texas

Michael Wright
Managing Director
Grubb & Ellis Consulting
Los Angeles, California

Thomas Wright
Broker
Davis Coleman Realty
Heber, Utah

Keith Yang
President
Cal Venture Properties
Marina del Rey, California

Susan Yau (60)
Real Estate Analyst
Sunny Hills Palladium
Los Angeles, California

Smedes York (5)
President
York Properties
Raleigh, North Carolina

Karl Zavitkovsky (12)
Managing Director
Bank of America
Dallas, Texas

Sam Zell (41, 83)
CEO
Equity Office Properties Trust
Chicago, Illinois

CONTENTS

Chapter 1
A Real Estate Career: The Big Picture

Like many people, you may not realize that real estate is so much a part of your life. Think about it. You live in a house or an apartment. You shop at malls, buy food in supermarkets, and have your teeth cleaned in a professional building. You work in an office building. You stay in hotels or at a resort. You eat in restaurants, attend the theater, have season tickets to a sporting event, work out in the gym, belong to a tennis club. Maybe you keep some of your paraphernalia in a public storage facility.

You are a constant user and perhaps even an owner of real estate. But have you ever considered real estate as a career?

This book is designed to help you answer that question. It is intended to help you decide whether you want to pursue a career in real estate, as well as to help you learn about the many career opportunities available—so that you can consider the available choices and decide on a suitable career path. You can find a very meaningful and fruitful career in real estate if you start by determining how your skill sets, strengths, goals, and desires match the various career opportunities that are available. Career planning is essential, whether you are in school, fresh out of school, or at midca-reer. Some people—not only students, but also people with 20 years of professional experience—do not give sufficient thought to career planning.

While *The Inside Track to Careers in Real Estate* is intended mainly for students and professionals in the United States and students and professionals from other countries who are interested in studying or working in the United States, the increasing globalization of real estate suggests that more career opportunities in real estate are becoming available to students and professionals worldwide. Thus, this book also looks at opportunities for American students and professionals to work outside the United States.

This book is about careers in the private sector. It does not cover government sector careers, although the public sector at the city, county, state, or federal level offers interesting and rewarding career opportunities related to real estate development. To be sure, many private sector real estate career paths can be enriched by public sector experience with, for example, a city planning and zoning department. Such public sector experience can increase your value to private sector employers by giving you, for example, firsthand knowledge of how the project approval process works.

What Is Real Estate?

What is real estate? According to the investorwords.com glossary, it is land, including the air above it and the ground below it, and any buildings or structure on it. But real estate in a broad sense is not merely property. It is also an industry made up of thousands of companies producing products and providing financial and property services, an investment class, and a highly regulated enterprise.

An Industry

Development is the part of the real estate industry that produces a multiplicity of products, the most common of which include office towers and business parks, shopping centers, warehouses, hotels, single-family houses, townhouses, and apartment buildings. These products are created by developers and construction contractors working with architects, investors, and consultants in a variety of specialties. They may be built and held for long-term investment, or they may be sold to investors or ultimate users. Decisions to create these products are primarily driven by the market—the households, the businesses, and the other entities that buy or rent space.

A Mix of Businesses Centered on the Use of Land

Thousands of companies large and small develop, build, buy, own, rent, lease, manage, and sell properties. Their scope of business may be local, regional, national, or global. The development and management of properties is a complex undertaking that involves a host of service-providing businesses as well, including brokers, asset managers, facilities managers, project managers, lawyers, and many others. Like developers and operators, these service providers may operate on many levels, from local to global.

An Investment

Real estate is, like stocks or bonds, an important asset class for investors. Pension funds and other institutions as well as small partnerships and individuals invest billions of dollars in real estate every year, either through direct investments in properties or through indirect investment vehicles like mutual funds or real estate investment trusts (REITs).

A Highly Regulated Enterprise

In most places, the development of property is subject to building codes, zoning and subdivision codes, environmental laws, planning laws, and citizen participation requirements. The zoning and entitlement process for a large residential subdivision or a commercial project is often complex and protracted.

Why Choose Real Estate?

People have gone into real estate by accident, design, or necessity. Some real estate professionals have started fresh out of school, others at midcareer. Some have come from liberal arts undergraduate programs, others from graduate programs in real estate, and others from a variety of careers, such as teaching or high technology.

To help finance his studies for a doctorate in psychology, James Chaffin worked as a real estate broker in Hilton Head, South Carolina. Today, as president of Chaffin/Light Associates, he builds resort and recreation communities, using his grounding in psychology to assure that they meet the quality-of-life needs of his market.

Some planning classes at USC's School of Public Administration had sparked Richard DeBeikes's interest in real estate development, when, in his senior year, he flew to the USC/Notre Dame game. On the plane he was seated next to Jerry Jamgotchian, an executive at Ernest W. Hahn Inc., a shopping center developer and owner (which was sold in 1980 to Trizec Properties). As a fellow Trojan, Jamgotchian offered DeBeikes an opportunity to intern at Hahn, and thus started him on a career in real

estate. Later, DeBeikes became a junior partner, in the Halferty Development Company (Jim Halferty is another USC graduate), running its Irvine, California, office; and eventually he opened his own firm, DeBeikes Investment Company.

A history major in college, Larry Webb became a teacher for a few years, and then decided that he wanted a different career. He began his real estate career with a consulting, marketing, and research firm that gave him an opportunity to learn about real estate. He went on to work for various homebuilding companies, and today is CEO of John Laing Homes, one of the largest private homebuilders in the United States.

Why do people choose to go into real estate? The reasons are numerous. To some people its appeal lies in the challenges and opportunities for entrepreneurship that it offers. To others, the idea of building something and the durability of buildings are important. Still others look forward to the opportunity to help shape the urban environment or to engage in public issues. Its monetary rewards (commensurate with the risks) are not unimportant.

Q&A: Donald J. Trump

Wharton School graduate. World-famous developer. Office, hotel, residential, casino, and golf course owner. Best-selling author. Philanthropist. Star and coproducer of NBC's The Apprentice.

"Tenacity is absolutely necessary. If you don't have it, don't go into real estate."

What's the biggest challenge graduates face in pursuing a career in real estate?

Academic credentials can serve real estate professionals well, but there is no substitute for the skills and acumen that come from exposure to the industry. Acquiring that experience—and learning from it—will be the biggest challenge for every graduate.

What counsel would you give new graduates pursuing a career in real estate?

Decide where your true passion lies. Don't try to please someone else in making a career choice. Make sure it's your own choice. Then focus on it and simply don't give up. Tenacity is absolutely necessary. If you don't have it, don't go into real estate.

If a gradate is interested in development, what's the best way to get experience?

Work for a real estate developer and learn everything you can. Like a great photographer who translates a vision into reality through photographs, a developer has a strong vision that he realizes through his projects.

What are companies looking for from new graduates?

I look for people who are committed and loyal, people who take their work seriously and are disciplined. I don't have time for people who aren't responsible to themselves, to me, and to the positions they hold. Look at it this way: What kind of person would you like to have working for you? Be that kind of person.

What will make people tomorrow's leaders in the real estate industry?

Those who have vision and discipline will succeed. One is useless without the other. With both, you have a likely chance of becoming a leader, provided you've learned and sharpened your instincts through your experiences.

There follows a list of common reasons that real estate professionals give for their choice of career.

To Build

Developers like to build. In fact, they tend to have a passion for building, for applying their imagination, talents, and resources to the creation of buildings. They like building something of value, whether it is a massive mixed-use project like London's Docklands; a large-scale planned community like Irvine, California, or Columbia, Maryland; a standout skyscraper like Chicago's Sears Tower; a small-scale office building, shopping center, or apartment project; or single-family housing.

Alan Merson was fascinated by buildings and construction from a very early age. That interest led to a career in construction, and today he is a vice president of Morley

Builders, a private, employee-owned construction company in Santa Monica, California.

Darryl Brown also had an early interest in development. When he was in college, he and a friend were driving through a neighborhood when they saw a piece of land they thought would be perfect for development. However, they had no money and no development experience. But their instincts were right. Brown checked out the site several years later and found that it had been completely developed. Today he's housing director at West Angeles Community Development Corporation, a church-affiliated community development corporation in Los Angeles.

To Feel a Sense of Accomplishment

Developers who are passionate about their work take great satisfaction in seeing what they have created. Wade Cable,

Q&A: **Donald Bren**

Chairman of the Irvine Company (beginning 1981) and majority shareholder (from early 1990s). Homebuilder in Orange County, California, 1958 to 1963. Founder of the Mission Viejo Company (1963), developer of the 10,000-acre new community of Mission Viejo. With a group of investors, purchaser of the Irvine Company from the Irvine Foundation (1977).

The Irvine Company
Developer of the nation's premier master-planned community on the 93,000-acre Irvine Ranch in central Orange County, California. Most of the company's land and property holdings are in Orange County, but it also owns investment properties in Los Angeles, San Diego, and Silicon Valley. Its portfolio includes approximately 400 office buildings, 35 retail centers, 80 apartment communities, two hotels, five marinas, and three golf courses.

"I believe few careers can compete with real estate development for personal satisfaction."

Would you recommend real estate as a career path, and why?
Absolutely, and for several reasons. First, unlike some industries, it's not going away. Real estate will be here in perpetuity. As our country and world grow, so does the demand for real estate of all kinds—homes, apartments, offices, industrial space, and retail centers. It is a significant and comparatively stable segment of our economy. And, as an investment, it continues to create wealth for many, many people. I believe few careers can compete with real estate development for personal satisfaction. First, developers create spaces that people need and want—places to live, work, shop, and play. We have the satisfaction of filling basic human needs. Further, each project is different and challenges our creativity, imagination, and good sense as businesspeople. We have the opportunity to start with a dream or an idea, and guide its evolution into a completed project. Nothing is more satisfying than seeing ultimate users enjoying real estate projects that we have created.

What are the most important characteristics for success for an entrepreneur or a professional working for a company?
Success starts with proper academic training and on-the-job experience. A background in business and finance—marked perhaps by a law degree, an accounting degree, or an MBA—makes an excellent foundation. I have found exposure to art, architecture, landscape architecture, design, and politics to be invaluable. Success comes to those who can exert leadership, think big, and take reasonable and well-reasoned risk, who have the courage to make decisions, and who are disciplined. Real estate can be a very difficult and challenging business. Successful professionals must have the determination to invest the extra time and energy necessary to pursue creative, out-of-the-box solutions to the enormous challenges—whether an architectural issue, a community concern, or a complex business decision—that present themselves.

What's your perspective on opportunities in the real estate industry for young people?
As far down the road as I can see, I see unlimited opportunities. Even if opportunities for large-scale master planning and development in areas like Southern California diminish, our region and the nation as a whole are experiencing massive redevelopment and infill development. It is an exciting and challenging industry that will test our ability to innovate, to adapt to new demands, to change our ways and directions. Young professionals who can adapt quickly to a constantly changing business environment will be rewarded. It is difficult and unusual for young people to go directly into real estate development; the more usual route is through entry-level positions in real estate finance, property management, or leasing. This is an industry that offers wonderful opportunities for creativity, resourcefulness, and rewards to match the risks.

A Sense of Accomplishment

Stan Ross
Whatever career path you choose in real estate can give you a sense of accomplishment. Working for a developer or homebuilder, you are part of a team that creates office buildings, shopping centers, hotels, or housing. Working for an investor or lender, you provide the capital that developers and owners must have to start projects or acquire properties. Working for a broker, you help investors and owners buy and sell properties or lease space in their buildings.

In my career as an accountant, I took particular satisfaction in helping clients solve business problems and capitalize on business opportunities. In the late 1960s and early 1970s, when many large corporations were looking to diversify their businesses, some of these were considering the acquisition of large development companies that were involved in either commercial property or homebuilding. But the senior managers of these corporations generally were not familiar with the real estate business. I helped them understand how a real estate business could fit with their strategic plans, business operations, and investment goals, so they could make an informed decision about such acquisitions.

Over the course of my career, I also felt a real sense of accomplishment from helping a number of financially troubled real estate companies resolve problems with their investors and lenders, restructure their businesses, and return to financial health.

As you contemplate a career in the real estate industry and learn more about the opportunities it offers, think about what career path would give you a sense of accomplishment. What do you want to achieve that matters to you?

president and CEO of William Lyon Homes, a homebuilder, likes homebuilding "because you have a sense of visible accomplishment. You start with a raw piece of land and in the end you have produced a home for a family." Smedes York, president of York Properties, a family-owned, full-service real estate business in Raleigh, North Carolina, says that he takes pride in driving by projects his company has developed. Bret M. Nielsen, vice president for leasing and acquisitions at Caruso Affiliated, a Los Angeles–based developer, is fascinated by how developers can turn empty land into tangible assets, much like an artist can turn a blank canvas into a painting.

Because Real Estate Is Durable
Commercial buildings and homes are built to last, often for decades. And with recycling, upgrading, and remodeling, their useful lives can be further extended. In a fast-changing world, the durability of real estate appeals to many real estate professionals.

Because Real Estate Is In Demand
Real estate, like any other business, goes through cycles. Demand for office space or shopping centers fluctuates with changes in the economy and other supply and demand factors. But beneath the cyclical shifts, demand for real estate will grow in the long term, based on continued growth in the U.S. population and the economy. With population and economic growth comes added demand for places to live, work, do business, shop, lodge, congregate, and play.

This was clear to Jona Goldrich when he moved to California in the 1950s. Crossing the state border, he noticed a billboard that proclaimed: "1,000 people are moving to California every day." With his mind made up to go into real estate, Goldrich started the trash collection business that financed his first investment, an apartment building. Today he's the CEO of Goldrich & Kest Industries, a multifamily and commercial property acquisition, development, construction, sales, and management firm based in Culver City, California.

To Be Challenged
Whether real estate professionals are developing a project, acquiring a property, obtaining and structuring financing, managing a property portfolio, negotiating a lease, or engag-

ing in many other kinds of activities, the work is challenging. The idea of challenge attracts many professionals to real estate. They are drawn by the opportunity to find solutions to complex problems. Or by the multifaceted nature of a real estate career, as Joshua Steiger, a principal of Cantilever Capital, a firm that invests, develops, and manages a private portfolio, puts it: "There are many facets to developing, owning, and managing real estate, and the hardest part is making sure everything is working smoothly."

Because Real Estate Offers Variety

Real estate professionals have the chance to work with a variety of clients and customers. These may include large corporations and small businesses, large retail companies and small retailers, pension funds and other institutions that own real estate, the owners and managers of multifamily properties, and single-family-home buyers. Real estate also offers a variety of work. No development project, real estate transaction, or property management assignment is exactly the same as another.

Career Profile: Dale Anne Reiss

Dale Anne Reiss, global and Americas director of real estate, hospitality, gaming, and construction at Ernst & Young, passed on an engineering career and found success in accounting and real estate.

Dale Anne Reiss started as an engineering student at the Illinois Institute of Technology (IIT). "Before long, I realized I was a lousy engineer," she says. She changed majors and went on to earn a bachelor's degree in economics and accounting from IIT and an MBA in finance and statistics from the University of Chicago.

The Wrong Place

After graduating from IIT at age 18, Reiss started in a training program with a bank, then moved to another financial institution, where an officer who noted that she was a diligent worker, gave her some valuable advice: "He advised me to leave. He said that because I was a woman, I could never get ahead at that institution—no matter how hard I worked." Rather than languishing at that job, Reiss decided to look for opportunities elsewhere.

And the Right Time

Reiss found a job with the City Colleges of Chicago, a system of seven community colleges, which was undergoing a repurposing and restructuring process. "It was like being part of a startup company," she recalls. At age 19, Reiss was in charge of establishing polices and procedures and managing grant funding for City Colleges. One of her responsibilities was to determine the costs of proposed union contracts for the use of a judge who was arbitrating City

Colleges' contract negotiations with the unions. "The chancellor would walk into my office, dump these inch-thick union demands on my desk, and tell me to cost them out as quickly as possible. It was a great learning experience."

While continuing to work, Reiss enrolled in the MBA program at the University of Chicago, taking night classes. With her MBA in hand, she sought other job opportunities, but "the economy was in a recession and it was difficult for a woman to get a private sector job." She was headhunted for the position of director of accounting and finance for Chicago's department of public works, a position in which she would manage about 80 people. She accepted the job offer. "In those days, government was the best place for women and minorities to get leadership positions," Reiss notes. On the job, she spent a lot of time in the field, inspecting the city's bridges, tunnels, sewers, and streets and getting her "first direct experience with real estate and infrastructure."

A Goal Realized

While working for the city, Reiss turned 21 and was eligible to take the CPA exam, which she had wanted to do since the time she had studied for her MBA. She passed the exam, but to be licensed as a CPA she had to work for a public accounting firm. Thus, she joined the Chicago office of Arthur Young & Co., eventually becoming a principal in charge of the firm's financial planning and control practice, a position that gave her broad exposure to a variety of industrial companies.

Because Real Estate Offers Opportunities for Entrepreneurship

Real estate has a long history and tradition of entrepreneurship and easy entry. While some real estate practitioners say that there are not as many opportunities for entrepreneurs as there were in the past, the opportunities are there—and will be in the future. Bill Shoptaw, CEO of The Shoptaw Group, an Atlanta-based multifamily investment and asset management company, explains the attraction of being an entrepreneur: "I wanted to take control of my own destiny instead of working for someone else. The risk and excitement of entrepreneurship have kept me in this business."

Because the Rewards Are Commensurate with the Risks

Real estate offers monetary rewards commensurate with the risks that individuals and companies are willing to take. Entrepreneurs can realize very attractive returns from their investments in projects they develop, which usually are financed not only with the entrepreneur's capital, but also

She was then recruited to the position of controller and senior vice president at Urban Investment & Development, a private, diversified real estate development and investment company owned by Aetna Life & Casualty. "Urban Investment was a precursor to today's public real estate companies, and a great place to learn about every aspect of real estate," Reiss says.

Aetna eventually put Urban Investment up for sale, and hired Kenneth Leventhal & Co., a California-based CPA firm specializing in real estate, to represent its interests in the sale. When Stan Ross, KL&Co.'s comanaging partner, came to town, Reiss asked him why KL&Co. did not have a presence in Chicago, where a number of the nation's leading real estate companies were headquartered. The firm had been thinking about establishing a Chicago office, and it did in 1985. Reiss was brought in as managing partner. The Chicago office built up a strong regional client base. In 1995, KL&Co. merged with Ernst & Young. And when Ross retired in 1999, Reiss succeeded him as leader of E&Y's real estate group.

Career Lessons

If she were embarking on a career today, Reiss would start in finance and accounting. "Much of real estate is about generating dollars from bricks and mortar, and understanding the underlying economics of real estate is essential to entering the business."

But she understands that there are many avenues into real estate. "Decide what interests you—whether it's finance or architecture or construction or something else—and develop a foundation of knowledge and experience in your area of choice. Build on this foundation by learning about other areas," Reiss advises. "I'm not a construction manager, but I have ruined more shoes walking around construction sites than I can remember, and I can talk about construction. I'm not an architect, but I can talk about architecture." She believes that to succeed it is necessary to have a curiosity about this business and a willingness to learn and to be flexible and adaptable in planning a career. "You should have a plan, of course, but life is unpredictable. An opportunity may unexpectedly come along, and you must be responsive. If you are, opportunities sometimes have a way of finding you."

Reiss gives much of the credit for her success to the extensive professional relationships and networks that she developed over her career. "Many people have helped me along the road, but none were mentors in the formal sense." Reiss calls "mentoring" an overworked term. "What mattered was that these people were accessible, that they gave me advice, guidance, and support, and that I learned from them."

One of the biggest challenges that Reiss faced in her career was being a woman. Accounting and real estate were not considered good career paths for women. "For most of my career, I was the only woman in the room. That was a challenge, but it was also an opportunity to prove myself." Her advice to women now pursuing a real estate career is to be willing to take risks. "Women are raised to be risk-averse, and that's unfortunate. It's only by taking risks that you create opportunities for yourself."

with equity from investors and a high level of borrowing. An entrepreneur must understand the risks and be prepared to invest his or her own capital in the business. Working for a real estate company in a position that offers a competitive salary and compensation package can also be highly remunerative.

To Help Shape the Urban Environment

People have been drawn to real estate by the opportunity to join, work with, or advise real estate organizations whose projects, buildings, and portfolios of real estate assets have far-reaching effects on the urban environment. It is buildings—office buildings, civic buildings, shopping malls, industrial buildings, apartment buildings, and houses—that make up the bulk of the fabric of cities and towns. Buildings are also important cultural symbols. It is buildings and their role in determining where people live, work, shop, and play that, to a considerable degree, determine the economic vitality and quality of life of cities.

Because Real Estate Affords Opportunities to Participate in Civic Enterprises

Many key public issues of the day—including urban revitalization, growth management, affordable housing, economic growth (business attraction and retention), and environmental protection—are in large part involved with real estate. Real estate professionals have the opportunity to become major players in land use planning and growth management efforts, in urban revitalization programs, and in environmen-

tal stewardship. One form of participation in civic enterprises is public/private development partnerships. The number of such partnerships between the public and private sectors is growing. They are used to execute a variety of projects, from the conversion of decommissioned military bases to private use; to the privatization of airports and other public facilities; to the development of office, retail, hotel, or housing uses in conjunction with public facilities such as convention centers, sports stadiums, or mass transit stations.

Because Real Estate Affords Opportunities for Public Service

Many real estate professionals work for organizations—nonprofit or for-profit—that provide a public service. These include organizations that build or buy housing for low-income families or elderly people; that build and operate shelters for abused children or homeless people; that buy or develop space in inner-city neighborhoods for startup businesses; that acquire, preserve, and rehabilitate historic properties; that buy, clean up, and redevelop environmentally contaminated properties; or that advise and assist building owners in the use of energy-saving technology. Two nonprofit examples are Architecture for Humanity, a New York–based organization that has helped design and build housing for Kosovo refugees and mobile health clinics in Africa; and Common Ground Community, a housing and community development organization that focuses on innovative solutions to the problem of homelessness in New York City.

Real Estate's Surprising Breadth

As a career choice, however, real estate sometimes seems to be overlooked. People in a career-planning mode—college and university students, recent graduates starting out in the job market, and professionals thinking of a midcareer change—tend not to have given the same thought to real estate careers as to careers in law, business, finance, or other fields. And even those who are thinking about real estate tend to be unaware of the breadth of the real estate industry and thus not fully aware of all the career possibilities.

Many of them think that real estate is just about housing, or that everyone involved in real estate is a developer.

In fact, real estate offers more career choices today than it ever has. For starters, career opportunities can be found in working for any one of the following types of organizations:

- large public real estate companies, which are coming to resemble corporate America in their organization and structure;
- small private entrepreneurial organizations, which are unique to real estate;

- companies that invest regionally within the United States, nationally, or globally;
- companies that specialize in a single product or related products, such as office buildings, shopping centers, hotels, industrial real estate, apartments, or homebuilding;
- companies that develop or own multiple real estate products;
- nonprofit organizations that own and develop real estate;
- companies that finance real estate;
- corporations with their own real estate departments; and
- companies that provide real estate services, such as design and architecture firms, brokerage companies, and various consultancies.

Q&A: **Raymond C. Mikulich**

Recognized leader and innovator in real estate finance. A managing director of Lehman Brothers and cohead of Lehman Brothers Real Estate Private Equity Group (with more than $4 billion in capital for real estate merchant banking and mezzanine lending). Participant in hundreds of financial transactions.

"You don't have to choose one end of the spectrum or the other; often it chooses you."

What's the outlook for the development business?

Development will become a less significant component of the real estate industry and national GDP (gross domestic product). In the United States, obsolescence requiring replacement will become less of a factor, particularly when compared with older markets, such as Europe. Because the development business will be less robust, profitability will be lower. The most profitable development pursuits will be land entitlement and the envisioning of novel products or uses for sites. Design and creativity will continue to be valuable—and rewarded.

Where are there opportunities to make money?

Developers have to build a lot of space to make money. Asset managers have to manage a lot of space to be profitable. This argues for size, efficiency, and economy—if you can deal with the diseconomies and inefficiencies that set in; it is hard to maintain a creative environment within a huge development business or massive asset management portfolio.

What are the opportunities for the entrepreneur today?

Opportunities for the creative individual to go out on his/her own, be creative, and make something happen are shrinking. Financing sources are more conservative. You're not going to find guys like me betting on a young kid to succeed in the real estate equivalent of an Internet startup. One option might be to buy an established business. I'm thinking of the analogy of a dentist who wants to have her own practice; she'd be smart to find an experienced dentist with an established practice who plans to retire.

How would someone who wants to go into real estate finance go about deciding what direction is most appropriate?

Any job search starts with a very healthy self-assessment. You must think about what you like to do. Real estate finance, like many careers, offers a spectrum of opportunities, ranging from sales or origination on one end to pure execution—lawyers, accountants, financial modelers—on the other. If you're personable, good with people, and quick on your feet and could be characterized as a salesman, you are likely a client person. Alternatively, if you really like to sit down at a computer and figure out how the numbers work, you are likely a person who can come up with a new twist on a financial structure. There's plenty of room in the middle for the hybrid personality, which characterizes most of us. You don't have to choose one end of the spectrum or the other; often it chooses you.

—continued

Q&A: **Raymond C. Mikulich**
continued

What do you look for in a job candidate?

What is most lacking and hardest to find in finance operations today is a finance person who is knowledgeable about real estate, someone who knows enough to discern a good piece of real estate from a bad one or at least to ask the right questions. Real estate finance is about understanding the risk, and then assessing, allocating, attributing, and pricing that risk.

What do you ask job candidates in interviews?

I interview a lot of people and always ask them first why they want to be in real estate. I look for one very simple answer from them: "I like the tangibility. I like looking at it." If they don't tell me that, if that answer doesn't just roll off their lips, then they don't love the business and chances are they're not going to have a long-term career in real estate.

What is more important, education or experience?

Quality experience will carry you longer than education. Anyone who wants to work in the real estate industry after graduation should get some experience in the industry before graduate school.

What are the personal qualities of successful people in the real estate industry?

As in any industry, the people who succeed are smart, hardworking, and committed. In entrepreneurial development, they're also risk takers. But even in institutions, the successful people tend to be risk takers. They also tend to be proactive, thoughtful, and aggressive—but not belligerent—and to question the way things work. Innovation earns a very big premium in real estate, so creativity is probably the characteristic that will make the largest difference in a person's career. Of course, there is no tolerance today for a lack of honesty and integrity.

Key Trends in Real Estate

Let's begin to look at real estate careers by considering some key trends in real estate. Why consider trends? Because they will help you understand the real estate business and the opportunities and challenges that will define its future. Some of the most successful people in real estate (and in business in general) are trendspotters who have used their insights to start businesses, launch new products or services, move their companies into new markets, and advance their careers. Today's trends are tomorrow's opportunities. Your awareness of trends will enable you to make more informed decisions about the specifics—the job, the company, the educational requirements—of your real estate career.

Here's an example. Over this and the next decade, the baby boom generation—which accounts for about 60 percent of the workforce between the ages of 25 and 54—will retire, and the next generation of workers is too small to replace them. Between 2002 and 2012, according to projections from the U.S. Bureau of Labor Statistics (BLS), the working-age population (adults 16 to 54) will grow by 6 million, while the 55-plus population will grow by 18 million. Assuming that the economy grows at a normal 3 to 3.5 percent annually, a skilled-worker gap will start to appear in 2005, and reach 5.3 million workers by 2010 and 24 million by 2020, according to the BLS.

Think about what this trend might mean to you in terms of employment opportunities in real estate. For example, would a skilled-worker shortage mean less demand for office space, because companies cannot find workers? Would that mean less business for office developers and owners? Or would companies spend more on their facilities in order to attract and retain skilled workers? Would that mean more business for developers and owners? Would you want to be working for an office developer or owner in a decade? Would the kind of development it specializes in be a consideration?

WITH A VISION THINGS WORK OUT

Stan Ross
I had a career choice to make when I was a young manager for a national CPA firm in New York City. I had talked by telephone to Kenneth Leventhal, founder of an accounting firm bearing his name, about moving to California to work for him. My sister had just gone west, but I wasn't sure I wanted to make the move.

I met with Ken in New York. He told me that his vision was to build an accounting firm specializing in real estate. It would provide services to clients in every sector of the industry. He convinced me to join his firm.

As I recall, when I arrived in California, I asked Ken: "Where are the 300 people that are supposed to be working for you?" He said that I had misunderstood him, that what he had said was that we could grow the firm to 300 people.

Shortly thereafter, Ken and I visited a major real estate company. When we returned to our office he said: "I thought you said you knew real estate." I said that he had misunderstood me, that what I had said was that I wanted to learn real estate.

Anyway, we cleared the air and went on to build the leading accounting firm in the country specializing in real estate.

It just goes to show that a career path can sometimes take unexpected twists and turns. Especially, it seems, in real estate.

The aging of the baby boomers is creating long-term opportunities for developers and builders of seniors housing, retirement communities, assisted-living facilities, and other product targeted to older people. What will be the best markets and locations in the United States for such facilities? How much product will be required? How will builders meet the specific requirements and needs of the seniors market?

ONE SECRET OF SUCCESS

Stan Ross

If you learn to apply your powers of observation, perception, and analysis, you can develop the insights and analytical skills that can create value for your organization—whether by finding ways to improve routine business operations or realizing how a market trend could mean new business opportunities.

Let me give you an example from early in my career.

When I first began in accounting, I worked for a company where my job was to look at canceled checks to verify that they were properly signed and endorsed. A few days and many checks later, I began to doze on the job. Surely, I thought, there must be more to accounting than this—and I began to look at the checks from a different perspective. I compared the dates on which the checks had been written with the dates on which they had cleared the bank. I found that a number had been written to vendors who, for whatever reasons, took their time about depositing them. As a result, the company had a lot of money tied up in uncashed checks for prolonged periods of time during which it could have made other, temporary uses of the money. As a result of my observations, the company entered into deferred payment schedules with many of its vendors.

That experience taught me that there is value to be found—if you look for it—in even routine tasks.

The best companies are very good at studying demographic and economic trends, analyzing real estate markets, looking for opportunities, and developing plans for future development or investment. "Successful companies excel at anticipating and adapting to changes in their markets," notes Robert Larson, former CEO of the Taubman Company, a retail developer (now Taubman Centers, a retail real estate investment trust). These companies value people who can help them manage change, and experience has shown that the best ideas can come from anyone in the organization. Real estate professionals who have exceptional skills in identifying, monitoring, and interpreting demographic, economic, and real estate trends will have high value in the marketplace—either in a real estate company or a consulting or research firm that provides economic and demographic analysis to real estate companies. Some may even be able to establish new niches in the industry.

The following list of some of the trends that define today's real estate industry and are shaping its future has been compiled with the help of interviews with a number of senior executives and mid- and entry-level professionals in the real estate industry. The interviews were conducted by USC student research teams. The list is not meant to be inclusive, but rather to highlight trends that may indicate growth opportunities—new markets, new products or services, or growth in existing product or service lines—for real estate companies. You may find some of the best opportunities in companies that are responsive to these trends, but every organization will have a need for professionals with the insights, knowledge, and skills to contribute to its growth. "Increasingly, real estate is a value-added business," notes Karl Zavitkovsky, former managing director for Bank of America's commercial real estate banking group's central division. "The key is coming up with real solutions that differentiate your products." Professionals who can help a company arrive at such real solutions will be highly valued in the marketplace.

Industry Consolidation

The real estate industry is evolving from a local, fragmented, project-focused, and entrepreneur-driven business into a consolidated, global, institutionalized industry. If you had started on a real estate career in the 1950s or 1960s, your choices would have been limited mainly to small private companies owned by entrepreneurs. Your business would probably have been concentrated in a local market and focused on a few projects.

You can still work for such companies today. But because of consolidation and the growth of public companies, you are just as likely to work for a large company that operates throughout a region or throughout the United States. Large public companies develop and own extensive portfolios of projects and property investments. Some of these companies focus on a single product market, such as office buildings or shopping centers, while others are diversified. If you started your real estate career with a large development organization, you typically would move through different departments to gain experience, and move up the corporate ladder over time.

Globalization of Real Estate Investment

The flow of real estate investment capital into global markets is on the rise. Opportunity funds, investment bankers, pension funds, and other investors are making direct investments through partnerships with local investors or developers, or they are providing investment capital globally. "Globalization will be the strongest trend over the next ten years," says Joseph F. Azrack, former chairman of AEW Capital Management, a real estate investment adviser. "Global debt markets are maturing, and global equity markets are becoming more transparent."

Developers have been slower to globalize. One reason is that it is difficult to acquire local market knowledge and experience. If U.S. developers do venture overseas, it usually is as a participant in joint ventures with local developers.

What does globalization mean for your real estate career? If you have an interest in living abroad and can discuss real estate and finance in a foreign language, you may find an opportunity with a global investor or real estate services company or, less commonly, with a global developer.

Institutional Ownership of Property Assets

The ownership and management of investment-grade real estate is shifting from individuals or small partnerships of developers and investors to large real estate investment trusts and real estate operating companies, pension funds, private equity funds, and other institutions that control large portfolios of assets. While many small investors are still active in the market, real estate increasingly is owned by large institutions.

U.S. pension funds are a leading real estate investor, every year putting billions of dollars into development projects and property acquisitions in the United States and, increasingly, around the globe. Private equity funds or opportunity funds also raise billions of dollars in capital from investors for the development or acquisition of real estate. In addition, public REITs sell shares to raise capital for investing in commercial properties. REITs are now the biggest owners of malls in the United States.

In considering a real estate career, you might consider becoming a real estate investment adviser or portfolio manager for a pension fund or a private equity fund. Or you might go with a firm that advises funds on their property investments. You also could work for a REIT.

Increasing Financial Sophistication

The flood of capital into real estate investment, means that many developers now have ready access to the capital markets and are able to compete with other types of investments for capital. Before they had relatively ready access to investment capital markets, developers and builders typically financed their projects out of their own pockets, often with the help of family and friends or business partners and with the backing of a friendly lender. While many developers still finance projects in this way, the largest developers and builders now can access capital markets to raise capital from investors or borrow money to finance their projects, just as big corporations do. This relative ease of availability of capital allows new entrepreneurs and developers to develop or acquire real estate.

Developers and investors are using increasingly sophisticated financing structures. Development has traditionally been financed on a project-by-project basis, meaning that the financing was collateralized by the project itself. If a developer borrowed $2 million to finance the construction of a small office building, the building was collateral for the loan. If the developer defaulted, the lender usually would foreclose, assume ownership of the property, and try to sell it for at least $2 million or the amount of the loan. Today, large developers and builders can raise financing backed by their balance sheets and investment-grade credit ratings, just like corporate borrowers, and at substantially lower costs than project-based financing.

In raising capital and developing projects or buying properties, real estate companies and investors must continually adapt to new accounting and tax rules or changes in existing rules. In the past, real estate was a heavily tax-sheltered business. While the tax benefits are not as great today, decisions about buying, owning, operating, and selling real estate are still driven to a considerable degree by tax considerations—federal, state, and local. Accounting rules and regulations likewise influence decisions about real estate investment and ownership.

The increasing sophistication of real estate finance means that real estate professionals need, more than ever, a solid foundation in finance. Gary M. Tenzer, executive vice president and principal with real estate investment banker George Smith Partners, describes his firm's future hiring needs: "We will need finance professionals who have backgrounds similar to those of their counterparts at commercial lending institutions, investment banks, and opportunity funds. They will need a formal education in real estate finance and a sound understanding of real estate and development issues."

All in all, trends in real estate finance along with the growing size of real estate businesses will heighten demand for real estate professionals with a multidisciplinary education that includes finance as well as tax, accounting, real estate economics, and computer applications courses.

Niche Development

Despite the trend towards bigness, thousands of small real estate companies owned by individual entrepreneurs or small partnerships continue to operate successfully in local and regional markets. As has been noted, a growing number of large development and homebuilding companies operate in many markets, generate millions of dollars in revenue, and employ thousands of people. Nonetheless, no single developer or builder dominates its market.

Small developers and builders continue to successfully operate in single markets like Atlanta or Cincinnati, and in niche specialties, such as development on vacant or under-

used land in or near urban areas. "While larger developers are able to weather the time and expense of prolonged approval processes, smaller developers have opportunities in infill/redevelopment locations or unique development situations," notes Joseph Davis, president and CEO of the Irvine Community Development Company, the subsidiary of the Irvine Company responsible for residential community development on The Irvine Ranch.

We are seeing more partnerships between big and small developers to leverage their respective strengths. "More joint ventures are being formed between big developers, who are better at raising money, and small developers, who are better at getting entitlements," observes John Loper, vice president in the California division of the Fritz Duda Company, a diversified real estate investment and development company.

Thus, despite the trend toward consolidation in the industry, if you would prefer to work for a small organization, you have a choice of thousands of small real estate companies across the country.

Complex Entitlement Process

The increasingly complex regulatory environment is a challenge for real estate companies. Developers and homebuilders often must work with a number of different local, state, and occasionally federal agencies to obtain entitlements for their projects. The process sometimes can take years—and significantly impact development costs. As Renée McDonnell, senior vice president with IHP Capital Partners, an investment firm that provides equity financing mainly for residential development, notes: "A rigorous entitlement process, tight land inventories, and infrastructure constraints, especially in California, have forced severe land price increases, which translate into higher housing costs."

Some entrepreneurs with experience in the entitlement process have started consulting firms to assist developers in getting project approvals. You may be interested in this type of work. If so, it is certain that large developers and entitlement consultancies will be looking to hire professionals with the necessary skills to navigate the project approval process. These skills include a knowledge of laws and public policy issues that affect development; an understanding of the complexities of zoning laws, environmental regulations, and other elements of the entitlement process; articulateness; the ability to work with public officials; and the confidence and demeanor needed for representing proposed projects before various government agencies, public meetings, and community groups.

Sophisticated Information Technology

Real estate practitioners have acquired the technology and devised the analytical tools they need to collect, classify, evaluate, manage, and use information far more efficiently and productively than in the past. The adoption of database technology has enabled real estate companies and investors to create sophisticated platforms for the measurement and benchmarking of asset performance, for managing assets, and for evaluating investments. The adoption of advanced computer communications technology allows them to better collaborate on projects and share information.

Information technology is a powerful—and evolving—tool. Real estate companies that are the fastest and most adept at applying it to, for example, evaluating deal opportunities or making investment decisions will gain a competitive edge. A company that has acquired customized state-of-the-art information technology can analyze 100 prospective investments today in less time than was required to analyze ten deals a decade ago.

Q&A: Kenneth Leventhal

Founder in 1949 of Kenneth Leventhal & Company. Practice concentrated in helping clients find innovative solutions to complex real estate situations. Recognized authority in the field of nonjudicial reorganizations. Trustee at the University of Southern California (USC). Benefactor of The Elaine and Kenneth Leventhal School of Accounting of the University of Southern California. Recipient of an honorary doctorate from USC in 2000.

Kenneth Leventhal & Company

National certified public accounting firm, which in 1995 merged with Ernst & Young LLP. The firm played a role in the total business needs of its clients, rather than confining itself to traditional CPA services only. From its beginning, it helped clients to find ingenious ways to finance their projects and manage their businesses. The Leventhal firm gained far-reaching influence and prominence because of its aggressive leadership in the dynamic real estate field. Fortune magazine described it as having an "attention-getting track record of financial innovation."

"Scores of people who took entry-level jobs with Kenneth Leventhal & Company are now household names in the building industry."

Why did you elect to build an accounting firm specializing in the real estate industry?

In 1949, the accounting profession was dominated by eight major firms. I decided that to start a new firm I would need to offer a specialty, and I looked for an industry that had easy ingress, was capital intensive, and was entrepreneurial and unstructured. Real estate was such an industry. The population in California was growing exponentially every year and the demand for housing was immense. Young, entrepreneurial builders were in need of good accounting and business advice.

What personal characteristics are important for success in accounting?

Integrity, technical excellence, and interpersonal skills are as important today as when I started my firm.

Is accounting a good starting point for a real estate career?

Yes. Scores of people who took entry-level jobs with Kenneth Leventhal & Company are now household names in the building industry and some have made the *Forbes* 400 list.

For students who are not accounting majors, what courses would be most helpful in preparing for careers in real estate?

Enroll in the MRED (Master of Real Estate Development) program at the University of Southern California.

Keeping up with information management technology is an important function for many real estate companies. Therefore, there will likely be ample career opportunities for professionals who are skilled in the application, use, and customization of information technology.

Building Green

In the past decade, sustainable development or "green" building has become a trend affecting all areas of real estate development, in the United States and globally. Green building aims to design, construct, and manage buildings in ways that respect the environment, use natural and nonrenewable resources efficiently, conserve water and energy, and create healthy and comfortable environments for their tenants and other users. Developers and clients engaged in every type of construction project—from corporate headquarters complexes to small office projects and government facilities, from shopping centers to warehouses and schools, from hotels to apartment buildings and single-family houses —have climbed onto the green-development bandwagon.

The trend toward green building is driven partly by increased awareness of the environmental impact of building and buildings. In the United States, buildings produce an estimated 30 percent of the nation's greenhouse gases and consume 12 percent of its potable water. Developers and owners and tenants are coming to realize that building green can have substantial economic benefits. Buildings consume nearly two-thirds of the electricity used in the United States; the inclusion of such energy-saving technologies as light-reflective materials, natural daylighting and ventilation systems, highly efficient mechanical and electrical equipment, or solar panels can produce energy cost savings of 20 to 50 percent. Through such savings developers can recover the added costs of green-building applications.

Employers also are realizing the advantages of occupying space in green buildings; studies have shown that healthy buildings raise employee productivity and lower absenteeism. Federal, state, and local governments offer various incentives to promote green building.

This trend is creating a growing need for expertise in sustainable development, and real estate professionals who are knowledgeable and experienced in green-building principles and practices will be in demand.

Resurgence of Urban Markets

Investors and developers are showing new interest in development and rehabilitation projects in inner cities and close-in suburbs. Various forces—including demographic trends, suburban growth controls, a growing awareness of the problems that have accompanied urban sprawl, the emergence of smart growth initiatives and incentives, and ever-worsening traffic congestion—are stimulating demand for residential, retail, and employment development in urban areas. Investors are seeing more opportunities in mixed-use projects located near transit facilities and in the acquisition of older or historic downtown commercial buildings for conversion to apartments for young professionals and a move-back-to-the-city crowd mostly made up of suburban empty nesters and households tired of long commutes. Investors are developing or buying apartment buildings and shopping centers in inner cities to meet demand and partnering with nonprofit organization and public agencies to develop office or industrial space for startup businesses. As residential land in the suburbs becomes scarcer, some suburban home-builders are turning to urban housing development.

This urban resurgence will create many development and investment job opportunities for real estate professionals.

Chapter 2
A Look at Development

Essentially, there are two main businesses in real estate: development and ownership/investment. The real estate services that are needed by developers and owners/investors—including financing, asset management, property management, brokerage, market and feasibility analysis, site and building design, and numerous other development and investment services—make up, in effect, a third line of business. This chapter looks at developers. The next chapter covers investors/owners as well as businesses that provide real estate services. Some companies both develop and own real estate, and some of these also provide various real estate services.

IS REAL ESTATE FOR YOU?

First, you have to decide whether you want a career in real estate. Start by doing research on career planning generally. Appendix A suggests books, articles, Web sites, and other resources.

Second, take the time to research the real estate industry. Again, appendix A is a resource. Of course, you can't learn everything there is to know about real estate. But learn enough to feel that you can make an informed decision about whether to invest your time, energy, talents, and money in pursuing a real estate career. Along the way, you'll develop a better idea of not only whether you want to work in real estate, but also what the options are and where you might want to work—in what sector of the real estate industry, for what type of company, in what type of position—and whether you might want to go into business for yourself.

Third, talk to people in real estate. Talk to brokers, property managers, project managers, and other real estate professionals. Visit some real estate projects and talk to people on the job site. Also talk to educators in business schools and real estate programs and to friends and relatives working in real estate. Their insights and comments could be helpful.

Fourth, attend meetings of local real estate organizations (see "Professional and Trade Organizations" in appendix A). Get the observations of real estate professionals in attendance on career opportunities in real estate. If your school has a real estate center or club, attend its meetings and talk to the attendees.

Fifth, take an introductory course in real estate at a local college or other institution. (To locate courses, try a Google search on introductory real estate course plus the name of your city.) Or enroll in an online course.

Finally, conduct a self-assessment. You need to go through this process, because finding the right career starts with having a clear understanding of your aspirations, interests, values, talents, and skills. Compare the idea of a career in real estate with other careers that might interest you. There are many good books and resources that can help you with the self-assessment process, some of which are listed in appendix A. (See also the questionnaire on deciding on a real estate career in appendix C.)

In the course of this six-step process, you may begin to develop professional relationships that can be of benefit to you, should you choose to embark on a career in real estate. The real estate people whom you interview and from whom you seek advice not only can help you with your career planning, but also can become mentors who can help you along your career path.

Development is a complex, diversified, and dynamic business, but real estate professionals have a way of looking at it—sector by sector—that can help you understand and analyze the business and find career opportunities. Real estate offers careers in many fields and to help you in considering a real estate career, this chapter looks at development and developers sector by sector.

REAL ESTATE CAREER DECISION TREE

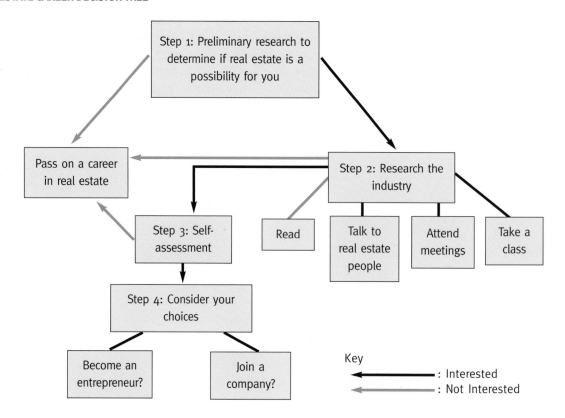

What Do Developers Do?

Developers can be individuals, small partnerships, or large companies. Some operate in a single market, such as Houston or Atlanta, while others focus on a larger region, such as the northeastern United States, or even on the entire country. A few U.S. developers operate globally.

Some developers maintain a small staff and outsource many development functions, while others employ a large number of professionals and perform most development functions in-house. Whatever their staffing policies, developers must know the local market—the city, suburb, or town where they plan to build—and establish good relationships with local land owners, lenders, investors, public officials, and other people who are essential to the success of a development project.

Developers start with the land on which they will build. To decide where to acquire land in a market, they first conduct a market study to determine the need for new (or rehabilitated) office buildings, shopping centers, housing, industrial parks, hotels, or other land uses. Their market research considers population and employment growth, other demographic

Q&A: Michael McKee

Vice chairman and chief operating officer of the Irvine Company (see company profile on p. 4), responsible for overseeing all company functions, including land development and asset management as well as administrative, financial, and legal affairs. Before joining the Irvine Company in 1994, managing partner of the Orange County office of Latham & Watkins, an international law firm, where he specialized in corporate finance matters with an emphasis on investment banker and public company representation.

"First jobs are always the most difficult. The most important thing is to get started."

What are some of the biggest issues facing the development industry today?

There is a need for broader understanding by public officials and the public as to how real estate really works. It's an organism that grows, changes, and adapts to its environment. Creating the right environment through intelligent land use planning and good design and architecture is essential to the health and growth of communities. Public officials and the public need to have a broader understanding of how the development process works. Development is an essentially organic process, changing and adapting in response to its environment.

What are some of the long-term concerns of the industry?

Changing the prevailing public perception that development is the enemy. Development must be seen as a friend. Cities, citizens, and developers need to cooperate in land use planning that achieves common goals and realizes common benefits.

Which real estate sectors have the greatest potential for long-term growth?

On the development side, large land banks are fewer and far between. The ability to do reuse projects, infill projects, and redevelopment will take on added importance. This is true for both residential and commercial development.

Which development companies will be most successful?

Companies that can deal with large-scale reuse and redevelopment. Companies that are able to conserve natural resources and address other environmentally sensitive issues. And companies that are able to grow internally or through joint ventures; this is because a number of development issues, such as infrastructure financing, are best addressed on a large scale.

What professional qualities characterize the most successful developers?

They have a very good sense of design and land use, and can see how to realize the most value from a piece of land. They know the communities where they plan to develop and what development products can create maximum value. They have a passion for what they do, and they sustain it throughout their careers. They work well with people, which is essential on large projects that may involve dealings with 40 to 50 government agencies.

What advice would you offer someone seeking a first job in the real estate industry?

First jobs are always the most difficult. The most important thing is to get started. Seek a position with a larger institution where you can meet lots of people. Success often comes from networking with work colleagues.

trends, the local economy, space supply and demand, and many other factors. Based on this market research, they evaluate a particular site—or alternative sites—for development.

Developers may find sites through land brokers, who specialize in finding owners who are interested in selling their land and finding buyers for these properties. Land brokers are highly knowledgeable about local property markets—what properties are for sale or might be for sale, who owns these properties, and who might be interested in buying them. They represent owners in finding buyers, negotiating terms of the sale, and closing the transaction. Developers may find properties through other sources as well, including other developers, real estate consultants, architects, accountants, lawyers, and government agencies.

CAREER TIP: If you think you would like to become a developer, think about how you would develop a property if you had the opportunity. Begin in your own neighborhood. Look around, find some vacant land or an old building that might be torn down, and think how you would develop the property from scratch. Apply your imagination. It's good preparation if you plan to work for a developer or start your own development business.

After deciding where they might want to build, developers decide what they might want to build, and whether to go ahead with the project. They conduct what's known as a financial feasibility study. They estimate the amount of capital required to acquire the land and develop the project (their costs) and how much money they can make from the project (their return).

Developers also conduct what are known as due-diligence studies to evaluate the risks of a development project. The use of sophisticated risk-analysis tools that are based on decades of experience enables them to quantify these risks. They cannot eliminate risk, but they try to minimize it.

The potential profits and the risks of land ownership and development are directly related: the greater the potential profits, the greater the risks. For example, if a developer pays $1 million for land that then appreciates in value to $2 million, it could simply sell the land for a $1 million profit.

But the developer may be able to realize substantially higher profits from developing the land and selling the completed office building, shopping center, or other product (or operating it for a time before selling it). However, the very high profit potential of development also entails high risks. Obtaining government approvals might take longer than anticipated, delaying the start of construction or even killing the project. Project costs might run over budget. Leasing might take more time than expected. The rents that tenants are willing to pay might be less than expected. Many things can go wrong, and developers have to decide how much risk they are willing to take to achieve their profit goals.

Once a developer has completed preliminary studies of a possible site, it may want to do further research and analysis before deciding on whether to go ahead with a project. If it prefers not to tie up a lot of money in buying the land or to have to sell the land if the project is a no-go, it may try to acquire what's known as an option to buy. Essentially, the developer persuades the seller to give the developer the right to buy the land for a specified period of time

Why would a landowner agree to tie up land in an option agreement? Because the developer gives the owner incentives, such as a payment for the option, a payment if it decides not to buy the property, or some of the profits from any development. To be sure, options are not always available. (In markets where developable land is much in demand, landowners may not offer options, giving developers no choice but to acquire land outright.)

During the option period, a developer conducts more detailed market and financial feasibility analysis and tries to assess the climate for obtaining the support of local business and community groups and project approvals from local and, if potentially necessary, state and federal agencies. The multiple approvals usually required for a development project—and the detailed conditions that must be met for approvals—make development a complex, difficult, and prolonged process.

If the developer decides to go ahead, it will exercise the option to buy and negotiate purchase terms with the owner. It might buy the land outright or it might enter into a partnership with the owner under which the owner typically would contribute the land and the developer would invest its own money. The developer usually would raise additional capital from other investors in exchange for interests in the partnership.

On some projects, developers may act as merchant builders. Merchant builders do not have their own money invested in a project; instead, they negotiate a contract with an owner to build a facility for a fee. The owner could be a corporation needing office or distribution space, a retail chain, or an apartment investor. The facility could be an office building or warehouse, a retail store, or an apartment building.

Developers are frequently redevelopers and renovators, especially in metropolitan areas where the supply of raw land is limited. In such areas, developers may acquire old, run-down, functionally obsolete, or partially vacant buildings, which they either tear down and replace or retain and renovate. For such properties, developers perform studies to determine the best use(s), such as rental apartments, condominiums, or a hotel; the market

for a new versus a renovated building; the cost of new development versus the cost of renovation; the projected rental stream from a new versus a renovated building; and what it will take to obtain approvals for a newly constructed building versus a rehabbed building.

CAREER TIP: Start as an assistant in a development company, helping with market analysis, feasibility studies, and due-diligence analysis. Take this opportunity to learn the development business and acquire experience in research, financial analysis, and other key areas of the business.

Old buildings—including those of historic value—usually can be acquired for substantially less than similar newer buildings in the same market, but they often require substantial investments in repairs and code compliance; electrical, air-conditioning, and heating systems upgrades; and energy efficiency. At the same time, market rental rates for older buildings may be lower than for newer buildings. To determine if they can meet their profit objectives, renovators must carefully compare the property's projected revenue stream from rentals and other sources with the cost of upgrading and operating the property.

Buildings of historical significance may be subject to preservation requirements. For example, their facades may have to be retained. But such special requirements usually do not limit their potential use. In fact, developers in New York, Chicago, St. Louis, Los Angeles, and a number of other cities are buying old or historic office buildings in prime locations and converting them to rental apartments or condominiums to meet an increasing demand for housing in downtowns.

DEVELOPMENT IS ABOUT VISION

Stan Ross
A key difference between people who are developers and people who are not is vision. Developers see opportunities in empty land or an underutilized or obsolete building. I learned this long ago when developer Ray Watt and I were looking at a raw piece of land. (Ray's company, Watt Communities, began in homebuilding in the late 1940s and is now a leading homebuilder and developer of commercial property in southern California.) As Ray and I were walking around the property, he turned to me and said: "Don't you see it?" I said: "See what?" He said: "Don't you see the housing, the town center, the schools, the lakes, the trees, the golf courses?" I replied: "All I see is rock, dust, and mud—and my shoes are dirty." Ray told me: "Stan, you made the right career choice in becoming an accountant."

What It Takes to Succeed as a Developer

Developers have a high degree of confidence, as they must. Their creations are highly visible, and their successes—or failures—are judged by their tenants and buyers, the businesses and employees that occupy their buildings, the store owners and shoppers in their retail centers, their bankers and partners, public regulatory agencies, and their neighbors, that is, by just about everyone in the community.

By nature, developers are optimists, more inclined to push ahead with projects than not. But they also are pragmatists. They have the discipline to say "no" when it becomes clear that a project won't work, for whatever reasons. (As a further safeguard, a developer's lenders monitor the project and may refuse to provide financing if they decide the project is not feasible.)

Q&A: Albert B. Ratner

Cochairman of the board of Forest City Enterprises. As a college student, drawn to real estate (a family business) at a time when no U.S. university offered a major in real estate. Instead, studied lumber merchandising and light house construction and graduated from Michigan State University in 1951 with a degree in forestry, going on to a lifelong career in real estate.

Forest City Enterprises

A publicly traded diversified real estate company that, under Ratner's direction, set out in the early 1980s to become a nationwide developer of major real estate projects. Today, Forest City holds more than $6.9 billion of completed properties (at cost) in its real estate portfolio, and has $1.2 billion of properties under construction and approximately $2 billion of properties under development. The company is active in 20 states and the District of Columbia and is involved in a number of major urban development projects, including the high-tech and academic MetroTech project in downtown Brooklyn, New York, the mixed-use Central Station project in Chicago, and the redevelopment of Stapleton International, Denver's former main airport.

"We have much to learn [about sustainable development] and young people will lead this effort."

Why did you decide on a career in real estate?

It was my family's business. For my generation, at least, real estate was the industry where people made millions and enjoyed doing it. We created great buildings and places that changed people's lives. Along the way, we met and partnered with some of the most interesting people in the world.

What does it take to succeed in real estate?

Whether you're an employee or an owner, you should have a passion for this business—the business of applying your imagination and creativity to a piece of raw land, designing and planning a project, and building a useful and desirable product. Passion means taking responsibility for the project's success.

How has the industry changed?

Today we know much more about sustainable development and about construction practices that are compatible with the environment. But this is just the beginning. We still have much to learn about applying good practices to the development process—and young people will lead this effort.

Where do you see opportunities in real estate?

According to some forecasts, the U.S. population will increase by 50 percent, or 133 million, over the next 50 years. That means there will be a huge demand for office, retail, hotel and resort, and other products—as well as for schools, hospitals, and other public facilities. Young people going into real estate will have a tremendous opportunity to apply their values in creating places for future Americans to live, work, and play.

Developers have patience. If they go ahead with a project, they must be prepared to wait months or years to start to realize a return on their investment of capital, time, and effort. And there are no guarantees. A project could be killed anywhere along the line for any number of reasons. Unexpected problems and challenges are inevitable with any project, and developers must be prepared to deal with them.

To obtain project approvals, developers have to be flexible and adaptable. Every project, large and small, affects a community to some degree. Public officials, community groups, neighbors, and many other stakeholders in the community want a voice in the project planning process. In order to win community support, developers must have the ability to work with a variety of people and the ability to communicate their vision for the project, address key issues, and seek solutions.

Product Sectors

Developers engage in either for-sale residential development or commercial development, which includes income-producing rental apartments. The "Real Estate Developers and Product" chart below shows the major products of residential and commercial developers, and the following sections provide further details.

Commercial Development

Commercial developers build income-producing properties. These may include shopping centers, office buildings and business parks, industrial buildings and campuses, rental apartment buildings, hotels, and mixed-use properties combining two or more different land uses, such as office and retail. These properties are called income-producing development because, once construction is completed, the developer or investor (if the project is sold to a property investor) earns income from renting space in the project and also from parking operations and the provision of other services. Each income-producing property sector is described in more detail in the following sections.

Retail. Most everyone has been to a shopping center. But what is a shopping center? Simply put, it's a group of retail and other commercial establishments that is planned, developed, owned, and managed as a single property.

REAL ESTATE DEVELOPERS AND PRODUCT

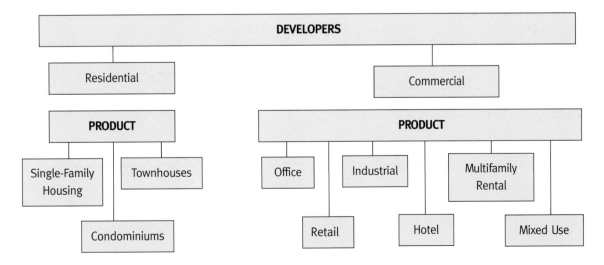

Company List: Commercial Developers and Investors

The following list of companies involved in commercial property development and investment represents only a small fraction of all such companies. Sources listed in appendix A tell you where to find more information about real estate companies and businesses, and the Web addresses of the companies on this list are provided in this appendix as well.

AEW Capital Management	Hines	RREEF North America
Apollo Real Estate Advisors	The Lefrak Organization	Silverstein Properties
Boston Capital	Legacy Partners	Trammell Crow
Colony Capital	Lincoln Property Company	Watson Land
Duke Realty	Lowe Enterprises	Westcore Properties

With consumer spending accounting for about two-thirds of the nation's GDP (gross domestic product), it's not surprising that shopping centers are big business. According to the International Council of Shopping Centers, there are more than 46,000 retail centers in the United States.

Shopping centers have a long history in the United States. They were preceded in the 1930s and 1940s by the large freestanding department stores that Sears Roebuck & Co. and Montgomery Ward started building. In the 1950s, the first shopping centers opened. They featured department stores as anchors surrounded by smaller stores. In the 1970s, the Rouse Company developed Faneuil Hall Marketplace in Boston, the first of the "festival" marketplaces developed in U.S. cities and a significant factor in the revitalization of downtown Boston. The 1980s brought factory outlet centers tenanted by manufacturers selling their own goods at discounted prices. Today there are more than 250 such centers in the United States. In the mid-1990s, the Mall of America was completed in Bloomington, Minnesota, a suburb of Minneapolis. The largest U.S. shopping mall, it includes an amusement park, nightclubs, and restaurants.

Shopping centers are either malls or strip centers. A mall is typically enclosed and features climate-controlled walkways linking the stores. A strip center is an attached row of stores or service outlets with on-site parking usually located in front of the stores. Open canopies may connect the storefronts, but a strip center lacks enclosed walkways. They are popular with shoppers because they are convenient and carry the basic necessities.

The "Retail Development Product" chart on the opposite page shows some of the many variations of strip centers and malls that make up the retail landscape. These include:

- convenience centers—containing a small number of stores anchored by a convenience store;
- neighborhood centers—typically anchored by a single supermarket;
- community centers—typically featuring two anchor tenants, such as a supermarket and a drugstore;
- regional centers—malls anchored by one or more department stores;
- super regional centers—larger than regional centers and typically featuring more anchors;
- fashion/specialty centers—higher-end, fashion-oriented stores with no primary anchors;
- power centers—centers dominated by a few large anchors, such as a discount department store or a warehouse club;
- big-box centers—centers anchored by major discounters and category killers, such as Wal-Mart, Home Depot, or Costco;
- theme/festival centers—tourist- and entertainment-oriented centers featuring a mix of stores and restaurants;
- outlet centers—manufacturer's outlet stores, typically in a rural location, with no primary anchors;
- lifestyle centers—high-end, leisure-oriented shops; and
- stores within a mixed-use project—the retail component of an integrated mixed-use development that also contains other uses, such as office space, residences, entertainment venues, or a hotel.

RETAIL DEVELOPMENT PRODUCT

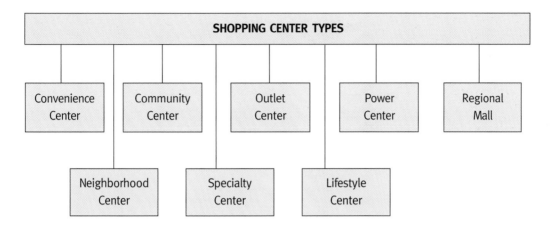

The development, ownership, and management of shopping centers is big business. Retail centers are developed by REITs (real estate investment trusts), private partnerships, and development companies. Retail developers decide where to build, what type of center to build, and how much square footage to include based on a thorough analysis of demographic trends, consumer spending patterns, market competition, vacancy rates, land acquisition and construction costs, financing availability and costs, and much other information. They pay close attention to the tenant mix, seeking to select tenants that will help the center maximize sales.

Most retail projects are developed on a preleased basis, meaning that the developer leases some of the space before starting construction. For most large projects, the developer first secures the anchor tenants, such as department stores, because they represent a commitment to leasing a large share of the space. Some retail projects are built on spec—meaning on a speculative basis, without preleasing. Such projects entail a much higher risk.

A number of retail developers focus on the redevelopment of existing centers. They specialize in renovation and the repositioning of a center in its marketplace to attract more customers and increase sales.

Office. The first skyscrapers built in the United States in the late 19th century were office buildings rising ten to 20 stories. Today's skyscrapers are of course much higher, and office buildings come in many shapes and sizes. Developers build huge multitenant office towers in the downtowns of major cities, mid- and low-rise office buildings in the suburbs

---

Company List: Regional Mall and Shopping Center REITs

The following list of regional mall and shopping center REITs (real estate investment trusts) represents only a small fraction of all such companies. Sources listed in appendix A tell you where to find more information about real estate companies and businesses, and the Web addresses of the companies on this list are provided in this appendix as well.

Caruso Affiliated	General Growth Properties	Pennsylvania REIT
CBL & Associates Properties	Kimco Realty Corporation	Simon Property Group
Developers Diversified Realty	The Macerich Company	Taubman Centers
Federal Realty Investment Trust	Mills Corporation	Weingarten Realty Investors
	New Plan Excel Realty Trust	Westfield America

OFFICE DEVELOPMENT PRODUCT

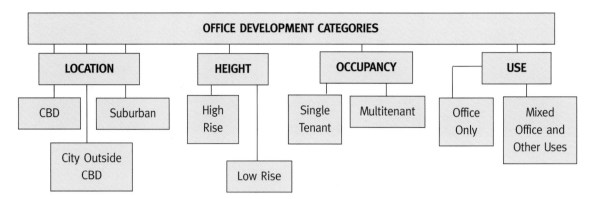

designed for multiple tenants or a single tenant, and build-to-suit properties for clients like a corporation or a group of health care professionals. Some office developments include other uses like industrial or retail. The tenants that occupy leasable space in office buildings cover a broad range from global corporations to small businesses and professional firms.

Overall employment is a key driver of demand for office space, but employment in specific office-oriented industries and businesses is an even more important demand driver. The finance, insurance, and real estate (FIRE) sector is one of the major generators of office-using jobs.

Professionals involved in office development and leasing typically segment the office space market into classes—A, B, or C—based on the location, age, physical condition, construction material, finishes, HVAC (heating, ventilating, and air-conditioning) system, and other qualities of available buildings. Class A buildings are the newest properties that attract the most creditworthy tenants, offer the best loca-

tions, and command the highest rents. Class B buildings are generally older, well-located, and well-maintained properties that exhibit little deterioration or functional obsolescence. They offer lower rents than class A properties. Class C buildings are usually the oldest buildings in a market. They are found in less desirable locations, are often functionally obsolete, and offer the lowest rents.

The developers of office space include private partnerships and companies as well as REITs. Developers may partner with institutions, such as pension funds or universities, to develop office properties. The institution typically provides much of the equity capital for the project and the developer contributes expertise and a share of the required capital.

In considering office projects in specific local markets, developers look at current and projected employment growth, trends in business growth, the costs of doing business and leasing space, the competitive market for office space, office vacancy rates, the supply of prospective tenants, and many other factors.

Company List: Office Developers and Investors

The following list of companies involved in office property development and investment represents only a small fraction of all such companies. Sources listed in appendix A tell you where to find more information about real estate companies and businesses, and the Web addresses of the companies on this list are provided in this appendix as well.

Boston Properties	Mack-Cali Realty Corporation	Shorenstein
Crescent Real Estate Equities	Maguire Properties	Tishman Speyer Properties
The Durst Organization	Rockefeller Development Corporation	Trizec Properties

INDUSTRIAL DEVELOPMENT PRODUCT

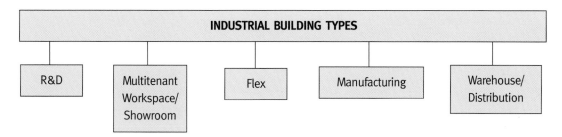

In markets with an excess of office space, developers may find opportunities in the redevelopment of existing office buildings—particularly older buildings in secondary locations, which often can be acquired at lower costs than better-located, newer buildings in the same market.

Industrial. Industrial real estate encompasses land and buildings used for or suited for industrial activities. The main product categories include:

- warehouses and distribution centers—buildings used for the storage and distribution of goods; such facilities include regional warehouses, bulk warehouses, distribution centers designed for heavy goods, refrigerated distribution buildings, and automated high-rack distribution buildings;
- manufacturing properties—buildings designed to accommodate manufacturing and related processes;
- flex space—buildings that can accommodate office, warehousing, and possibly R&D functions;
- multitenant workspace/showroom facilities—buildings designed for customer-oriented small manufacturing or assembly tenants; they often include showroom space for displaying the tenants' products;
- R&D and other specialized workspaces—buildings designed, built, and managed for specialized uses such as biotech or high-tech R&D or the manufacture of computer, pharmaceutical, or similar products.

The developers and owners of industrial space are mainly private partnerships and companies, REITs, and opportunity funds. They may be local firms specializing in a particular geographic market or national companies that oper-

ate in markets across the country. They may partner with institutions or other capital sources in joint ventures.

Industrial property is built either on a speculative basis or on a build-to-suit basis for specific corporate or business clients. Compared with most other kinds of property, industrial space can be constructed in a short amount of time, so industrial developers can sell or lease their buildings more quickly and adapt more quickly to changes in market demand and economic cycles. Also, the cost of building, buying, and managing industrial properties is often lower than for other types of real estate.

Although industrial development can be accomplished comparatively quickly and economically, it still requires detailed market, economic, and feasibility analyses. Industrial developers must determine the best location for a project, the demand for space, the type of product to be built, who are the prospective tenants (and whether to seek a build-to-suit client or to build on spec), the supply of space and vacancy rates in the market, the competing properties,

CAREER TIP: Working for an industrial developer can give you exposure to interesting product lines, such as state-of-the-art manufacturing or distribution facilities or R&D facilities for cutting-edge industries, such as pharmaceuticals or biotechnology. It can also connect you with the corporate world.

Company List: Industrial Developers and Investors

The following list of companies involved in industrial property development and investment represents only a small fraction of all such companies. Sources listed in appendix A tell you where to find more information about real estate companies and businesses, and the Web addresses of the companies on this list are provided in this appendix as well.

AMB Property Corporation
Bedford Property Investors
Cabot Properties
CenterPoint Properties Trust
EastGroup Properties

First Industrial Realty Trust
Highwoods Properties
Hillwood
Kilroy Realty Corporation
Koll Development Company

Majestic Realty
ProLogis
Rockefeller Development
 Corporation

---

and so on. Site selection is particularly important; access to freeways, arterials, and rail transportation is often a key determinant of a project's success. Industrial developers concern themselves with local retail sales as well, since retail sales are an indicator of demand for warehouse and distribution space for consumer goods.

Hotel. Hotels and resort properties are developed by private partnerships, private developers, REITs, and others. Some developers also own hotel properties. Developers or owners typically contract with an operator—which can be a global hotel chain or a firm operating only in a local market—to manage hotel properties. Operators manage the daily operations of the lodging facility, hire and supervise staff, and establish budgets and pricing.

The main types of hotel properties include:

- convention hotels—offering 400 to 500 rooms plus considerable banquet and meeting space along with many in-house or nearby dining and drinking options; usually connected to a convention center;
- commercial hotels—containing 100 to 500 rooms with banquet and meeting space that caters to smaller business groups; more limited food and beverage services;
- luxury hotels—offering fewer than 300 rooms with high-quality furnishings, amenities, and services; typically located in large metropolitan areas;
- budget/economy hotels—containing 50 to 150 rooms with limited services and no restaurants or meeting space; average room rates are typically 20 to 50 percent below the rates of full-service hotels in the same area; usually located along highways outside central cities; further segmented into upper-, mid-, and lower-price tiers;
- all suites—offering rooms that are larger than normal and have a living area and separate kitchen area; target markets are long-stay business travelers and families; further segmented into urban, suburban, and residential markets; and
- conference centers—ranging from 200 to 400 rooms and providing a large number of dedicated meeting rooms plus food and beverage services; marketed as self-contained, distraction-free environments for executive and professional meetings and events; typically located in rural or suburban office districts in or near major metropolitan areas.

HOTEL DEVELOPMENT PRODUCT

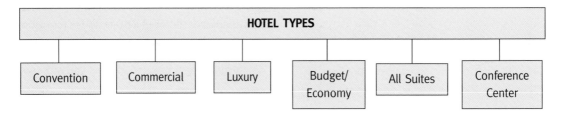

Company List: Hotel Owners

The following list of hotel owners represents only a small fraction of all such companies. Sources listed in appendix A tell you where to find more information about real estate companies and businesses, and the Web addresses of the companies on this list are provided in this appendix as well.

Accor North America	FelCor Lodging Trust	MeriStar Hospitality
American Property	Hersha Group	Corporation
Management Corporation	Hilton Hotels Corporation	Peabody Hotel Group
Baymont Inns	Host Marriott Corporation	Suburban Franchise Systems
Boykin Lodging Company	Innkeepers USA Trust	Tharaldson Lodging
Capital Hotel Management	InterContinental Hotels Group	Tishman Hotel Corporation
LLC	Jameson Inns	White Lodging Services
CNL Hospitality Corp.	LaSalle Hotel Properties	Corporation
Cooper Companies	Lodgian	Winegardner & Hammons
Equity Inns	Loews Hotels	

In deciding whether to develop or buy a hotel, developers and owners are concerned with the same types of market and feasibility issues, such as the right location for the property, that concern the developers of other commercial real estate products. The brand name (flag) of the operator is of special concern, because that name can affect how the hotel is perceived by the market, its ability to attract guests, and the room rates that it can charge.

Multifamily Rental. Multifamily buildings—defined by the U.S. Bureau of the Census as residential structures with five or more dwelling units—containing rental apartments are considered to be commercial real estate. (Condominium and cooperative apartment buildings are categorized as noncommercial residential real estate.) Multifamily rental developments can take many forms. They are commonly classified by size and density (the number of dwelling units per acre), and the main product types include:

■ garden apartments—the most common form of multifamily development in the United States; typically one- to three-story buildings with landscaped common areas; often clustered in small groups to resemble master-planned, single-family developments in scope and layout; their density is typically higher than the density

of single-family housing and lower than the density of mid- and high-rise apartments;

■ mid-rise apartments—three- to eight-story buildings;

■ high-rise apartments—eight-story or higher buildings; density may exceed 100 units per acre;

■ townhouse apartments—usually share a ground-to-roof wall; units typically include an individual garage, a walk-up entrance, and a private outdoor area; density is typically lower than the density of garden or mid-rise apartments;

■ special-purpose multifamily housing—including, for example, nursing homes, housing for seniors, mobile-home parks, and retirement homes.

Developers and owners of multifamily rental properties include private partnerships and companies and REITs. Some developers and owners specialize in this market. Private or institutional investors may participate in joint ventures with developers to build apartment projects, or they may acquire apartment developments that are up and running.

Apartment project developers and investors address many of the same market and feasibility questions that other developers address. Employment trends, which influence demand for rental units, are of particular concern. So are interest rates. When rates are low and for-sale housing is relatively affordable, households may elect to buy rather than rent.

Q&A: **Alan Casden**

Chairman and chief executive officer of Casden Properties LLC. Member of many advisory boards, including the National Multi Family Housing Conference, the California Senate Advisory Commission on Cost Control in State Government, and the President's Council of the California Building Industry Association. Long affiliation with the University of Southern California, starting with a cum laude degree from the Leventhal School of Accounting in 1968; member of the university's board of trustees; endower of the Alan Casden Dean's Chair at the Leventhal School of Accounting; endower of the Casden Institute for the Study of the Jewish Role in American Life; and creator of a major real estate forecast study within USC's Lusk Center for Real Estate.

Casden Properties LLC

One of the largest residential property developers in the United States, with a portfolio of about 90,000 multifamily apartment units representing a total acquisition and development cost of approximately $8 billion.

"Development is a highly entrepreneurial business with great growth opportunities, as well as an exciting process involving decision making."

What would you tell students who ask whether accounting and consulting are good career paths into real estate?

When I started as an accountant with Kenneth Leventhal & Company, most of our clients were real estate developers, including the largest homebuilders in the United States. Working with these clients gave me an inside look at the vision, goals, organization, and management of these companies. At the time, their finance departments were very unsophisticated. As outside advisers, we were able to help developer clients create more sophisticated financial tools and systems to analyze the financial implications of potential transactions, evaluate risks and rewards, and make better business decisions.

As an outside accountant, what did you learn about real estate companies?

Just talking with the executives of our client companies and sitting in on their management meetings was educational. As an auditor and a tax consultant, I was able to review potential transactions, see the decision-making processes, and suggest how to structure transactions.

Why did you move from accounting into development?

Development is a highly entrepreneurial business with great growth opportunities as well as an exciting process involving decisions from whether to buy a piece of land to what to build on it. The development business is like the motion picture business. Just as each picture—even a sequel—is different, each property is different in its location and other characteristics. Having to deal with constantly changing challenges is what sets movie producers and developers apart.

How did you decide what to develop?

I started by developing rental apartments and branched into for-sale homes. It took a lot of time and effort. I learned from other developers, especially the Irvine Company.

What are the most important factors for success in real estate?

One of the most important is an understanding of the financial implications of development. You have to determine whether your costs align with the expected sale price of the finished product. Because this is a dynamic equation, you have to update cost information and sales estimates throughout the development process. Many times, developers end up with higher-than-expected costs and struggle with the question of whether to raise sale prices or reduce costs. In selling, I always assume the worst, and I'm surprised if my sale prices are higher than I anticipated.

What do you look for in hiring graduates?

Quantitative and verbal reasoning skills, writing skills, and the ability to do research and make corresponding judgments.

MULTIFAMILY RENTAL DEVELOPMENT PRODUCT

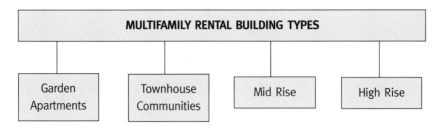

Conversely, when interest rates and the price of for-sale housing are relatively high, households are more likely to rent.

Mixed Use. A development that contains two or more integrated land uses is called a mixed-use development. Among the possible components of a mixed-use project are office uses, retail and entertainment uses, hotels, a resort, and housing (either single-family or multifamily housing). Some projects include office and retail uses; others combine a hotel with retail uses; and still others mix retail and entertainment uses with office space.

Mixed-use projects can be large complexes spread over many acres or buildings that occupy a single block. They can be found in many kinds of locations, including suburbs, inner cities, and resort areas. Some are built from scratch on raw land. Others reuse underutilized land (such as inner-city railyards) and buildings (such as train stations). Some mixed-use projects are structured as public/private partnerships and include public facilities, such as a sports stadium or a

convention center. Some are oriented to public transportation facilities like commuter-train stations, subway stops, or intermodal terminals.

Compared with single-use projects, the financing of mixed-use projects is more complicated. The projected rental stream, tenant base, and other performance measures of each component property type must be analyzed. Furthermore, lenders and investors must be able to separate out their collateral. The developers of these projects face the challenge of finding different types of tenants for each use. Despite the heightened challenges, mixed-use projects offer opportunities for developers and owners to attract a broader, more diversified tenant base and to generate more income than a single-use project could achieve.

For-Sale Residential Development

Residential developers develop land for housing construction. They buy the land; obtain government approvals to build housing; construct roads; install water and sewer lines,

---

Company List: Rental Apartment Developers and Investors

The following list of companies involved in multifamily rental property development and investment represents only a small fraction of all such companies. Sources listed in appendix A tell you where to find more information about real estate companies and businesses, and the Web addresses of the companies on this list are provided in this appendix as well.

Apartment Investment &
   Management
Archstone-Smith Trust
AvalonBay Communities
Boston Capital
BRE Properties

Camden Property Trust
Equity Residential
Essex Property Trust
Gables Residential Trust
Post Properties
Related Capital Company

Sentinel Real Estate
   Corporation
SunAmerica Affordable
   Housing Partners
United Dominion Realty Trust
Wachovia

streetlights, and other necessary infrastructure; grade and otherwise prepare the land for construction; subdivide the land into individual lots; and sell the land to homebuilders. In some cases, residential developers partner with homebuilders to construct the housing as well.

Homebuilding companies build and sell single-family houses, townhouses, or condominium apartments. Some are local operations that build 50 to 100 units a year; others are large, national companies that build thousands of homes annually in multiple markets.

Like other sectors in real estate, the homebuilding business is consolidating. The 20 largest builders have about a 22 percent share of the new single-family housing market in the United States, and they are continuing to increase their market share by acquiring smaller players. The largest companies benefit from size and economies of scale. Their homebuilding costs are usually lower and their access to capital is usually easier—and they can get it at lower rates. Smaller builders stay competitive by drawing on their knowledge of local markets; capitalizing on niche opportunities, such as a small but well-located tract of land that might not interest a larger builder; or specializing in a niche market, such as custom homes.

To finance construction, small homebuilders usually borrow from banks and other lenders. Large, public homebuilders typically raise capital in the equity or debt markets and may also obtain construction financing from lenders.

Homebuilding companies typically subcontract the construction work to carpenters, plumbers, electricians, and other tradespeople. Homebuilders manage the construction and sales process. Their specific activities include scheduling and maintaining construction timetables, supervising subcontractors, buying construction materials and supplies, marketing, and providing customer service to buyers. Homebuilders may have their own in-house marketing team, or they may outsource the marketing function to third-party brokers.

In markets where demand for housing is very strong, builders may presell houses by signing sales contracts with buyers before construction begins or while it is in progress. In other markets, houses are first completed and then sold. Builders are paid in full at the close of sale. Buyers typically

Career Profile: **Daniel Pfeffer**

Daniel Pfeffer, CEO of New York–based Midtown Equities, a private real estate development and investment firm, originally planned to be a doctor, but eventually he found his calling in real estate.

While he was studying under the auspices of an undergraduate fellowship in neurosurgery at New York Hospital Cornell Medical Center, Pfeffer had a chance to observe firsthand the construction of a medical building. For him, this was a revelational experience.

A Learning Process
Intrigued by the building process that he observed unfolding, Pfeffer decided to learn more about construction and real estate, a decision that led him to take a position with Kenneth Leventhal & Company, a real estate accounting and consulting firm, where he worked on REIT structurings and real estate dispositions.

In 1987, Pfeffer started with Manufacturers Hanover in its financial training program. Because of the global stock market crash that occurred at about this time, he spent the next five years on workouts and bankruptcy reorganizations, with a focus on hotel clients. This work taught him much about how companies operate and how they can get into trouble—and out of trouble as well.

While at the bank, Pfeffer began part-time studies for an MBA. He switched to a full-time program and, after earning his degree, joined a leading investment bank where he worked on REIT IPOs and other deals. After a few years, he tired of this work and moved to GE Capital, where he initially was involved in buying heavily discounted real estate securities and later in new business development.

A Change in Direction
One night, Pfeffer received a phone call from Joe Cayre, founder and chairman of Midtown Equities. Cayre had made his fortune in videotape movie sales, video games,

---

Company List: Homebuilders

The following list of homebuilders represents only a small fraction of all such companies. Sources listed in appendix A tell you where to find more information about real estate companies and businesses, and the Web addresses of the companies on this list are provided in this appendix as well.

Beazer Homes USA	John Laing Homes	Pulte Homes
Centex Corporation	KB Home	The Ryland Group
D.R. Horton	Lennar Corporation	Shea Homes
Hovnanian Enterprises	Lyon Homes	Toll Brothers
	NVR Inc.	

---

put a down payment on a house and secure a mortgage(s) from banks or other mortgage lenders to cover the balance of the sale price. Some large builders may provide buyer financing through a mortgage-financing subsidiary or an affiliated third-party lender.

record labels, and real estate. "Are you ready to become an entrepreneur?" Cayre asked. "I've been ready all my life," replied Pfeffer. He joined Midtown Equities as CEO.

Like many entrepreneurs, Cayre had been focused on creating businesses and doing deals. Midtown's investment portfolio contained a variety of attractive assets, but lacked a plan, a sense of direction. Pfeffer worked with Cayre to restructure and reposition the company, clean up its balance sheet, dispose of personal guarantees, and refinance or dispose of assets—a process that took a number of years. Finally, in Pfeffer's words, they "opened the company for new business."

This new business has involved investment in a number of development projects and property acquisitions in New York, Miami, Houston, and other U.S. cities. Among other projects, Midtown and its partners are developing a $1 billion mixed-use project in Miami on the site of a former railroad yard, one of the largest undeveloped parcels of land in the city. Attracted by the company's successful track record, developers and investors often pitch proposed deals, most of which, Pfeffer says, Midtown turns down for a variety of reasons.

Career Lessons

In Pfeffer's view, development is the most preferable choice of careers within the field of real estate. "Development," he argues, "is the most creative and opportunistic area of real estate." And he thinks that a knowledge of finance is a good route into development. "You must have a fundamental understanding of finance" in order to know where to get financing, how to negotiate with capital providers, and how to structure deals. As a developer, "you need to structure transactions that consider the perspective of investors and lenders. They'll be appreciative and more receptive to your proposals."

Q&A: John F. Shea

Chairman of J. F. Shea Co., a diversified family-owned company. Learned the real estate business from the bottom up, starting—when he was in high school—with a job in a Shea company parts warehouse.

J. F. Shea Co.

One of the oldest and largest private companies in the United States, with interests in homebuilding, civil engineering, construction contracting, commercial property investment, and other businesses. John F. Shea's grandfather started J. F. Shea Co. as a plumbing business in 1881, when Thomas Edison was beginning to use electricity to light commercial buildings.

"Starting out, you don't want to get locked into a job that's too narrow."

Your company is more than 100 years old. What's your secret of success?

There are three. Caring for our customers and employees. Diversification in businesses that fit our skills. Finally, lots of good fortune.

What businesses are you in today?

We are the largest privately held homebuilder in the United States. We are also involved in apartments, shopping centers, and commercial and industrial centers. We have long been involved in heavy engineering construction work—particularly in underground work—and have become one of the largest contractors in the country. We have been an investor in Venture Capital—a Shea division—for about 25 years.

What has been your biggest challenge?

Execution. Successful execution involves estimating construction costs, buying land, building efficiently, marketing, selling, financing, et cetera, et cetera. As a private company, we also find it difficult to accomplish growth and, at the same time, maintain an investment-grade balance sheet.

What's the best starting point in real estate—a small or a large company?

Starting out, you probably would learn more from a small company, unless you happen to find a big company that will train you, help you to learn, and give you a variety of jobs. You don't want to get locked into a job that's too narrow. Real estate is a vast industry, and it is advantageous to have a broad understanding of the business.

What does it take to succeed in real estate?

If you want to do well in real estate—or in any business—and be a leader, you must have excellent people skills. I've known people who were very bright but failed in business because they weren't able to connect with other people. You must have a solid understanding of finance. It's also important to get into the field and learn how to build from start to finish. Then, when you're talking to architects or contractors, you will understand what goes into building a home, an apartment complex, or a commercial development.

Where do you see future opportunities in real estate? In what product lines?

With the oldest baby boomers reaching retirement age and millions more to follow in coming years, active adult and assisted-living projects have very good futures. We're expanding our investment in active adult development and we're optimistic about it. One of the problems with developments for seniors, though, is high capital requirements.

Chapter 3
A Look at Real Estate Investment and Ownership, Financing, and Services

As has been noted, real estate comprises two main businesses: development and ownership. The last chapter looked at the development business. This chapter looks at the ownership business. It also covers the major supplementary real estate businesses that fall under the rubrics of debt financing and real estate services. Supplementary real estate businesses include the companies and professional firms that support the business activities of developers and investors/owners. Financing and real estate services—including accounting, appraisal, asset management, brokerage, consulting, design and engineering, law, marketing, property management, security, and information technology—offer a variety of real estate career opportunities.

Real Estate Investment Basics

In contrast to developers, who acquire land and build on it, investors acquire existing (built) buildings. Investors may be individuals, partnerships, real estate investment trusts (REITs), real estate companies, or pension funds. They buy, own, and manage office buildings, shopping centers, industrial and warehouse properties, rental apartments, and other income-producing real estate. They receive income from renting space and providing parking and other services to tenants.

Investors may focus on properties in a single market, such as Denver or Minneapolis; in multiple U.S. markets, such as throughout the Pacific Northwest or the Southeast; or in the entire United States. Many U.S.-based investors operate globally as well. Investors may own a single building or a large portfolio of properties. Some investors specialize in a certain type of property, such as retail; others invest in a variety of property types, such as multifamily, retail, and office. Some owners also are developers.

Regardless of how many properties they own or in how many markets they operate, investors and owners must have a thorough knowledge of local market conditions and they must carefully evaluate the potential profits and risks of each particular property. Buying a building usually is not as risky as developing a new building. But the tradeoff for lower risk is that an owner's returns (profits), although often attractive, are usually less than a developer's returns.

Many considerations go into an investor's decision on whether to buy specific properties. In considering a property acquisition, investors must address two important questions: Can tenants be found? Can the required rents be achieved? Most buildings that interest investors are already partially or mostly occupied. But can tenants be found for the remaining space? Will tenants sign new leases as their current leases expire, or will they move out, requiring the owner to find new tenants? How much rent will tenants pay? Relatively low rents may fill a building, but they may not generate enough income to cover the building's operating expenses and realize the owner's profit goals.

Investors also have to consider the cost of acquiring specific properties. A new office building located in a CBD and filled with blue-chip corporate tenants will have higher rents and command a higher price than an older building in a neighborhood outside of downtown. They must also consider the operating costs—including tenant-improvement allowances (the allowances that owners give tenants to refurbish their space as an inducement for signing a lease), utilities, maintenance, and security.

The ownership of income-producing properties is generally in the form of a partnership or a corporation. In a partnership (also called a joint venture), two or more persons agree to invest their capital in the acquisition and ownership of a property or properties. All of the partners are responsi-

---

CAREER TIP: You can jump into real estate quickly. Simply buy a building.

---

ble for the partnership's debts and liabilities. The income or loss from the property(ies) is passed through to the partners, and the partnership entities do not pay tax.

In a limited liability partnership (LLP), a general partner manages the investment for the partners and has unlimited legal responsibility for the partnership's debts and liabilities. The other partners are limited partners whose liability is limited to what they have invested. The limited partners are passive investors, meaning that they do not actively participate in the management of the partnership.

A corporation—a legal entity separate and distinct from its owners—is the most common form of business ownership for public real estate companies. For shareholders, a C corporation has the advantage that they are not personally liable for the corporation's debts and liabilities. A disadvantage of a C corporation is double taxation—it pays a tax on its corporate income and its shareholders pay income tax on dividends received.

By contrast, for tax purposes limited liability corporations (LLCs) are treated like partnerships. Their profits (and losses) are distributed to their members, who pay taxes on their share of the partnership's profits or take deductions on their share of its losses. The most common form of private ownership, an LLC is like a regular corporation. It is a separate legal entity that is managed by its members, who are not personally liable for its obligations.

Another form of ownership is the Subchapter S corporation (S corporation), which enjoys the benefits of a corporation but is taxed as if it were a partnership, thereby avoiding double taxation. All profits and losses of an S corporation flow through to the individual income tax returns of the shareholders, and the corporation itself pays no taxes. An S corporation must comply with numerous rules. For example, it can have no more than 75 shareholders.

In the past, most real estate investments were structured as partnerships created by investors (and developers) to own an individual development project or property. Such a property-by-property approach to investment enabled investors to limit their risks; if a single partnership failed, it would not bring down the other partnerships.

The partnership structure worked well for managing small, local projects that were financed mainly through local lenders and investors. But as developers and owners became involved in more numerous, larger, and more dispersed projects, they found themselves in charge of increasingly complex labyrinths of partnerships and cross-ownership structures. As a result, they sometimes had difficulty obtaining financing from lenders and investors who could not find their way through the labyrinth to see the big picture of the developer's or owner's overall financial soundness.

As their businesses continued to grow and their financing needs increased, some developers and owners restructured their partnerships and consolidated them under the umbrella of C corporations, thus creating ownership structures and balance sheets that were more transparent to lenders and investors. This gave developers and owners broader access to capital, which allowed them to raise larger amounts of capital and reduce capital costs.

Developers and owners today have a great deal of flexibility in their choice of ownership and investment structures. Depending on their development or investment goals, capital needs, and other criteria, they can use partnerships, LLPs, C corporations, S corporations, or LLCs to develop a small one-off project or a series of projects, to acquire a single property or a portfolio of properties, or to invest locally, regionally, nationally, or even globally.

WHO OWNS REAL ESTATE?

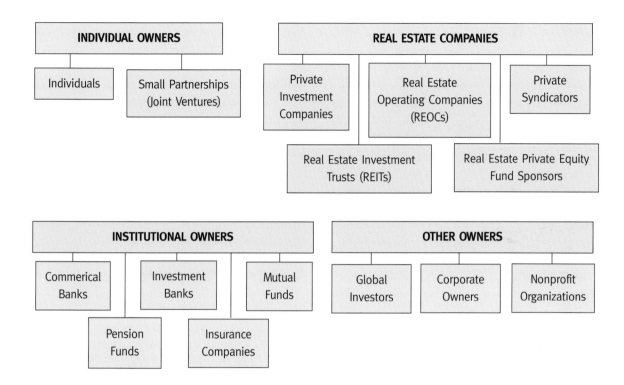

Who Owns Real Estate?

The owners of investment real estate cover a wide range of types, from individual investors and small partnerships, to real estate companies, a variety of major institutional investors, non–real estate corporations, and nonprofit organizations.

Individual Investors and Small Partnerships

Individual Investors. Across the United States, thousands of individuals own—either by themselves or with other individuals—apartment buildings, office buildings, retail centers, developable land, and other commercial real estate properties. These owners are of various ages, income levels, ethnicities, and educational backgrounds. They include both native-born Americans and immigrants. They

work in a variety of professions and trades. They may be retired or still in school or at-home parents.

Individuals invest in real estate for many reasons: to build wealth, save for retirement, create endowments for their children, supplement their incomes, diversify their investments. Many invest for the satisfaction of owning a piece of real estate. They may feel that real estate, as compared with, say, a Fortune 500 corporation, is something about which they have firsthand knowledge, because all of them are familiar with real estate in some way—from where they live, work, shop, travel, or play. As individual investors, they generally concentrate on a particular market, and—at least initially—own only a single property, such as an apartment building or a motel, or a small number of income-producing properties.

Some individual investors have used their initial experience in property investing to launch careers in real estate.

High-Net-Worth Individual Investors. In 2002, more than 2 million high-net-worth individuals (individuals with financial assets, not counting their real estate investments, of at least $1 million) lived in the United States, and they had an average of 15 percent of their wealth invested in real estate. In addition to directly acquiring properties, these individuals invest through private partnerships and public companies, such as real estate investment trusts.

Many high-net-worth investors hire advisers—either full-service financial consultants or specialized real estate consultants—to provide real estate investment guidance; or they invest in private real estate funds. Advisers develop customized real estate investment strategies for their high-net-worth clients and, in consultation with their clients, execute these strategies by buying, selling, and managing properties and arranging financing. These strategies are often closely linked with the individual's tax and estate plans.

Some ultrawealthy individuals establish their own real estate investment companies that serve largely the same functions as a third-party real estate adviser, except they have only one client. These personal or family investment companies frequently are driven by a social agenda in addition to a financial agenda. Magic Johnson's Johnson Development Corporation, for example, develops entertainment complexes, restaurants, and retail centers in underserved urban communities, as well as in suburban communities. Shamrock Holdings, the private investment entity of the Roy E. Disney family, has invested in the Genesis L.A. Real Estate Funds, which were created to raise capital for investment in real estate projects in low- to moderate-income neighborhoods in southern California.

Small Partnerships (Joint Ventures). When a limited number of investors contribute their capital and expertise to pursue small investment opportunities, such as the acquisition and management of a ten-unit apartment building or a small strip shopping center, they are participating in a joint venture or small partnership. The most common legal structures for these partnerships are LLPs, LLCs, and S corporations.

Joint venture participants include the general partner and the equity investors (limited partners), who may be high-net-worth individuals, other individual investors, or institutional investors. Before the general partner gets a share of the profits, the limited partners typically recover their capital investment and perhaps receive an initial return. Partnerships often hire or contract with professionals for a variety of services, including accounting, brokerage, construction and construction management, engineering, environmental impact studies, economic feasibility studies, insurance, legal services, market research and analysis, project financing, and property management.

Because of their small size, partnerships are able to quickly identify and capitalize on market opportunities, develop and implement investment strategies, and put together deal and financing structures.

Real Estate Companies

Private Investment Companies. Private investment companies, a.k.a. private real estate companies or real estate funds, are similar to small partnerships, but they operate on a larger scale. They typically have more investors, often including high-net-worth individuals as well as institutional investors, such as pension funds. They raise more capital than do small partnerships, and they invest in more and larger development projects and property acquisitions, which they either hold for income or resell for gain.

Like small partnerships, private investment companies are usually structured as LLCs, with a general partner and limited partners. Each has its own investment strategies and objectives, and these can vary widely from company to company. Private investment companies may be involved in every type of income-producing property, as well as in land development and redevelopment projects. They may also form joint ventures with government agencies to develop or acquire properties.

Typically, the partners in a private investment company require a return of the equity they've invested as well as a percentage of the partnership's profits. In addition to equity contributions by the partners, banks, or other financial institutions, these companies often provide financing to help cover development or acquisition costs.

Q&A: **Bruce Karatz**

Chairman and CEO of KB Home, a leading U.S. homebuilder. Graduate of Boston University. Law degree from the University of Southern California. Short stint with a law firm before joining KB Home in 1972; named CEO in 1985 and chairman in 1993.

"The people who move up the ladder in our company just love being in the game. Homebuilding is not a job. It's a way of life."

How did you develop an interest in real estate?

Through my dad. He developed some small hotel projects, including the Scottsdale Hilton, which still stands today.

What was your first brush with real estate?

In 1970, I joined Keating & Sterling, a law firm specializing in securities work. One day, a colleague who knew something about condo conversions in Philadelphia, where he grew up, and I decided to buy and convert three small apartment buildings in Santa Monica. But the idea fell through.

How did you join Kaufman & Broad?

In 1972, a headhunter called to say he was recruiting for an associate corporate counsel at Kaufman & Broad, a hot young company. I didn't know the company, and I told the recruiter that a company job really wasn't my thing. In those days lawyers who left law firms to go to companies were lawyers who didn't make partner. The recruiter asked how many clients I had brought into the law firm. After I said: "Wait a minute, I just started," he asked again: "Have you have brought in any clients?" to which I replied: "No." He said: "Well, I'm giving you an opportunity to meet with the CEO of one of the hottest companies in Los Angeles, and you're telling me you're too busy?" I was persuaded to go to an interview, and then they invited me back and made me an offer. I decided to accept. When I told my friends I wasn't getting paid much more than at the law firm, they thought I was cuckoo. But I wanted to get into the building business.

As a new counsel at Kaufman & Broad, what was your next move?

After a couple of months at the company, I decided I wanted to move from legal to operations. I was working late one night when the CEO stopped by and asked how I was doing. When I told him I'd really like to get into operations, he said: "Bruce, you just got here. Would you cool your jets?" Several months later, I was working late again and had the same conversation with the CEO, who said: "You're really serious, aren't you?" and responded to my "I am" with "Okay, you asked for it." He sent me down to our Irvine division as a land/entitlement guy. After I had been there a year, he asked me if I wanted to start up a business in France. At the time, K&B had an established business in Paris and I was assigned to develop our business in the provinces, which, management thought, offered an opportunity for growth.

How did that work out?

After two years, our Lyon and Marseille businesses were prospering, delivering as many homes in those two cities as the company was building in Paris. Then the president of K&B France, to whom I reported, resigned to start a competing business. When Eli Broad came to Paris to recruit a successor, I suggested to him that I was the right person for the job. He couldn't easily find a more experienced candidate, and so reluctantly made me president of K&B France, a position I held for five years before I returned to the United States to head up all the company's real estate activities. After another five years of hard work through the housing recession of the early 1980s, Eli Broad and I agreed to spin off the housing company and create two NYSE companies: K&B Home and Kaufman & Broad.

What does it take to succeed in homebuilding?

The people who move up the ladder in our company just love being in the game. If they're looking for land, they

—continued

Q&A: **Bruce Karatz**

continued

could spend all day and night at it. If they're developing property, they go out to the site and meet with everyone involved in the project, from the engineers to the graders. They understand the importance of building homes for people. This is not a job. It's a way of life.

Would you advise students who are interested in development to go with a large company like K&B or with a small entrepreneur?

With a bigger company. If you're ambitious and work hard, you will have more opportunities to move along faster in a large company than if you are working for a guy who may pay you more initially but is calling all the shots.

In a large company, does it matter where you start in order to get experience?

No matter what you're doing, figure out who the stars are in your department. Watch how they talk, what they do, how they manage, what they know. You can learn a lot if you view your position as a steppingstone for something bigger, even if you don't know what it is. Do everything you are asked to do—and more. Does someone need help on Saturday? Or with selling homes in a new community the company just opened? If you're on a mission to advance in your career, you could learn more in two years than most people learn in four, five, or six years.

Will such extra effort be noticed in a big company?

Absolutely.

What other personal or professional characteristics are important?

Fully complete the job assigned to you. That sounds elementary, but it's amazing how many people do only 85 percent of a job. If you want to be on a fast track to success, you have to be the go-to person. Regardless of the complexity of the project, people need to know that you are going to get it done.

Is there any special knowledge required in the homebuilding business?

In California, the most important skills in this business are probably land evaluation and buying, engineering, and land development and entitlements.

How should a graduate go about trying to get an interview at a company where he or she wants to work?

Research the company. Learn as much as you can. Find people who know senior people at the company. Ask them to be your advocate and to lobby for you. When people I respect call me, I can tell very quickly whether they're recommending somebody they really know or if they are just making a call. If somebody I respect says: "Hey, this is really a great kid who wants to be in real estate," I always follow up.

What can you tell students who plan a career in real estate?

The beautiful thing about real estate is that it will never go out of style. You picked the right business. As for the question of how well you will do, who knows? There's no way to know.

What opportunities are there in real estate globally?

There will be huge opportunities overseas. It takes a special kind of person to flourish in a foreign environment, because real estate is, like most businesses, still very much relationship-oriented. You have to be able to handle relationship building along with foreign languages and foreign cultures. Nonetheless, overseas opportunities can be worth pursuing, as shown by the example of a number of people at K&B who have had successful real estate careers in France—which some would say is the most difficult country to work in.

Company List: REITs and REOCs

The following list of leading real estate investment trusts and real estate operating companies represents only a small fraction of all such companies. Sources listed in appendix A tell you where to find more information about real estate companies and businesses, and the Web addresses of the companies on this list are provided in this appendix as well.

Archstone-Smith Trust
Boston Properties
BRT Realty Trust
Colonial Properties Trust
Cousins Properties
  Incorporated

Crescent Real Estate Equities
  Company
Equity Office Properties Trust
Equity Residential
First Union Real Estate
  Investments

Forest City Enterprises
Kimco Realty Corporation
Simon Property Group
Starwood Hotels and Resorts
Vornado Realty Trust

bonds, and other types of investments. That perception has changed over time with the growth and consolidation of the real estate industry; the emergence of large developers and owners; the increasing use of the corporate structure in owning and managing real estate; real estate's high rates of return; the shift of real estate from private to public ownership; and the development of more sophisticated investment and financing structures.

Furthermore, institutional investors—including pension funds, investment banks, life insurance companies, and com-

to Los Angeles, where the company had invested in property and wanted a presence. "It was during my time there that I realized that I enjoyed the real estate business and running an office on my own. I also knew that I wanted to be CEO some day."

Career Lessons

Bucksbaum suggests that students who may be interested in working for a retail developer or owner start by working for a real estate brokerage firm or other company that specializes in the leasing of retail space. "Leasing is a good way to learn about tenants, and good tenants are essential for the success of a retail asset." Working for a property management company—"a very good way to learn the ins and outs of managing a retail property"—is another possibility. Opportunities may also be found in working for consulting firms that provide advisory services to retail developers and owners.

Bucksbaum says that while real estate firms still tend to give more weight to a candidate's experience than education, a candidate's educational background is becoming more of a factor in hiring decisions. "It's almost mandatory to have a strong background in finance, especially if you work for a public company, and if you want to move into upper management."

What qualities does it take to succeed in a professional career with a developer and owner like General Growth? You must, says Bucksbaum, be able to build relationships with people, to communicate effectively, to pay attention to detail, and to be aggressive in the pursuit of opportunities. But you also have to have the discipline to take a pass. "Know when to back out of a deal. Don't let your pride get in the way." And don't become complacent. "Never be satisfied," he says. "Always try to do better."

Company List: Real Estate Private Equity Fund Sponsors

The following list of leading opportunity fund sponsors represents only a small fraction of all such companies. Sources listed in appendix A tell you where to find more information about real estate companies and businesses, and the Web addresses of the companies on this list are provided in this appendix as well.

AEW Capital Management
Apollo Real Estate Advisors
Blackrock
Blackstone Real Estate
    Advisors LLC
Colony Capital
Hines

J. E. Robert Companies
Legg Mason Real Estate
    Services
Lubert-Adler
Morgan Stanley Real Estate
Prudential Real Estate
Investors

Rockwood Capital
    Corporation
RREEF North America
Starwood Capital Group
Walton Street Investment
    Company

---

mercial banks—now possess the technologies, methodologies, databases, and analytical tools they need to evaluate prospective real estate investments. Whereas real estate was once only of marginal interest to institutional investors that invest in and own real estate, it is now an integral part of their portfolios. The playing field on which real estate competes with stocks, bonds, and other investments has leveled out, and real estate is attracting increasing amounts of capital from institutional investors.

Pension Funds. Pension funds invest large pools of capital, consisting of the contributions of employers and employees to fund employee retirement benefits. They allocate certain percentages of their total investment capital to specific investment classes, such as equities, fixed-income securities, and real estate. In-house staff or outside consultants are used in making allocation decisions, while outside advisers or investment managers are typically hired to actually invest and manage a fund's investments.

The amount of capital that pension funds invest in real estate varies based on the performance of the economy, the performance of the stock market, the inflation rate, and many other factors. The long-term trend appears to be toward increased pension fund investment in real estate. Real estate's appeal to these funds it that it is a relatively stable investment that generates a consistent income from rents and other sources, offers competitive yields in comparison with bonds and other fixed-income securities, and helps the funds diversify their portfolios.

Investment Banks. Investment banks primarily help clients raise capital, facilitate corporate mergers and acquisitions, and trade securities. They act as intermediaries, bring-

---

CAREER TIP: Get to know the companies listed on the opportunity funds sponsors list on this page. Because they manage some of the most active funds in the marketplace, they may offer many different career paths.

---

ing together those who need capital and those who have it. They also lend and invest their own capital. They buy and sell stocks and bonds and other securities for clients or for their own accounts. They also provide financial advice, market research, and other services.

Many investment banks have sections dedicated to real estate activities, including the issuance of securities backed by mortgages on commercial or residential properties, the sale of REIT stocks, and the origination of bonds and preferred stock for real estate companies. Investment banks may also invest in income-producing real estate, either directly or through special purpose funds.

Life Insurance Companies. The premiums that insurance companies collect from the insurance policies that they issue are invested in various assets—equities, fixed-income investments, real estate, and other assets—in order

Company List: Commercial Real Estate Investors

The following list of leading investors in commercial real estate represents only a small fraction of all such companies. Sources listed in appendix A tell you where to find more information about real estate companies and businesses, and the Web addresses of the companies on this list are provided in this appendix as well.

Boston Properties	LaSalle Investment	RREEF North America
Brookfield Properties	Management	Starwood Capital Group
CB Richard Ellis Investors	Prudential Real Estate	TIAA-CREF
Heitman	Investors	UBS

to generate returns and build reserves for meeting insurance claims. They also make loans to companies and businesses, including real estate developers and investors. In some cases, insurance companies may provide developers or investors with both equity capital and loans for developing projects or acquiring properties. On the other hand, many insurance companies have disposed of their equity investments and now provide debt financing only.

Real Estate Mutual Funds. Mutual funds are investment funds operated by investment companies. They raise money by selling shares to the public and invest it in stocks, bonds, money market funds, and other investments. They constitute an indirect source of capital for real estate development and acquisition; that is, they invest in real estate securities, including the shares of public REITs or REOCs, rather than investing directly in real estate.

In return for buying shares in a real estate mutual fund, shareholders receive an equity position in the fund and, in effect, in each of its underlying securities. Shareholders generally are free to sell their shares at any time. A fund's share price fluctuates daily, depending on the performance of the securities held by the fund. For real estate investors, mutual funds offer a number of benefits, including diversification, professional money management, liquidity, and convenience. However, they charge fees and often require a minimum investment.

CAREER TIP: If you want to learn about doing deals, an investment bank is a good place to start.

Commercial Banks. Some commercial banks, for example Bank of America, sometimes joint venture with developers to buy land and develop commercial properties. However, the primary roles of banks in real estate are lending for construction or property investments and general corporate financing.

Company List: Investment Bankers

The following list of leading investment bankers in commercial real estate represents only a small fraction of all such companies. Sources listed in appendix A tell you where to find more information about real estate companies and businesses, and the Web addresses of the companies on this list are provided in this appendix as well.

Bank of America	Goldman Sachs	Merrill Lynch
Bear, Stearns & Co.	Greenwich Capital Markets	Sonnenblick-Goldman
Credit Suisse First Boston	JP Morgan	UBS
Deutsche Bank	Lazard LLC	Wells Fargo
Eastdil Realty	Lehman Brothers	

CAREER TIP: If you work for an institutional investor, you will have the opportunity to learn its investment philosophy, investment strategies, how it makes investment decisions, and how it manages its portfolio.

Other Investors

Global Investors. Individuals and institutions from around the world invest in U.S. real estate. They include wealthy individuals, private partnerships, pension funds, investment banks, and other investors. In recent years, Australians and Germans have been among the most active buyers of U.S. real estate, followed by Dutch and United Kingdom investors, according to the Association of Foreign Investors in Real Estate.

Commercial real estate in the United States attracts global investment largely because the U.S. commercial real estate market is the largest and most open such market in the world and it contains a large supply of investment-grade real estate. The U.S. market offers a wide range of investment options, stable investments, and ease of investing, and makes it possible for foreign investors to diversify their portfolios and realize competitive returns on their investments.

Global real estate investors consider real estate investment opportunities not only in the United States, but also in other real estate markets. In deciding whether to invest in the United States, they consider a number of questions: How do returns on U.S. real estate investments compare with real estate returns in other countries? How much capital should be invested in U.S. real estate versus in other real estate markets? Where should capital be invested in the United States? In what types of properties?

Corporate Owners. Corporations are among the largest owners of real estate in the United States, but most of them are not in the real estate business. They're in the business of producing airplanes, automobiles, consumer goods, computers, and many other products or in the business of providing consulting, banking, entertainment, investment, and many other services.

Corporations are among the largest users of real estate as well. They occupy industrial space, office space, retail space, and other buildings in order to conduct their businesses. They make up much of the tenant base and client base of developers and owners, who build, rent, and sell space for business uses.

A few corporate real estate (CRE) trends have emerged in recent years. A number of companies have moved excess real estate, a depreciable asset, off their books by selling properties not required for their core businesses—thereby reducing costs, raising capital, and strengthening balance sheets. Other companies have been expanding and buying properties. Still others have sold properties that are needed for their core operations to third-party investors, and then leased them back. These sale-leaseback transactions achieve the same goals as outright property sales, but allow the companies to retain control of the property. (In chapter 4, we look at CRE career opportunities within the real estate departments of corporations.)

CAREER TIP: If you want to learn about real estate finance, you could start by working for a commercial bank, investment bank, or insurance company.

Nonprofit Organizations. A nonprofit organization is an incorporated entity formed for educational, charitable, or similar purposes. Under the federal tax code, only specific types of organizations qualify as tax-exempt nonprofits. Most nonprofit organizations own or lease space for their own use. A number of nonprofit organizations are involved in real estate development or ownership as a means of furthering social and community goals.

A nonprofit might, for example, invest in housing development in order to help provide housing for low-income households or for the families of police officers, teachers, firefighters, and other professionals who cannot otherwise afford to live in the community they serve. Or a nonprofit might invest in the development of retail centers in underserved low-income neighborhoods or the conversion of deteriorated buildings in inner-city economic development areas to space that is suitable for occupancy by small startup businesses.

Some nonprofits form partnerships with for-profit developers to develop projects that meet specific social needs, such as a drug rehabilitation center or a shelter for abused women. Various federal, state, or local government agencies may provide financing for nonprofit real estate investment and development projects.

Debt Financing

Debt financing is another way of obtaining capital for real estate development and acquisitions. Real estate investors can obtain commercial property loans from a variety of sources, including friends and family, banks, mortgage REITs, credit companies, and a number of other sources that provide debt financing as well as equity capital. The major loan sources are described in the following section, which is followed by a section describing types of debt financing for commercial real estate.

Loan Sources

Individuals. Individuals—including friends, family members, and high-net-worth third-party lenders—may provide loans to help developers and investors finance development projects or property acquisitions, particularly when the project/acquisition is relatively small (and local).

Small Partnerships. In pursuing investment opportunities, the partners in small partnerships may prefer to provide debt financing than to provide equity, which carries a higher risk.

Private Investment Companies. As has been noted, private investment companies, which operate like small partnerships but on a larger scale, often provide loans as well as equity to help cover development or acquisition costs.

Commercial Banks. Commercial banks have long been a primary source of construction financing. Local and regional banks tend to focus on development projects in their markets, because they are knowledgeable about local market conditions and can closely monitor these projects. National and international banks finance the projects of developers with a track record in successful major projects in the United States and overseas.

Savings and Loan Associations. Although once very active in financing commercial real estate and in participating—through subsidiaries—in joint ventures with developers, savings and loan associations (S&Ls) scaled back their lending following the S&L crisis of the 1980s. S&Ls now focus primarily on home loans and apartment financings. By law, they are not permitted to participate in real estate joint ventures.

Mortgage REITs. Mortgage REITs (see earlier "Real Estate Investment Trusts" section) lend money directly to real estate owners or extend credit indirectly through the acquisition of loans or mortgage-backed securities. They generally extend mortgage credit only on existing properties (and not on development projects).

Commercial Mortgage Brokers. Commercial mortgage brokers act as intermediaries between borrowers (investors in and developers of commercial real estate) and lenders (commercial banks, insurance companies, and others) in arranging mortgage financing. They collect fees for their services. Compared with residential mortgages, commercial mortgages are typically more complex and less standardized.

Credit Companies. The credit company subsidiaries of some large corporations provide financing for commercial real estate development and acquisition. Compared with commercial banks and some other lenders, some credit companies may be more willing to lend on higher-risk projects, although they may charge higher interest rates and fees.

Life Insurance Companies. Life insurance companies provide real estate loans directly to large borrowers and indirectly to smaller borrowers through intermediaries, such as mortgage brokers. They tend to focus on Class A, investment-grade properties.

Pension Funds. Pension funds are a leading source of financing. They provide both construction loans and long-term financing.

Investment Banks. Investments banks are also among the leading sources of construction and long-term financing.

Other Lenders. Other sources of debt financing include opportunity funds, private syndicators, and global investors.

Types of Debt Financing

The development, construction, and ownership of income-producing property are financed by a variety of loans, including land development loans, construction loans, permanent loans, and mezzanine debt.

Land Development Loans. Commercial or residential land development is financed with short-term loans covering the costs of preparing the land and constructing infrastructure. These loans are repaid from the developer's sale or refi-

nancing of the real estate. Land development loans are generally nonrecourse debt, meaning that the borrower is not personally liable for them. However, the lender may require the developer to provide a letter of credit or other collateral, in addition to a mortgage on the property. In some cases, the lender requires the developer to personally guarantee the loan, with the terms and conditions of such a guarantee negotiated between the developer and lender.

Construction Loans. Developers obtain construction loans from banks and other construction lenders to cover the costs of building and leasing income-producing properties. Lenders provide such loans based on detailed analysis of the developer's financial strength and management capability; an evaluation of the project's feasibility, tenant mix, and pre-leasing schedule; and other information. Construction lenders generally require lien-free completion guarantees. Interest rates usually fluctuate with the prime rate.

Permanent Financing. Long-term mortgage lenders—including life insurance companies, pension funds, opportunity funds, and investment banks—provide permanent financing to the developers and buyers of income-producing properties. They carefully scrutinize the developer and the project (or the investor and the property acquisition) before providing permanent financing.

Developers use permanent mortgage financing to pay off construction loans. The term of the permanent loan, the interest rate, and other conditions are negotiated between the developer and lender. Loan terms typically range from a few years to a decade or more. Loans may be fixed-rate loans with an interest rate that remains the same throughout the loan period, or variable- or adjustable-rate loans with

---

Company List: Direct Real Estate Lenders

The following list of direct real estate lenders represents only a small fraction of all such companies. Sources listed in appendix A tell you where to find more information about real estate companies and businesses, and the Web addresses of the companies on this list are provided in this appendix as well.

Freddie Mac	GMAC Commercial Mortgage	L. J. Melody & Company
GE Commercial Finance Real	Corporation	Northstar Capital
Estate	Holiday Fenoglio Fowler LP	Wachovia
	KeyBank Real Estate Capital	Washington Mutual

interest rates that fluctuate based on changes in long-term mortgage interest rates or other criteria. Permanent loans come in many varieties. Participating loans, for example, give the lender a share of a property's cash flow.

Mezzanine Financing. Mezzanine debt is financing that is used to bridge the gap between the equity in a project or acquisition and the permanent mortgage financing that is available. For example, the permanent lender might provide financing covering 75 percent of the cost of developing or acquiring a building; and the equity capital provided by the developer or investor and its partners might cover 10 percent of the total cost. The remaining 15 percent of project costs might be covered by mezzanine financing, which is available from some of the same lenders that provide permanent financing.

Real Estate Services

Because real estate development and ownership are such complex and varied businesses, they make use of an array of related services. The firms that develop, invest in, and manage real estate assets may have professionals on their staffs who can provide needed real estate–related services or they may outsource some or most of the real estate services that they need. A list of key real estate service providers follows.

Sales Brokers

Commercial property brokers may be sales brokers, leasing brokers, or tenant representation brokers. Brokerage firms may specialize in one or the other of these specialties, or they may be full-service firms that provide all types of brokerage services.

Sales brokers who specialize in income-producing properties bring together property buyers and sellers for the purpose of completing a sale. They may work for a brokerage firm or independently. They are licensed by the states where they do business.

Brokers find prospective buyers through, for example, listing networks; direct communication with other brokers; relationships with accountants, lawyers, bankers, and others who can refer buyers; and advertising, newsletters, direct mail, and other forms of marketing. They are paid a commission by the seller for marketing and selling a property. Usually, the commission is an agreed percentage of the sale price. Some brokerage firms prefer to pay their brokers a salary that is based on the performance of a brokerage team or the company itself.

The buyers of income-producing properties sometimes hire commercial brokers to find prospective properties for purchase and to negotiate acquisitions.

Leasing Brokers

Leasing brokers help find tenants for available space and represent owners in negotiating leases with tenants. Brokers may specialize in particular types of space, such as office space, shopping centers, apartments, or industrial space. The leases for large blocks of office or other types of space can involve millions of dollars in rent payments over the lease term, and the conditions and terms of the lease can be quite complex. A key part of the leasing broker's job is to negotiate the terms of a lease with the tenant or its representative. They generally are paid a commission.

Tenant Representation Brokers

Tenant rep brokers represent the tenant in lease negotiations. Some brokers and brokerage firms specialize in tenant representation.

Property Managers

Commercial real estate owners have their own property management divisions or they contract out property management functions. Property managers are responsible for maximizing the rental income of managed property, increasing the net operating income (income after operating expenses), and the efficient operation of property—all of which maintain or add to property value.

Property managers oversee all aspects of property operations, including the physical plant, financial flows, tenant relations, market positioning, and the public image of the property. They collect rents and pay bills—mortgages, taxes, insurance premiums, payroll, and maintenance expenses—

on schedule and keep the property in compliance with government laws and regulations, such as the Americans with Disabilities Act or local building codes. They are the owner's liaison with tenants, the maintenance staff, vendors, suppliers, and the public.

Asset Managers

Whereas property managers are responsible for the day-to-day operations of individual properties, asset managers are responsible for the performance of real estate portfolios owned by investors. Asset managers focus on long-term strategic financial planning for multiple properties. They evaluate portfolio performance, advise owners on development or acquisition and disposition strategies, manage the acquisition and disposition process, and identify opportunities for future investments.

Architects

Developers, investors, and users employ project architects to design houses, office towers, hotels, hospitals, sports stadiums—you name it. A project's design is the product of the architect's imagination, talent, and experience, but it is also shaped by the client's requirements—the amount of space required, how the space will be used, market preferences (if the client plans to lease space or eventually sell the building), the costs of construction and operation, and many other considerations. The design must also comply with the requirements of public agencies, zoning codes, and building and safety codes, and often it must take into account community and neighborhood preferences. In some cases, architects not only design the building but also manage its construction. The project architect usually hires structural,

CAREER TIP: Brokerage is one of the traditional starting points in real estate. It provides training in structuring deals and in buying, selling, or leasing properties. If you are good—and if you are willing to risk working on commission—you can also make some money.

mechanical, and electrical engineers as subcontractors and manages their work.

Land Planners

For large land development projects, developers may employ land planners. Land planners develop plans for the location, orientation, and design of buildings, open space, traffic circulation, and various uses and amenities—with the main objective being to make full use of the development site's potential. The land planner typically prepares several alternative plans based on the developer's initial concepts. The developer works closely with the land planner as well as with the team's marketing, economic, engineering, and political consultants to ensure that the final plan is efficient, marketable, financially sound, and politically feasible.

Real Estate Consultants

A developer seeking to take a project through the entitlement process, a pension fund evaluating the performance of its real estate portfolio, or a company planning to sell an office building may turn to a consultant for advice and assistance. Real estate consultancies may provide a full range of

---

Company List: Brokerage Firms

The following list of brokerage firms represents only a small fraction of all such companies. Sources listed in appendix A tell you where to find more information about real estate companies and businesses, and the Web addresses of the companies on this list are provided in this appendix as well.

CB Richard Ellis	Jones Lang LaSalle	Staubach
Coldwell Banker Commercial	Kennedy Wilson	Studley
Colliers International	Marcus & Millichap	Transwestern Commercial
Cushman & Wakefield	Newmark Knight Frank	Services
The Gale Company	PM Realty Group	Trammell Crow
Grubb & Ellis	Sperry Van Ness	

CAREER TIP: If you don't want to work for a developer or owner, get on-the-job experience in real estate by working for a company that provides services to developers and owners.

services—including market analysis, feasibility analysis, real estate research, site selection, environmental impact statements, and so forth. A number specialize in a particular product category, such as apartments or retail. Clients value consultants because they maintain extensive market databases and provide special knowledge or expertise that can be used to develop more business, reduce costs, improve the performance of investment portfolios, or achieve other business and investment goals.

Appraisers

Appraisers prepare estimates of the fair market value of properties using various methodologies. Appraisals are performed when properties—from single-family houses to high-rise office buildings—are sold, mortgaged, insured, or taxed. Appraisers (self-employed individuals or appraisal firms) may be hired by sellers, buyers, or lenders. Lenders usually require an appraisal before they will provide financing for the purchase of a property. Pension funds, opportunity funds, REITs, and other investors and owners employ appraisers to provide valuations of individual properties or portfolios of properties before acquisition or disposition.

Appraisers can be found through professional organizations, such as the American Society of Appraisers or the National Society of Real Estate Appraisers, or various online directories. Some brokerage firms and real estate consultancies also provide appraisal services.

Accountants

Accountants basically prepare, analyze, and verify financial documents in order to provide information to clients. Beyond this function, many accountants offer a variety of business and professional services. Some accountants offer specialized knowledge and experience in real estate. Frequently they are called upon to perform due-diligence assessments of property dispositions or acquisitions or real estate company mergers and acquisitions. Many accountants are tax specialists and assist clients in tax planning and structuring real estate transactions.

Real estate companies, developers, and investors seek a range of accounting, auditing, tax, and consulting services from public accountants (self-employed individuals or accounting firms), who usually are CPAs (certified public accountants). Publicly held companies that file reports with the federal Securities and Exchange Commission (SEC) are required to submit financial statements that are prepared according to a set of accounting standards known as "Generally Accepted Accounting Principles" (GAAP), and many of these financial statements must be examined and reported on by a CPA. The Sarbanes-Oxley Act of 2002 (SOX), designed to protect shareholders and the public from accounting errors and fraudulent financial practices, has increased the reporting and compliance requirement of public companies.

Many public and private real estate companies employ internal auditors to examine and evaluate their financial and information systems, management procedures, and internal controls to ensure that the company's records are accurate and that its controls to protect against fraud and waste are adequate. Internal auditors are also used to evaluate the efficiency and effectiveness of company operations, and to

Company List: Property Managers

The following list of property managers represents only a small fraction of all such companies. Sources listed in appendix A tell you where to find more information about real estate companies and businesses, and the Web addresses of the companies on this list are provided in this appendix as well.

CB Richard Ellis
Colliers International

Cushman & Wakefield
Jones Lang LaSalle

Company List: Asset Managers

The following list of asset managers represents only a small fraction of all such companies. Sources listed in appendix A tell you where to find more information about real estate companies and businesses, and the Web addresses of the companies on this list are provided in this appendix as well.

CIGNA Realty Investors	Lend Lease	RREEF North America
Heitman	Principal Real Estate	TIAA-CREF
INVESCO Real Estate	Prudential Real Estate	UBS
JPMorgan Asset Management	Investors (PREI)	

ascertain the compliance of these operations with corporate policies and procedures, laws, and government regulations.

Lawyers

Lawyers assist and advise developers on many fronts, from the negotiations on buying or selling a property or a portfolio of properties, to devising the terms of sale or lease contracts, representing the developer before public agencies, interpreting zoning and building codes, litigating, and much more. The increasing complexity of real estate development, acquisition, ownership, and management puts real estate companies and investors increasingly in need of legal services. Some law firms (or lawyers) provide real estate advice as part of an array of client services. Others specialize in real estate.

Construction Contractors

Developers and owners typically hire construction contractors to build or renovate properties. Construction contractors often specialize in a product type, such as office buildings, shopping centers, or warehouse buildings. A negotiated contract includes the contractor's fee and any performance incentives. The contractor usually does not have an equity interest in the project.

Depending on the size and scope of the project, the developer or owners may hire architects, engineers, and other specialists in addition to the construction contractor. In turn, the general contractor may subcontract work to specialist contractors such as electricians. Managing the construction process is one of the most challenging aspects of development and rehabilitation. Projects must be completed on schedule—often on tight deadlines—and within budget, and they must meet design and construction specifications.

CAREER TIP: If you're interested in working for a development company or becoming a developer, you could start by getting a job with a construction contractor. It's a good place to start learning about development.

Company List: Accounting Firms

The following list of accounting firms represents only a small fraction of all such companies. Sources listed in appendix A tell you where to find more information about real estate companies and businesses, and the Web addresses of the companies on this list are provided in this appendix as well.

Deloitte & Touche USA LLP	KPMG	PricewaterhouseCoopers
Ernst & Young	McGladrey & Pullen	

Chapter 4
Career Paths: What's Right for You?

Real estate offers many career opportunities—so many, in fact, that the choices can seem overwhelming. Do you want to work for a developer or a homebuilder? Be an entrepreneur? Work for a large company or a small company? A public company or a private company? In what sector? Multifamily, industrial, retail, or . . . ? In corporate real estate? This chapter is designed to give you a perspective on careers in the industry that can help you in considering the career options, figuring out where your interests lie, evaluating your professional skills, and thinking about what career might be right for you.

If you're in school or just starting out after graduating, you may have only a general idea of what you want to do. As you build up work experience in the real estate industry, you'll develop a better picture of where your opportunities are and where you want to be in five, ten, or 15 years.

POSSIBLE CAREER GOALS

Begin with a self-analysis. "You need to take a hard look at yourself, at why you are attracted to real estate, at your interests and skills," says Robert Larson, former CEO of the Taubman Company, a shopping center developer and operator (now Taubman Centers, a retail real estate investment trust). "Then decide what areas of real estate most interest you, and what your goals are."

advises Ming Lee, a principal of Strategic Partners LLP, one of the real estate investment funds managed by CB Richard Ellis Investors.

But where will you start? You most likely will decide to work in one of the types of businesses listed in the "Business Lines" chart shown below and discussed in detail in chapters 2 and 3—that is, for a developer or homebuilder, an owner

---

Business Lines in Commercial and Residential Real Estate

COMMERCIAL REAL ESTATE	RESIDENTIAL REAL ESTATE
Development	*Development*
Ownership and Investment	*Homebuilding*
Financial Services	*Financial Services*
Providers include:	*Providers include:*
▶ Commercial Banks	▶ Commercial Banks
▶ Mortgage REITs	▶ Mortgage REITs
▶ S&Ls	▶ S&Ls
▶ Private Investment Companies	▶ Private Investment Companies
▶ Credit Companies	▶ Credit Companies
▶ Life Insurance Companies	▶ Life Insurance Companies
Real Estate Services	*Real Estate Services*
Providers include:	*Providers include:*
▶ Property Managers	▶ Asset Managers
▶ Asset Managers	▶ Brokers
▶ Sales and Leasing Brokers	▶ Consultants
▶ Consultants	▶ Appraisers
▶ Construction Contractors	▶ Accountants
▶ Appraisers	▶ Lawyers
▶ Accountants	▶ Architects
▶ Lawyers	▶ Construction Contractors
▶ Architects	▶ Property Managers

* Commercial real estate comprises the development, acquisition, ownership, management, and sale of income-producing properties, including office, industrial, retail, hotel/resort, multifamily rental, and mixed-use properties.

** Residential real estate comprises the development, construction, and sale of single-family houses, townhouses, condominiums, and other owner-occupied properties.

Perhaps you will decide that your primary goal is to become CEO or CFO of a company engaged in development or homebuilding, to manage a portfolio of properties, to become an entrepreneur, to build personal wealth, to contribute to society by, for example, heading a nonprofit organization that develops affordable housing—or any number of other possible career goals. "Use each job as a steppingstone to gain experience and to figure out what you want to do,"

or investor, a financial services company, or a real estate services company. The advantages of working for different types of real estate companies and what you can expect to be doing at such firms as an entry-level professional are discussed in this chapter.

Alternatively, you may decide to enter the field of corporate real estate (CRE) or work outside the United States, career choices that are discussed in Q&A format in two sidebars—"Working Outside the United States" and "Corporate Real Estate"—at the end of this chapter. If you think you would like to become a real estate entrepreneur, you can turn to chapter 6 for suggestions on how to get started and advice from people who have tried and succeeded and from people who have tried and had less luck (so far).

As was discussed in chapters 2 and 3, some commercial developers and investors specialize in a single property type such as retail, while others own and develop more than one type of real estate product. And some develop or acquire mixed-use projects that combine two or more property types, such as office/residential buildings or office/

hotel/retail developments. An entry-level position with a diversified developer or investor will put you in position to learn about different commercial development products and projects. Homebuilding as a career also offers a great deal of variety. You could work for a residential land developer or a builder of for-sale housing product: single-family houses, townhouses, condominiums, or co-ops. Some residential developers are diversifying into emerging, niche housing markets, for example, urban housing for young professional and empty-nester households or active adult communities for retirees and preretirees.

Making the Most of Your First Job(s)

Regardless of where you begin your real estate career, you should, as Ming Lee advises, consider your first assignments as steppingstones on the way to your long-term goals. You can make the most of your first job(s) by paying heed to some simple rules for advancement, as follow.

Learn from Experience
Focus on gaining broad knowledge and experience in the essentials of real estate. Explore all key facets, including design, construction, financial analysis, acquisition and sales, deal structuring, financing, negotiation, property leasing and management, valuations and appraisals, entitlement and community relations, and technology. Be curious, or as Bentley Kerr, a project partner with the privately held southern California land development company Bluestone Communities, advises: "Understand the reasons why decisions are made." Try to figure out what was the thinking behind a decision to acquire a particular property; to undertake a development project; to finance an investment.

Begin as a Generalist
So that you can use your experience to develop an across-the-board picture of real estate, try at first to be a generalist, not a specialist. If you specialize too soon, you may get pigeonholed and fail to develop the skills that can qualify you for higher-up positions. After you develop a solid grounding in real estate, you can decide on a specialization.

Take Initiative
Ask to work in areas of the firm or on a project team outside of your job or department. Learn not only your job, but also the job on the next step up the career ladder. In the process, you will develop a better idea of what interests you—and, equally important, what doesn't.

Ask Questions
Learn by asking. Ask about your job responsibilities, your supervisor's expectations of you, the business of the company, why your colleagues chose real estate as a career. Don't be hesitant to ask what you may think are naive questions. There are no stupid questions. And listen to the answers.

Develop Core Skills
Focus on developing the core skills that employers seek—analytical, interpersonal, leadership, managerial, financial, and communications. (We look at these skills in more detail in chapter 8.) Having these core skills enhances your value in the marketplace. Unlike specific product or business knowledge, these skills are transferable. If you can demonstrate to prospective employers that you have these skills, you can find entry-level positions anywhere in real estate.

Work with Mentors
Look to seasoned real estate professionals for advice and counsel on how you can develop your talents and progress in

your career. Some companies you can work for offer formal mentoring programs. Others may encourage mentoring through informal relationships and networks.

Create Relationships

Real estate is not an overwhelmingly big industry. Over time you will have opportunities to get to know many professionals in the industry. Seize those opportunities. Use your business contacts to build long-term relationships that can potentially help you throughout your career.

Be Realistic in Your Expectations

Real estate professionals just starting out "need to guard against hyperinflated expectations," says Ki Ryu, development manager with TMG Partners, a Santa Monica, California, developer. "It's important to keep to the fundamentals and work hard early on—and to not think that success will happen overnight."

Put Compensation in Perspective

Consider compensation in the context of your other career goals. The best entry-level job for you may not necessarily be

MAKING CONNECTIONS

The theory called "six degrees of separation" postulates that anyone on earth can be connected to any other person on the planet through a chain of acquaintances that has no more than five intermediaries. To be sure, in advancing your career, you don't have to connect with everyone, everywhere, but you should connect with as many people as you can who can possibly help you along the way. Begin to develop a contact list while you are still in school or early in your career. This list should include:

- people you meet at industry events, networking receptions, student or alumni get-togethers, meetings of professional organizations, and other meetings;
- personal and professional friends and acquaintances;
- people you work with;
- people you work for;
- mentors;
- professionals whose names you have heard mentioned who are involved in areas of the industry that interest you;
- friends of friends and other contacts working for prospective employers; and
- the names of companies (and contacts, if known) that you might approach about employment.

If you manage your contact information effectively, you will have constructed a network of people who may help you. Constructing a good network takes time and organization, but it's well worth the effort. Don't add names just for the sake of it. Who is on your list is more important than the number of people on it.

There are many techniques for developing a good list. For example, you may exchange cards with people you meet at networking events or industry meetings. Note on the back of each card where and when you met this person, as well as pertinent matters of mutual interest, such as a friend in common or the same school. Then put all this information on your list.

Another technique: You usually can't meet everyone at a meeting, reception, or event. But you can get a list of attendees from the sponsor. Check the list for people you didn't meet but may want to contact, and follow up with a note introducing yourself, saying you were at the meeting, and maybe making a comment on what was discussed. Some of these overtures will lead to further correspondence and perhaps even an opportunity someday to meet.

Again, contact files don't just happen; they take work. Develop, maintain, and use your contact list. It can pay off in a career opportunity or a new business opportunity.

the top-paying job. "Go to work for a good company," advises Brian Prinn, vice chairman of Lowe Enterprises, a full-service real estate development and investment company. "It's important to work with people who are respected in the industry, and to learn from them." The experience of working in an excellent company will help you to develop as a professional and advance in your career—and eventually increase your income. (Compensation is discussed in more detail in chapter 9.)

Stay Challenged

Move on when the timing's right. The time may come when you feel you have learned all you can at your current company and are starting to feel bored on the job. Or when you feel you're getting too comfortable on the job and losing your drive. These are signs that it may be time for you to move on to a new career opportunity.

What Company?

Large or Small?

Whether you opt to work for a developer, owner/investor, lender, or real estate services company, you generally will have a choice of working for a large organization or a small one. The chart "Large or Small Organization?" on the fol-

CAREER TIP: The company that you start with, whether it's big or small, should have a solid reputation inside and outside the real estate industry.

lowing page lists some of the advantages and disadvantages of working for one or the other. Large companies, for example, may offer attractive, defined career paths, but their more formal organizational structures might put limits on your freedom to try your own directions. In a large company, you may have opportunities to work in different divisions, operations, or departments, but you may also face more competition for the positions to which you aspire.

Public or Private?

You also can choose to work for a public company or a private company. Public companies are generally larger. With their access to the public capital markets,

public companies may be able to raise investment capital at lower costs than some private companies. Many public companies are focused on a single product line, and most are focused on quarterly and annual earnings, dividends, shareholder value, and their stock price. Especially since the passage of the Sarbanes-Oxley Act of 2002, they operate under strict reporting and accountability standards and internal control requirements that affect everyone working for the company.

Private companies usually are more concerned with long-term results and tax-advantaged investments. Generally, they are less structured and produce fewer financial reports and analyses. Although they are not subject to Sarbanes-Oxley, an increasing number of private companies adhere to the law's reporting and internal control standards in order to stay competitive in attracting investment capital.

CAREER TIP: As an employee of a public company, you can learn the discipline of meeting stringent accounting and reporting requirements. As an employee of a private company, you can can learn how to think like an entrepreneur.

Large or Small Organization?

LARGE ORGANIZATION

Advantages	*Possible Issues*
▸ Formal training opportunities	▸ Little one-on-one mentoring
▸ Defined career paths	▸ Lack of career autonomy
▸ Opportunities to work in different areas	▸ Internal competition for positions
▸ Stable organization	▸ Bureaucratic work environment
▸ Job security	▸ Limited opportunities to realize talent
▸ Brand-name recognition	▸ Innovation less encouraged
▸ Steady, dependable compensation	▸ Few equity opportunities
▸ Company well capitalized	▸ Accountable to numerous investors/lenders
▸ High deal flow pipeline	▸ Need to replenish deal pipeline
▸ Structured work environment	▸ Nonentrepreneurial work environment

SMALL ORGANIZATION

Advantages	*Possible Issues*
▸ On-the-job experience	▸ Little formal training
▸ Informal work environment	▸ Little direction
▸ Flexible, adaptable organization	▸ Less stable organization
▸ Many equity opportunities	▸ Less steady, less dependable compensation
▸ Flexible career choices	▸ Absence of defined career paths
▸ More employee responsibility	▸ Greater employee accountability
▸ Opportunities to use initiative, talents	▸ More job pressures
▸ Company focus on niche markets/products	▸ Company dependence on small markets/products
▸ Entrepreneurial training	

Choosing a Starting Point

As must be clear by now, just as there are many possible careers in real estate, there are many starting points for a career in real estate. This section reports on the advantages of particular types of companies for jobseekers hoping to start a real estate career, and describes entry-level positions at those companies for college graduates with a bachelor's degree and little or no experience in real estate. (See chapter 7 for a discussion of education for a real estate career and the value of a bachelor's or graduate degree for people thinking of a career in real estate.)

CAREER TIP: Do your homework. Picking the right company and mentor is as important as the position.

Starting at a Development Company

J. Ronald Terwilliger, chairman and CEO of Atlanta-based developer Trammell Crow Residential, sees development—and particularly housing development—as a promising career for professionals just start-

THE POWER OF PRESENTATIONS

Stan Ross

Over the years, I have found that one of the best ways to network is to give talks at the meetings of industry or professional organizations or other groups. I always focused on technical topics, like mortgage-backed bonds, property exchanges, or sale-leasebacks. You might think that presentations on these subjects would send the audience into a comfortable nap. But when I explained these topics and why they mattered in simple terms—for example, when I explained that mortgage-backed bonds were a new tool for financing commercial development, property investment, and homebuilding—I got the attention of developers, builders, lenders, and anyone else in the audience in need of capital, which was almost everyone. The whole idea was to give the audience take-home value.

When I started giving speeches, I worried that I might not be getting across. But based on feedback from audience members, I found that I had made a connection. People called to ask if I could meet with them, talk some more, and maybe put them in touch with others who might help them solve a problem or find a business opportunity. I continued to make presentations, with the same good results.

How are you in front of an audience? I started small, by talking to local chapters of accounting organizations and real estate groups, before moving on to larger audiences. If you're still in school, begin by speaking to a student or alumni organization or a council of a professional organization like the Urban Land Institute. If you've recently begun your career, you might want to join an organization like Toastmasters International that helps aspiring professionals develop their public speaking and leadership skills. Once you feel comfortable speaking before small, informal groups, you can begin making presentations to larger organizations.

ing out. "Development is creative, rewarding, and entrepreneurial. And there is a fundamental need for shelter," he says. Working for a developer, you'll get an inside look at how to evaluate markets for future development, select possible sites for development, acquire sites, obtain entitlements, and plan and manage construction.

Entry-level professional jobs. In many development companies, you would begin as an analyst, providing support to other professionals. You would, for example, do computer runs and conduct various types of analysis—financial, cash flow, present value, internal rate of return (IRR), and so forth—under direct and full supervision, with little autonomy. After a year or two, or perhaps even sooner, you would move up to associate, and perform some independent data gathering and market research, due-diligence assessments on projects, and report preparation. After another six months to a year, you would move into a specialty—such as marketing, sales, land acquisition, or construction—as, for example, a director of land acquisition or a construction project manager. As a construction project manager, for example, you would need to have a full understanding of the development and construction process and be able to supervise a number of people; and you would report directly to a division head. Or, instead of a specialty, you could choose the finance track where you would continue to work on projections, financial statements, detailed analyses, forecasts, and support of the organization's treasury and finance functions—and still have the opportunity to move into development at a later time.

Starting at a Construction Firm

James Klingbeil, CEO of the Klingbeil Company, a developer, owner, and manager, says there are too few "mules" in real estate today. "By that I mean people who have actually built a house, developed land, or fixed up an old apartment building." His advice to people thinking of a real estate career is to get some hands-on experience in construction. Construction jobs have been a rite of passage for many people who went on to careers in development or ownership. The firsthand experience that such jobs offer in building product from the ground up can be valuable. You might try to get a job as a laborer or, if you can find the work, as a helper to an electrician, plumber, or other craftsperson. You might do some framing or find work doing on-site cost monitoring and progress reporting.

Starting at a Homebuilding Company

It's no surprise that Jeffrey Mezger suggests that new graduates consider a career in homebuilding. His father was a land developer and custom-home builder, and he's CEO of KB Home. "When you hand a couple the keys to their first home and see their emotional reaction, you realize that you're helping to create the American dream—you're providing people with a home."

Entry-level professional jobs. You could start as an analyst, helping senior analysts and managers decide on potential land acquisitions, estimate the costs of land improvement, and structure sale prices for new houses; and assisting with budgeting, feasibility assessments, financial reporting, and project management tasks. After learning on-the-job about land acquisition, contract bidding, cost monitoring, subcontractor oversight, and on-site monitoring and supervision, you could move up to project associate or manager.

Starting at an Owner/Investor Organization

Working for a corporate or institutional property owner/investor, regardless of the type of property, will give you a broad perspective on portfolio planning and management, the acquisition and disposition of assets, and financial reporting and analysis; and key skills in raising capital, investment analysis, and tax planning.

Entry-level professional jobs. You typically would start as an analyst, with many of the same kinds of analytical responsibilities you would have at a development company. Similarly to starting out at a development company, you would be exposed to a variety of assignments and responsibilities, but with more emphasis on due-diligence assessments and financial analysis. After learning the basics, you could advance to an associate position, and then move on to a specialty or a finance track.

Starting at an Asset Management Firm

Working for a company that provides third-party management of portfolios of properties for owners and investors is an interesting alternative to working directly for an

owner/investor. Susan Yau, an analyst with Sunny Hills Palladium, a Los Angeles–based asset and property management firm, is responsible for 16 to 18 of the properties in the firm's portfolio. She regularly visits the properties to review their condition and maintenance, manages their bookkeeping and cash flow accounting, handles monthly rent reconciliation, and prepares quarterly financial reports and annual budget forecasts. "My long-term goal is to expand into new avenues of real estate finance, and my current position is helping me to achieve that goal," she says.

Entry-level professional jobs. You typically would begin as a general analyst or leasing agent; or as an associate on specific properties working on such operating issues as rents, taxes, utility operations, and maintenance.

Starting at a Brokerage Company

Brokerage exposes you to all aspects of two key real estate functions—selling and buying transactions and leasing. As a sales broker you find owners interested in selling properties, market the brokerage firm's services to owners, contract with the owner to sell the property, market the property, find and qualify buyers, negotiate sales terms, and finalize the

CAREER TIP: Understanding tenants, leasing, and marketing is critical to a successful commercial real estate project.

sales contract. As a lease broker, you find owners with available space, market the brokerage firm's services to owners, market the property, find and qualify tenants, and negotiate and finalize leases. Brokerage trains you in people skills. And it provides networking opportunities that build up your Rolodex. Brokerage can be a steppingstone to other real estate businesses—particularly development. Ray Bayat, a commercial broker with Grubb & Ellis for seven years, leveraged his experience and relationships from the brokerage business to moving into development full time, not only for the opportunity to create wealth, but also for the challenge.

Entry-level professional jobs. Usually you will work for one or two years as an apprentice to an experienced broker. A broker-trainee at one brokerage firm says that he spends most of his time searching for potential buyers of properties listed by the firm. His chief responsibility is to figure out whether the buyer profile is right for the particular seller. The rest of his time is spent working on specific deals, cold-calling, or assisting senior brokers on their deals.

CAREER TIP: Working for a real estate consultant can offer you a quick start to a real estate career because it exposes you to many different projects, organizations, and management styles.

Starting at a Consulting Firm

Lynn Sedway, founder and executive managing director of the Sedway Group, a San Francisco–based consulting arm of CB Richard Ellis, suggests that beginning real estate professionals work for a time in consulting. "Consulting provides wide exposure to real estate and

enables you to develop valuable analytical and writing skills," she notes, "and from there, you can go on to many other areas, such as providing investment advisory services to institutional investors."

Entry-level professional jobs. You usually begin as an analyst. Your responsibilities could include basic market research, the analysis of sale comparables, fair market value analysis, writing reports, and preparing spreadsheets.

Starting at a Financial Services Firm

Most real estate professionals agree that a strong background in finance is important to a career in real estate. Some suggest that any real estate career would benefit from experience with a bank, insurance company, opportunity fund, investment bank, or other organization that provides financing to real estate companies. Marc Bromley, retired chairman and CEO of Gables Residential, a multifamily REIT, believes that "the financial arena is a good place to start. Capital is so important. If you distinguish yourself in finance, developers will offer you a job."

Entry-level professional jobs. You could start as a financial analyst with a commercial bank or investment bank. Joseph Kim is with Secured Capital Corp, a real estate investment bank. He started as an analyst and has been promoted to associate. He compares the two positions: "As an analyst, I was doing more of the grunt work—making rent rolls on ARGUS [property management software], graphs, presentations, some due diligence—and learning as I went along. On each deal, I'd assist another analyst. My work was 80 percent quantitative, 20 percent qualitative. Now, as an associate, I'm doing more of the complex modeling, calculating different debt structures and investment structures. I've helped to close a lot of financing deals and a couple of joint venture deals."

Or, you could start as an assistant loan officer at a commercial bank. In this position, you would learn from a senior loan officer how to market the bank's loan services to prospective clients, advise clients on the bank's various loan programs, help clients structure loans that meet their requirements, and negotiate and finalize loan terms. You would gain a perspective on the lending process that could help you to analyze and evaluate loans and—later in your career—to obtain financing for your company. A position as assistant loan officer would also give you exposure to loan documents and regulations affecting real estate.

Starting at a Property Management Firm

Property management provides valuable experience in dealing with tenants and property operations. You could work for a property management company or for an investor/owner or asset management organization, such as large pension fund adviser, that employs its own property managers.

Entry-level professional jobs. You typically would start as an assistant to a property manager, where you would be in a position to learn about establishing good tenant relations, marketing space, qualifying prospective tenants, negotiating and administering leases, property maintenance, working with suppliers, and financial reporting and management. From there, you could move up to a property manager position or move into other professional areas.

Starting at an Appraisal Firm

A job with an appraisal organization or an appraisal job with a financial institution (or with a county assessors office) can help you understand the process of valuing real estate, which is essential in buying, selling, owning, or financing properties. An understanding of cost and revenue components, the assumptions on which valuations are based, and

alternative valuation methods—comparable sales, replacement cost, and residual value analysis—can stand you in good stead in any real estate career.

Entry-level professional jobs. You might start as an appraisal assistant or trainee in an appraisal firm or financial institution, some of which may offer part-time work to college students. You would typically assist with market, due-diligence, and discounted cash flow analyses; appraisals; and pro forma assumptions for financing and sales.

Starting at an Accounting Firm

Working for a period of time at an accounting firm whose clients include real estate companies can give you a solid understanding of key facets of real estate, from the develop-

ment process, to real estate company management, financial reporting, accounting, taxes, and auditing. You would learn how to prepare cash flow analyses and projections. A number of people who started off in the accounting field have moved into the senior management ranks of development companies and other real estate organizations.

Entry-level professional jobs. College graduates are usually hired as analysts. (Some accounting firms also provide part-time work or internships to college students.) You could choose an accounting career path, which would expose you to many different companies and facets of real estate.

Accounting is not all number crunching; it also offers opportunities to work in the field visiting development sites and completed properties. You could also work on transactions, work that involves the interplay of economics, tax, accounting, and reporting to investors.

CAREER TIP: Accounting is a big-picture start to a real estate career. It gives you a complete financial perspective on real estate development projects and processes.

Starting at a Law Firm

Working for a law firm that specializes in real estate can provide good experience for a real estate career. You can, for example, work on drawing up contracts for the sale or leasing of property, get some experience in contract negotiations, become familiar with various key laws and regulations that affect real estate, and learn how to manage litigation. Perhaps you are thinking of earning a law degree. A number of successful real estate professionals have one.

Entry-level professional jobs. Some real estate law firms hire college graduates who have an interest in real estate, and some offer part-time work or internships to students. A hands-on introduction to legal work, whether as a student intern or a graduate beginning your career, can help you decide whether you want to earn a law degree and whether you would like to pursue a career as a real estate lawyer.

Starting at an Architecture Firm

Some knowledge of design and architecture—and, perhaps more important, some understanding of the real-world market and cost implications of design alternatives—will increase your value to development companies and other employers in real estate businesses. By beginning your career at an architecture firm, you buy a front-row seat to the entire development process from design through construction, and you get to see how developers' visions are translated into architectural ideas and how architectural ideas become finished buildings.

Entry-level professional jobs. Some architecture firms hire college graduates who have an interest in real estate, and some offer internships or part-time work to college students. Your work with an architecture firm—as is true for jobs in other professional organizations, such as an accounting firm or a law firm—provides an excellent opportunity for deciding on whether you might want to study for a degree in architecture.

Q&A: Working Outside the United States: Opportunities and Challenges

While many U.S. corporations operate worldwide, the number of well-capitalized U.S. developers and investors that develop or buy and sell properties in Europe, Asia, and other parts of the world is relatively small, but growing. Opportunities for American real estate professionals to work outside the country are limited, but as real estate evolves into a more global business, many American investors and developers are moving into global markets. Over time, more overseas opportunities for American real estate professionals may open up, particularly in emerging markets such as China. Every country involves a different set of rules, regulations, costs, construction methods, and barriers to entry.

Four of the interviews of real estate professionals conducted for this book focused on the interviewees' knowledge of career opportunities outside the United States and their experiences in working in other countries—the challenges and rewards and what it takes to succeed. A compilation of their comments in these Q&As follows. The four interviewees are:

—continued

continued

John Dawson, *vice president for worldwide development at McDonald's Corporation*, which operates in 120 countries. Dawson coordinates all development activities outside the United States, which involve planning for the opening of new restaurants and the relocation and closing of existing restaurants. The 15-year McDonald's veteran worked his way up in the corporation before expressing an interest in its international operations. He is based in the United States and spends two weeks of every month traveling overseas.

Gene Kohn, *principal and cofounder of Kohn Pedersen Fox Associates (KPF)*, an architectural firm. At an Urban Land Institute conference in the mid-1980s, Kohn heard an economist warn that "if you are not global by 1990, half of you will be out of business." Heedful of this advice, he and his partners decided to move the New York–based firm into the international arena, and soon KPF was hired by an investment banking client to design a building in London. The firm has since expanded in Europe and moved into the Middle East and Asia. "Going global was critical to our survival," Kohn says.

Bob Pratt, *senior director of design and construction for Tishman/Speyer Properties*, a leading owner, developer, and manager of properties throughout the United States, Europe, Latin America, and Asia. In 1986, Pratt was working for Lehrer McGovern (now Lehrer McGovern Bovis), a New York–based firm that was hired to manage construction of London's Canary Wharf. He joined the firm's team in London and spent five years in London and five in Malaysia.

Jack Rodman, *managing director in the Beijing office of Ernst & Young*. In 1985, while a partner with Kenneth Leventhal & Company (an accounting firm that later merged with Ernst & Young), Rodman went to Japan to examine a surge in Japanese investment in U.S. real estate. He subsequently began to travel to Asia on client work, developed an expertise in advising Asian banks and governments in the management and disposition of portfolios of nonperforming or bad loans, and in the late 1990s moved permanently to Asia.

What is the best preparation for overseas work?

Dawson: Understand your organization's U.S. business thoroughly before moving to another country to help export that business to a foreign market.

Rodman: Offer some special experience, knowledge, or skills; this is what foreign partners or clients seek in bringing in U.S. real estate expertise.

What skills are required for working internationally?

Dawson: Strong interpersonal, analytical, and communication skills. A deep interest in and ability to adapt to other cultures.

Pratt: Professional experience and technical skills. For example, my architectural training and my experience working on major construction projects in New York were great preparation for me. But the most important skill is the ability to listen to the local community.

What are the biggest differences between working in the United States and working in a foreign country?

Kohn: Approvals generally are harder to obtain. In Germany, city planning is more difficult. In England, preservationists play a large role. European and Asian clients want great buildings and are willing to spend more. The status of the architect is higher elsewhere than in the United States.

Pratt: In terms of construction, the biggest difference for an American going overseas is the structure of the delivery process. You must understand how this process works locally and understand what you are trying to achieve. Then you have to decide to either work within the country's system or try to change it.

Rodman: As a third-party real estate adviser, you carry less weight in Asia than in the United States, so you have to perform particularly well. The Koreans, the Chinese, and the Indians demand a huge amount of expertise.

What are the most challenging aspects of working in a foreign country?

Dawson: Different paces and different styles that can frustrate your efforts to get your point across. It can be a challenge to make sure your point is clear.

Rodman: Trying to persuade banks to make decisions that may cause near-term pain but are in their best long-term interests—for example to take write-downs from sales of bad loans in order to clean up their balance sheets.

Pratt: The first year overseas is a major transition. Not until your second or third year do you become effective in conducting business in the local culture.

What have been for you the most rewarding aspects of working in a foreign country?

Rodman: In the international marketplace, you compete with the best in the world. It feels great when you win.

Dawson: Seeing success in different cultures. Being part of a team. Being valued for the skills you contribute and not the position you hold.

Pratt: Exposure to different cultures and work methods. Discovering that the American way is not the only way to do things.

How does your firm staff overseas positions?

Rodman: In general, the Americans sent overseas by Ernst & Young are senior managers with specific knowledge and an understanding of specific processes. It is uncommon to send an American to Asia for a junior assignment, although the firm will occasionally send a young consultant who has special skills. Ernst & Young uses Americans to train local people to do the firm's ordinary work.

What would you tell a young real estate/construction professional interested in working overseas?

Pratt: It is absolutely worthwhile. Overseas work is broadening in a professional sense, and it helps you create an international network. You don't even realize how much you have learned until you have been back for a few years.

Rodman: You have to ask yourself why you want to go overseas. It is a great experience if you can get in and get out while you are young. You risk needing to start again from scratch when you return.

Dawson: Clearly understand your career aspirations, and then choose the business you want to work in and target companies involved in that business that work internationally.

Q&A: Corporate Real Estate

Corporate real estate (CRE) represents a possible career choice for students interested in real estate. It is an alternative to working for a developer, owner, or real estate services firm or becoming an entrepreneur. CRE offers a growing number of career opportunities for professionals with the requisite knowledge, experience, and skills in business and management as well as in real estate.

Corporations are among the largest owners of real estate in the United States. In fact, if the real estate assets of the largest corporations were spun off into separate companies, those companies would be among the largest owners of real estate in the world.

However, rather than being in the real estate business, corporations are users of real estate. They own or lease office buildings, manufacturing plants, warehouse and distribution centers, and other facilities that support a variety of business operations from management and administration to manufacturing, distribution, and sales.

Corporate real estate directors are the professionals who manage corporate real estate assets. In the following

—continued

continued

interviews, three CRE directors talk about their roles and responsibilities and what they look for in evaluating prospective candidates to work in their departments.

Q&A: Stephen Barker, *president of Boeing Realty*, a wholly owned Boeing Company subsidiary that directs Boeing's real estate strategies, acquisitions, dispositions, development, and leasing worldwide. A certified public accountant (CPA). Began with Boeing Realty in 1993 as controller; named president in 2003. Formerly CFO for a developer and a senior consultant with Ernst & Young's real estate practice. Graduated from California State University, Northridge, and did postgraduate studies at California State University, Fullerton.

What's your mission?

Our job is to understand the long-range strategy and needs of Boeing's core businesses and to provide the best real estate advice—and, more importantly, to make sure that the company's business needs and real estate are aligned. We manage real estate to help Boeing remain flexible, agile, and adaptable in a fast-changing market and to improve the company's bottom-line performance.

How does that pay off for the company?

The efficient use of real estate assets mitigates operating costs and helps the business units remain competitive. A long-range view of the entire Boeing enterprise allows us to balance current and long-range needs across the occupied portfolio.

How are you organized?

Of the approximately 65 people in our unit, about half are concerned with creating value through the redevelopment of surplus properties. The others provide strategic real estate services to Boeing's business units and manage relations with outside service providers. I report to the president of shared services.

How do you recruit people for your team?

We prefer people with experience on the institutional rather than the brokerage side, such as someone with a master's degree in finance who has worked for a pension

adviser, a public accountant, or someone from the corporate real estate group of a large company. We require a solid understanding of real estate—we're not a training ground—and a strong business background.

Why is a business background important?

Our people must understand the business of our internal customers. And they must be able to translate real estate into the language that businesspeople understand. That means being able to explain not just the details of subleasing space, but also the accounting and financial implications of real estate decisions or how a transaction will impact a customer's financial statements.

What types of services do you outsource?

We outsource appraisal, brokerage, and some transaction management to real estate services providers. Their representatives sit in our shop and work with our team. In addition, we pick the best brokers in local markets to manage transactions.

How do you see corporate real estate changing over the next five to ten years?

I think the change will come more on the service-provider side. Service providers will have to focus more on what's important to their customers. They all talk about their resources—their "tool boxes"—but it usually comes down to the people assigned to work on your account. We'd like to see more breadth of experience in those people.

How can service providers change to meet the expectations of CRE directors?

In the traditional brokerage environment, the execution of transactions is a high-level skill, but for corporations transactions are more of a commodity. To truly tap into the billions of dollars of property held by corporations, service providers must deliver solutions that address the changing business environments corporations operate in. One service provider that had lost out on a potential engagement with Boeing Realty asked what it could do differently. I recommended it hire some bright MBA candidates or recent graduates and put them through a yearlong training program during which they would rotate through transaction management, capital markets, asset management, and other strategic-service areas. When finished they would be ready to work in the CRE environment and would be experienced in tapping into the resources of the real estate services provider.

Will you continue to focus on the same mission?

Helping our business units succeed will always be the primary focus. The tactics we use to accomplish that will vary with the situation. People buy Boeing stock for its future business, and we are part of that future.

Q&A: **Larry Ebert,** *head of corporate real estate for Capital One*, a diversified financial services provider with a real estate portfolio of about 5 million square feet, mostly in the United States, including a 1 million-square-foot campus in Richmond, Virginia. Recruited to present position in 2003. Formerly real estate lawyer for Mead Corporation; director of real estate for Boise Cascade; executive director of the International Development Research Council (a predecessor of CoreNet Global, an organization of corporate real estate executives); and national director of real estate for Ernst & Young. Law degree from Ohio State University.

How many people are in your department?

When I joined the company, we had about 235 people. Now we have a core group of about 90.

How did you manage that?

We've moved from a tactical model that concentrated on specific services, such as transactions or facilities management, to a strategic model. We're focusing on business solutions that support the strategic goals of our company and its operating units. We're outsourcing noncore real estate processes, such as transaction management or facilities management.

What types of services do you provide to the company and the operating units?

1) Strategic planning—for example, advising Capital One on how to leverage its real estate to increase productivity and reduce costs or to attract and retain employees. 2) Strategic analysis—such as analyzing the workplace environment to determine its effect on employee innovation and creativity, which are central to our business. 3)

Portfolio planning—planning the development, acquisition, and disposition of facilities. 4) Construction management—for projects such as our new headquarters building in McLean, Virginia. 5) Account management—creating customized sets of real estate solutions and services for the operating units. 6) Risk management—such as meeting reporting and compliance requirements under the Sarbanes-Oxley law.

What skills do you look for in hiring people?

General business skills; strong management skills, particularly in solving business problems; and basic real estate knowledge.

Where have you recruited from?

Generally from other corporate real estate departments—we prefer experienced people. We haven't hired anyone right out of school, although we might if we saw a candidate who matches up with our requirements. For instance, we're recruiting an analyst for our planning group—a position that's heavy on quantitative analysis and statistics, that typically would require a graduate degree, and for which a knowledge of real estate is helpful but not necessary.

What is your process for recruiting and evaluating applicants?

We discuss our requirements with the company's human resources department, which finds prospective candidates. Applicants are given a battery of standardized tests relevant to the position they are seeking. Depending on their test results, they are then interviewed by hiring managers. It's a rigorous process.

What are you planning?

We've been working closely with our IT group on technologies to enable employees to work anytime and anywhere. We're also collaborating with IT on setting up an Internet-based, self-service real estate platform through which managers and employees can ascertain what facilities are available for use and make reservations for using available space. The intent is to provide fast, user-friendly real estate services. Technology will become increasingly important to the management of our real estate.

—continued

continued

Q&A: Robert Schuur, *manager of finance and planning in the corporate real estate department of Southern California Edison Co.,* one of the largest electric utilities in the United States. Responsible for financial reporting, budgeting for expense and capital investment, financial analysis of proposed projects, Sarbanes-Oxley compliance, and interface with the state's Public Utilities Commission and other regulatory agencies. Also responsible for the department's business process improvement efforts.

How is Edison's corporate real estate department structured?

We have about 200 people, a staff that has been declining because we have become more efficient. We've redesigned our business processes to increase productivity, for example, through better pooling and sharing of information. We're also outtasking more activities. Within the department, ten people report to me, including two supervisors. I report to the director of corporate real estate.

What professional skills are required in your position?

The ability to organize and multitask. Knowledgeability in multiple disciplines including finance, accounting, and real estate transactions. The ability to interface with internal and external clients. A talent for managing people, including people who have more professional expertise in specific areas than you do.

What education is required for a position in corporate real estate?

A bachelor's degree in business, finance, real estate, or economics would be most relevant. Increasingly, it seems that to advance in our organization it's almost mandatory to have an MBA or other master's degree.

How do you recruit people?

We mainly recruit from within. Many of our directors and managers are homegrown. I'm an exception—recruited in 1996 from a brokerage firm, Cushman & Wakefield. In the future, I expect we may recruit more people from the outside. On occasion, we recruit temporary help for specific projects, for example, a real estate professional (CPA) with an MBA degree. We recruit through our human resources department. We determine our requirements for a position and submit the skill and other requirements to HR, which typically conducts the search and the initial screening of applicants. Finding someone can take two weeks to two months, depending on the position, the skills required, and HR's workload.

Where do people usually start in corporate real estate with Edison?

It depends to some extent on the person's experience. If you join us right out of school, you usually will start as an analyst primarily doing budget-related work. These entry-level positions require an understanding of accounting and budgeting and an ability to learn and use Edison's specific systems and procedures. If you have experience as a broker or property manager, you might start as a facility manager or an agent. Agents interface with our tenants, who operate a variety of businesses—ranging from nurseries to ministorage facilities to parking garages—as secondary uses on land used for SCE's electric transmission and distribution system.

What would be the next step up from these positions?

You could go into project management, where you would gain experience in managing larger projects involving, for example, facility construction or land rights management. Or you could go into facility operations where you would manage facilities managers or help plan the company's space requirements and occupancy needs to support its current and future operations.

How would someone interested in a position with Edison approach the company?

Information on the company and positions available can be found on Edison's Web site. If you are interested, you can apply for positions through the Web site. We recruit on college campuses in southern California. You can better your prospects by developing a business relationship with someone in the company who can teach you about the organization and keep you informed on positions that may become available.

Chapter 5
On the Inside: Real Estate Jobs

What's life like on the inside, working for a real estate company? This chapter provides a series of short career profiles of real estate professionals, some of whom have just started their careers and some of whom are further along. The profiles are grouped under the business heads with which you are now familiar—developers, investors and owners, and financial and real estate services providers. These slices of life in real estate may be useful to you in your career planning. To complete this look at the world of real estate jobs, chapter 6 tells the stories of a number of real estate professionals who are entrepreneurs working for their own companies.

While the real estate professionals profiled in this chapter work in different positions and have different educational backgrounds and different career aspirations, they also have much in common—the qualities that have helped them to find work they like and to advance in their careers. They are critical thinkers, they are focused and resourceful, and they possess drive and energy. They use multiple skills in their jobs. A financial analyst must have not only excellent analytical skills, but also the ability to communicate well with clients, coworkers, and team members. A broker must have not only outstanding sales skills, but also the ability to analyze and understand sales or lease transactions, which are often highly complex.

Working for a Development or Construction Company

Director of Financial Analysis for the Irvine Company

Brian Clarke is director of financial analysis for the residential land development division of the Irvine Company, a developer of master-planned communities on The Irvine Ranch in Orange County, California. A CPA, Clarke previously worked for Kenneth Leventhal & Company, an accounting firm that specialized in real estate (see company profile on page 4), and as a controller for a small, upscale homebuilder. These work experiences helped him land his present position.

At the Irvine Company, Clarke is responsible for financial forecasting for a number of projects in various stages of planning and predevelopment. He also assists in lien allocations and disclosures for assessment and community-facility districts that use municipal bond financing to cover infrastructure costs, both before and after these districts are formed.

Clarke meets frequently with project managers to get updates on planned Irvine projects for his pro forma forecasts. He also performs cash flow modeling as part of the forecasting process. Twice a year, he prepares five- and ten-year forecasts. "A lot of the financial forecasting focuses on determining the proper land residual value and assessing highest-and-best-use scenarios for these projects," he explains. He must bring to the job both a micro and a macro perspective: "It's important to understand the nuts and bolts of a project, but you also have to see how everything fits together to form a community."

Clarke hopes eventually to move into a project management position with his employer. He is still learning the business, he says: "I feel I still have a lot to learn about the land development business. I want to make sure that I have a firm grasp on every aspect of the entitlement process, construction phase, and ultimate disposition of the land parcels. I also want to learn more about the product decision-making process, what makes a community project successful, and what are some of the common pitfalls to avoid."

Development Controller at DDC Stowe LLC

Bill Kuhnert is development controller with DDC Stowe LLC, a company that is developing resort real estate at the base of Stowe Mountain in Vermont. Before moving to the development side of the resort business in 2004, Kuhnert worked on the operations side as a finance manager for Vail Resorts Development Company, a developer of ski and golf resort communities.

As is true in many small companies, his responsibilities at Vail Resorts were not precisely defined but were similar to those of a controller's. "People were assigned different responsibilities, based on the company's needs and an individual's strengths," he notes. At Vail Resorts, Kuhnert focused on reporting results, establishing accounting systems for new projects, and forecasting financial performance for new and planned projects. The company only recently moved into the golf resort business, and Kuhnert worked with the operating managers of the golf resort communities and clubs division to set up financial forecasting and reporting systems. One of his biggest challenges was to make clear to the company's executives how accounting and performance forecasting systems used for the resort golf business differ from the systems used for the ski resort business.

Kuhnert says that his experience at Vail Resorts was invaluable in preparing him for his move to the development side of the business. "In the resort business, you must have a strong grasp of operations before you can be successful in the development side," he observes. Long term, he expects to build upon his experience to take on more senior roles, such as chief financial officer.

Director of Acquisitions for the Olson Company

Ryan Aeh is director of acquisitions with the Olson Company, a builder of urban communities. He began with the company, which is based in Seal Beach, California, as a land acquisition associate and was promoted to his present position, in which he is responsible for helping the company find new land development opportunities; managing its site acquisition efforts; maintaining relationships with redevelopment agencies, municipalities, and property owners; and acting as the community representative for projects as they are being planned and developed.

Aeh became interested in real estate as a USC undergraduate studying planning and development. An internship with a city planning department heightened his interest. "From meeting frequently with developers while a city planning intern, I decided I was more interested in development than planning," he says.

What does it take to succeed in his position? "Part of the job is trying to convince owners of land or existing buildings to sell their property to you," Aeh says. "You need to be outgoing and have people skills, and you have to be persistent. And the ability to manage time and to multitask is essential." His immediate goal is to continue his on-the-job learning about aspects of the development business, including sales, marketing, and operations.

Project Manager and Planner at Cimm's/L&R

Steven Mongeau is project manager and planner for Cimm's/L&R Construction in Glendale, California. Founded by brothers Larry and Ralph Cimmarusti, Cimm's is one of the largest owners/operators of Burger King and Tony Roma's franchises and owner of L&R, a general contractor and construction manager. Mongeau originally thought he would like to be a city planner, and interned in a city planning department for a year while he was studying for a graduate degree in planning at USC. This changed his mind: "I didn't like the bureaucratic aspects. My real interest was in economic development," he says.

Since joining Cimm's/L&R in 2000, Mongeau has managed various commercial and residential projects, such as the conversion of the historic Van De Kamp's bakery in Los Angeles into a community college, and worked with an internal design team on formalizing design guidelines and value engineering in planning new restaurant construction for the Original Roadhouse Grill, a small restaurant chain that Cimm's has acquired. He is now project manager for the company's Burger King and Tony Roma's franchises, helping to find new sites across the country, obtain entitlements, and work with architects to design and build restaurants or remodel existing ones. He also manages the company's general contracting division and helps the company with new business development.

Associate at Tishman Speyer Properties

Stephen Anderson is a financial analyst in the San Francisco office of Tishman Speyer Properties, a global real estate owner, developer, and operator, where he performs financial analysis for the company's $500 million condo development project on the San Francisco waterfront and for new office acquisitions and developments.

Before joining Tishman, Anderson was a real estate adviser in the New York office of Ernst & Young, a global busi-

ness services firm. This experience, where he had the opportunity to assist senior consultants in advising clients on large development projects and financial transactions, taught him much about real estate finance: "I learned just from being in the room during client meetings and observing," he notes.

Anderson learned of his current position at Tishman from an online ad and a contact from USC. He interviewed with Tishman executives in New York and San Francisco. "My experience in New York counted for a lot when I applied for this job," he says. One of the aspects of this position that attracted him is the company's "horizontal organization. It's not obsessed with titles or rank." Anderson is using his work at Tishman to deepen his knowledge of property development and acquisition. He hopes some day to apply that experience in starting his own company to develop infill properties in southern California or Brooklyn.

Working for a Real Estate Investor or Owner

Vice President for Real Estate Investment Banking at Eastdil Realty

Anthony Malk is a vice president in the Los Angeles office of Eastdil Realty, an investment banking firm that structures real estate transactions as investments and places them in investment markets around the world. A CPA and an MBA, he worked in the commercial real estate group of a national accounting firm and for a REIT before joining Eastdil as an associate.

As a recent MBA, Malk wanted to work for Eastdil because, the company "offers a great way to learn the real estate business if you are coming out of business school. It's given me the opportunity to work on teams with people who are on top of their game."

His day as a vice president varies, but he generally spends up to half his time analyzing numbers and up to 30 percent of his time helping to write offering packages for the sale of real estate. He particularly enjoys getting out in the field to look at properties. "I'm able to acquire experience working on different types of transactions and different uses," he said. "I get to deal with very smart people in every sector of real estate and to really understand what is going on."

His long-term plan is to stay at Eastdil and move up to managing director. "In 15 or 20 years, I'd still like to be in real estate," Malk says, and adds: "People who leave this firm after a long career here have a lot of different options."

Director of Acquisitions for IPC US REIT

Zachary Vaughan is director of acquisitions for Toronto-based IPC US REIT, a Canadian real estate investment trust that focuses exclusively on the ownership and management of U.S. commercial properties. His job is to identify and evaluate acquisition opportunities for IPC. Vaughan's father was a real estate lawyer who developed properties on the side, and he knew early on that he wanted to be in real estate. After graduating from the University of Western Ontario, he worked for a real estate asset management firm in the United States for a few years, learning the U.S. real estate market. This experience helped him obtain his current position.

Vaughan needs to keep abreast of property markets. His daily tasks include talking with brokers and other people in the know, reviewing industry publications and other sources

REAL ESTATE OFFERS MANY OPPORTUNITIES FOR PUBLIC SERVICE

Students interested in real estate often ask about opportunities to work for a company (or start a business) that provides tangible benefits to the community. In their view—as well as in the view of many people in the real estate industry—real estate is not just about making money (although that's obviously important), but also about helping people.

In a broad sense, much real estate activity is involved with promoting the general public good by providing needed housing, commercial, and public-use facilities. In a narrower sense, some real estate activity is specifically directed to markets or facilities that serve a specific development need, such as housing for low-income people, shelters for the homeless or for battered spouses, community centers, inner-city retail complexes, or urban infill and redevelopment.

So how can you identify opportunities to contribute to the public good through real estate work?

REAL ESTATE COMPANIES

Many for-profit companies focus on community-sensitive work. Phoenix Realty Group, for example, creates and manages smart growth equity funds that raise capital from pension funds, life insurance companies, and other investors to, for example, finance the development of affordable housing for middle-income professionals— police officers, firefighters, teachers, and other providers of essential services—who often cannot afford to live in the communities where they work. Other for-profit companies work with nonprofit organizations to develop projects that benefit communities. And others join with public sector entities to develop joint public/private projects with public-use or public-purpose components.

In your research on job possibilities, if you pay attention to the specific businesses conducted by real estate companies, you will find many that are involved in areas that can satisfy your desire to contribute to the public good.

COMMUNITY DEVELOPMENT CORPORATIONS

Community development—the revitalization of local communities under the leadership of residents—is a growing field that offers career opportunities. Community development efforts generally focus on the economy (jobs and incomes); the community's physical character (housing, stores, parks and public spaces, transportation facilities, and the environment); and the community's social bonds.

Community development often is carried out by community development corporations (CDCs), which are usually created and controlled by residents. CDCs typically are incorporated as nonprofit, tax-exempt organizations and their boards include residents, municipal officials, bankers and other investors, real estate professionals, and other people plugged into community resources. CDCs involve themselves in a variety of projects, such as the development of affordable housing, the development of retail centers, business attraction, and after-school programs.

There are thousands of CDCs across the United States, and they are supported by a large network of banks and other financial institutions that provide equity and debt capital; nonprofit organizations that invest in community development initiatives; for-profit developers and other businesses that partner with CDCs on specific programs and projects; and local, state, and federal government agencies that provide funding and subsidies.

National networks of support to CDCs are provided by a number of organizations, including the Local Initiatives Support Corporation, Enterprise Community Partners (formerly the Enterprise Foundation), and NeighborWorks America.

Community development organizations offer a number of career opportunities in community lending, development planning, property management, research and public policy, community services, housing development, construction, rehabilitation, and other fields. Many universities have created programs for students interested in community development careers. To explore your interest in the field, you might work as a volunteer or an intern for a CDC.

PUBLIC SECTOR

Public sector work is not within the purview of this book, but real estate students should be aware that there are many opportunities for real estate–related planning and development careers in the public sector in which they can use real estate skills to create tangible social benefits.

of market information, evaluating offering memorandums from brokers, and running financial analyses on potential property acquisitions. "I need to be resourceful in learning about markets, because most of the time the buildings we're interested in are located in markets we've never been to," he says. "I need to be able to pick up the phone and speak to the head of a brokerage company to get information." If a site inspection is warranted, Vaughan visits the property. In fact, he spends about 40 percent of his time traveling.

Acquisitions Manager at SARES-REGIS Group

Stephen Lanni is acquisitions manager in the multifamily acquisitions for the investment and development group at the SARES-REGIS Group, a commercial and multifamily real estate investment and development company headquartered in Irvine, California.

As a college graduate with a major in real estate finance and marketing, Lanni started out his career as an analyst in the Los Angeles office of Jones Lang LaSalle (JLL), a global real estate services firm. JLL provided a week's basic training to help new analysts learn the company and further develop their real estate knowledge and software skills and Lanni was trained and shown the ropes, including help with his Excel modeling skills, by other analysts and associates. At JLL, he says, "the senior professionals liked to throw you into the fire to see how well you can perform, but they would

never let you get burned. Everyone, from analysts to senior vice presidents, was easily accessible for questions and always willing to help you out."

He worked up to senior financial analyst at JLL, and was part of an acquisition and disposition team that helped a major bank find sites for new banking centers in southern and central California. "I helped find pad sites in grocery-anchored shopping centers, bring in project management from JLL to complete due diligence on the sites, submit site analysis packages to the bank, buy or lease the land, and get the center up and running," Lanni says, adding that "everything we did was team-oriented. Everyone worked together and helped each other to make sure the client was happy."

At SARES-REGIS, which Lanni joined in 2004, he works directly under the president of multifamily acquisitions for investment and development on land and property acquisitions for rental apartment and attached for-sale housing development, for conversion to condominiums, and for multifamily investment transactions. He says that many of his college real estate courses—including principles, finance, and case studies—have helped him to develop the technical knowledge and critical thinking skills that are essential in his current position. "I joined SARES-REGIS to broaden the scope of my knowledge of the real estate business and to gain skills on the investment and development side," Lanni says. His long-term goal is to own and operate his own real estate investment and development company.

Associate Director of Investment Research with CB Richard Ellis Investors

Shubhra Jha is associate director of investment research with CB Richard Ellis Investors, the investment management affiliate of CB Richard Ellis, a global real estate services firm. She started her career as an architect in India, with a bachelor's of architecture degree earned in New Delhi. Then she was "inspired to consider a career as an analyst" by a class in market analysis taught by the late Rena Sivitanidou, associate professor in USC's School of Policy, Planning, and Development, where Jha earned a master's in urban planning. "Having a background in planning and architecture, I saw how market demand ultimately drives the planning and design of a building," she says, and "it was at that point that I decided that market analysis was what I wanted to do."

At CB Richard Ellis, Jha is responsible for monitoring commercial property market trends in major U.S. metropolitan areas, producing economic forecasts and real estate market reviews for proposed acquisitions, preparing annual market summaries for assets in the firm's portfolio, and assisting with the production of specialized studies on economic and real estate market trends. "A lot of my work involves taking the market data and models we purchase and changing them to reflect our knowledge of individual markets," she explains. "My education in market analysis really comes into play here, as most companies take the purchased data and use it unaltered."

Working for a Financial or Real Estate Services Company

Relationship Manager at Wells Fargo Bank

Gail Tubbs is a relationship manager with Wells Fargo's real estate merchant banking group in Los Angeles. He got into banking not by design, but because an opportunity came up through a USC alumnus he met while he was at USC studying for an MBA. "I didn't imagine myself ending up in banking or at a large institution," he says. "It was not planned, but now that I'm here I enjoy it very much."

He has found real estate to be rewarding work. "One of the great things about real estate," he says, "is that there is no normal day." Tubbs works on financial analysis and loan underwriting, monitoring the progress of real estate projects, and processing requests for loan draws. He needs to pay attention to details, to carefully document and support his activities to meet regulatory and internal control requirements. Tubbs also works the phone. For example, he helps clients structure potential real estate deals for financing. "Our business is built on financial services," he says, "but it's really a people business. Relationships are important." On many days, he's in the field, looking at properties that the bank has financed or is thinking of financing.

One aspect of working with real estate that he likes is that "you're not just dealing with financial instruments or pieces of paper. There's actually a tangible asset."

Sales and Leasing Agent for Colliers International

Ronald Tong is a sales and leasing agent in the Pleasanton, California, office of Colliers International, a global brokerage firm. An undergraduate degree in economics and a law degree were good preparation for this work. His economics degree helps him to understand the impact of economic indicators such as employment growth on demand for space. His law degree helps him land leases: "Leases are complicated contracts, and having a legal background has helped me in putting leases together. More importantly, law school honed my negotiating skill, and that is perhaps the one skill that can make or break you in this line of work."

—continued on page 78

Career Profile: **Ken Rock**

Ken Rock, senior cost manager with Tishman Speyer, a leading owner, developer, and manager of properties throughout the United States, Europe, Latin America, and Asia, has gone from design work, to construction management, to development management and he would like to eventually manage a real estate portfolio.3

Goal-related education has been a staple element of Ken Rock's real estate career to date.

Pre-MRED

Ken Rock's path into real estate was a traditional one: construction. He majored in engineering at Stanford University and spent his junior year at the school's overseas study center in Berlin, where he participated in a program that offered students an internship with a German company. Rock's internship with a small German architectural firm piqued an interest in working internationally. He went on to earn a master's degree in construction management at Stanford.

Rock decided to seek employment in Berlin: "Since I had been a student in Berlin in 1988, the Berlin Wall had fallen, Germany had reunified, and a construction boom was underway. I decided to explore opportunities there for employment in the real estate and construction business." Before leaving the United States, he compiled a list of American companies in Berlin and people to contact for networking. "An American architect referred me to a British engineering company that had just established a Berlin office. I met the managing director. He liked my educational background and the fact that I spoke decent German and was familiar with Berlin, so he hired me."

Rock worked for the engineering firm in Berlin and later in London. After a time, he says, "I grew tired of working only on the design side of construction projects. I wanted to work for an owner's organization and to have responsibility for managing the overall development process." He therefore joined Tishman Speyer as a construction manager in Berlin to work on the development of a large, mixed-use project. He subsequently worked for the company in San Francisco.

Post-MRED

After six years in construction management, Rock decided he would be more interested in the business side of real estate. "I also wanted to learn more about development, and specifically about the entitlement and approval process and about how to create pro formas," he says. He enrolled at USC to study for a master's of real estate development degree (MRED).

After graduating, Rock joined the Schuster Group, a small, entrepreneurial development company based in Seattle that specializes in value-added projects. He attributes his success in finding employment with Schuster to a combination of his work experience and the analytical skills he developed in the MRED program. His work at Schuster was mainly to manage development projects, and "my construction management and financial skills were most important in this work."

After a year with Schuster, Rock found that he missed the environment of a large firm, working on large projects, and being part of a team, so he returned to Tishman Speyer to work on a large commercial development project in New York City. Long term, he says, he would like to advance to a position as senior manager of a real estate portfolio, dealing with both existing product and new development. And he might want to work internationally again. For now, he is pleased with where he is: "I'm having fun, and enjoying being back on a large project again."

Career Profile: **Marinel Robinson**

Marinel Robinson, principal of DeComa Structural Industries, a Torrance, California-based industrial and commercial engineering and contracting firm, has persuaded her partners to refocus the firm on development.

Marinel Robinson felt that her construction firm could find new opportunities by expanding into development, and she went back to school to learn about the development business.

In on the Ground Floor

Robinson graduated with a degree in journalism from USC, but decided that journalism wouldn't pay enough for her to repay her college loans, move out of her parent's house, buy a car, and meet other expenses. So she took a job with DeComa, a construction firm that specialized in the structural upgrading, renovation, and conversion of commercial and industrial properties. The firm needed an office manager who could write, keep the books, and operate the computer. She went on to obtain her contractor's license and work her way up to a partnership position. She liked the business: "The art of building something that might serve a useful purpose was fascinating, and so were the financial and deal-making aspects of building."

Robinson felt that DeComa could find new opportunities by expanding from construction into development. To learn more about the development business, she returned to USC to earn a master's of real estate development (MRED) degree. Her enthusiasm for real estate struck her mother as "funny," given her maternal grandfather's career as an apartment developer in the Philippines. "Real estate must be in my DNA," Robinson says.

Becoming an Entrepreneur

After graduating from USC, Robinson decided to become an entrepreneur, not by going out on her own, but by convincing her partners to focus DeComa on development, a more entrepreneurial and higher-risk business, but one that potentially offered greater financial rewards. "We had been strictly engineers and contractors for ten years prior to my earning an MRED," Robinson notes. "Fortunately, my partners were willing to try something new."

To help raise startup capital for development, Robinson borrowed from family and friends. "That made me really nervous," she says, but "now, we're able to use our own money for small projects and then joint-venture for larger projects." The company's development projects have included the Toy Warehouse Lofts in downtown Los Angeles, the first for-sale artist lofts in Los Angeles; the Mission District Lofts in South Pasadena; and The Blair House, the first artist lofts in Torrance, California.

A few successful projects and good relationships have made raising money less of a chore. "I'm hoping that with good sense and some good luck, we'll always make a profit for our investors," says Robinson.

Career Lessons

"We still have a long way to go before we are fully committed to development work," Robinson admits. Meanwhile, every project undertaken has given her—and her partners—more experience and confidence in development. "Having a construction background makes all the difference in the world, and so does the finance experience," Robinson observes. "The gift of gab—of being able to convince the public and government officials that a project is worthwhile—comes over time."

As an entrepreneur, Robinson tries to emulate other entrepreneurs. "Most entrepreneurs I know have incredible street smarts, very little fear, and enough confidence to know that they will land on their feet—no matter what," she says. "They're also born leaders and visionaries. Vision is what sets them apart from the rest and keeps them a step ahead."

Has she had any second thoughts about being an entrepreneur? "In general, women in real estate development have two choices: Work for a large builder and be satisfied with marketing or design work. Or, work as an entrepreneur and have the opportunity to do it all. I chose to be an entrepreneur."

Career Profile: **Renata Simril**

Currently vice president for development with Forest City Enterprises, a publicly traded diversified real estate company (see company profile on page 22) and former deputy mayor for housing and economic development for the city of Los Angeles, Renata Simril has experienced development from the public and private sides.

The focus of Simril's career and expertise has been the development of economically underserved urban communities, as both a public official and a private developer.

A Focus on Urban Issues

Simril became interested in development at 19 when she was traveling through Europe. "I liked the fact that cities in Europe are so well designed and planned. They felt good to be in," she says. After serving as a military police officer in the U.S. Army, she earned a bachelor's of science degree in urban studies at Loyola Marymount University in Los Angeles and a master's of real estate development (MRED) degree at USC.

Since graduating, she has worked as an employee of the Los Angeles Community Redevelopment Agency; a council deputy for redevelopment on the staff of city council member Mark Ridley-Thomas; director of development for a national real estate development company; and vice president for Genesis LA Economic Growth Corporation, a nonprofit urban development organization. Simril served as deputy mayor for housing and economic development under former mayor James Hahn, where she was involved with economic investment, housing, workforce development, and community growth. As deputy mayor, she was the top negotiator on major development projects and was responsible for human capital issues and managing housing policies and initiatives.

After leaving the mayor's office in June 2005, Simril joined the Los Angeles division of Forest City Enterprises in its residential development group. At Forest City, Simril's two primary responsibilities are managing the development of 3800 Wilshire, a 22-story office building that is being converted into 238 condominium units; and helping to grow the company's development opportunities in southern California through public/private partnerships. Her experience in acquisition and predevelopment, her knowledge of public policy and planning, and her ability to navigate through the city's often cumbersome entitlement processes are important skills that she brings to this job.

"Forest City was one of a few private sector developers that I would consider working for, due to its long history of building community, its reputation in the industry, and its expertise and desire to work on large-scale public/private partnerships," Simril says. "Forest City excels at creating long-term, mutually beneficial relationships in its target markets, and it is a leader in the real estate industry. I felt that this would be a great place to apply my 13 years of knowledge and experience and an exceptional place to expand my knowledge of the real estate business."

Career Lessons

Simril advises students who are considering a career in real estate development to develop a thorough knowledge of all its aspects, but particularly finance. "This doesn't mean you must have a degree in finance. A few courses in school and experience as an analyst, junior loan officer, or appraiser can get you the knowledge you need. But you have to do more than simply model (calculate) numbers. Finance drives all deals, but pro forma analysis is only your best guess on how well your project will perform in the market 12 to 36 months in the future. So, you must do your due diligence and truly understand what the numbers are telling you."

Also, Simril tells students to appreciate the role that good urban design and land use planning play in establishing the framework for good development projects. And also to gain an understanding of the public aspects of the development process, including the politics of public decision making and community review of potentially controversial projects.

She considers lifelong learning to be an important success factor in the development profession. "Expose yourself to the different facets of development. Always be willing to learn—be it the newest financing technique, land use principles, or design strategy. A thirst for continuous learning is a key to longevity in this business."

continued from page 74

To identify opportunities in his market, Tong reads business journals and trade publications and talks frequently with clients and other people with information. "Beyond that," he says, "I review and prepare lease quotes, negotiate lease terms, and, if everything goes well, sell or lease some office space." Brokerage is an extremely competitive business, where success depends on the ability to build relationships with tenants and landlords, buyers and sellers. "Unless you know the tenants in your market, it's unlikely they will seek you out. You cannot afford to let any opportunity go by. If you aren't maintaining relationships with developers and landlords, your competitors will gladly take your place," says Tong. But simply knowing the right people is not enough. "Unless you come off as someone who is credible and has valuable ideas, why would anyone maintain a relationship with you? Every prospect has people like me offering to take them to lunch or to golf or to dinner. You have to bring value to the table."

Chapter 6
On the Inside: Becoming an Entrepreneur

Are you interested in becoming an entrepreneur—a person who organizes and operates a business and assumes the risk for it? In real estate, entrepreneurs have started every kind of business, from development to consulting, brokerage, asset management, property investment, investment banking, and many others. Susan Hudson-Wilson, for example, founded and was CEO of Property and Portfolio Research, a Boston-based real estate research and portfolio strategy services firm whose clients include institutional investors, developers, and public agencies.

On page 80 is a quick test to help you decide whether you are entrepreneur material or would be happier in a corporate career. Of course, you won't base your decision on a single test, which only complements other resources. Read the career profiles and Q&As in this chapter. They all tell stories of entrepreneurs. Peruse the books and articles listed under entrepreneurship in appendix A. Talk to entrepreneurs about their experiences. If you have the opportunity, work for an entrepreneur. These activities will give you the knowledge and experience to decide whether entrepreneurship is right for you.

Entrepreneurs possess a number of important attributes in common:

A vision or unique idea for a business. Isadore (Issy) Sharp had the idea to build what he called a motor hotel in downtown Toronto. It would combine the convenience of a motel with the service of a downtown hotel. Today he's chairman and CEO of the Four Seasons hotel and resort chain (see Q&A on page 85).

The persuasiveness to sell their vision. Entrepreneurs are able to persuade others to invest in their vision. The idea is what's valuable. Entrepreneurs who have good ideas and can communicate those ideas will be able to find money.

The passion to pursue their vision. Entrepreneurs believe in their vision—and in themselves. That belief drives them to overcome all odds to achieve their vision.

Initiative. Entrepreneurs are self-starters. They take the initiative. They are doers—energetic, enthusiastic, and hard working.

The ability to execute. Entrepreneurs don't just dream. They act on their vision. They create a plan to accomplish their goals. In short, they execute.

Adaptability. Entrepreneurs are quick reactors. They can readily adapt to the exigencies of the market, to opportunities that crop up, and to unexpected challenges. This gives them an edge over larger but slower-moving competitors in acquiring properties, closing transactions, and completing development projects.

The ability to manage risk. Starting a business is a risky endeavor. Successful entrepreneurs know how to assess and manage the risk involved in various tasks including business startup, raising capital, taking on partners, starting projects, obtaining entitlements, meeting budgets, and completing projects on schedule. "There's very little margin for error," says Sean Hyatt, development manager with AMCAL, a multifamily housing developer based in Agoura Hills, California. "You always have to be on top of your game."

Sense of timing. Real estate is cyclical. Entrepreneurs know when to buy (the market is at or near the bottom of its cycle) and when to sell (the market is at the top of its cycle). They always design an exit strategy up-front.

Are You Entrepreneurial?

Choose option "a" or "b" for each of the following
either/or statements.

1. I prefer
   a. ☐ a 50 percent chance of $100,000 and a 50 per-
      cent chance of $0.
   b. ☐ $50,000 guaranteed.

2. I am
   a. ☐ willing to put all my personal assets at risk for a
      large potential reward.
   b. ☐ not willing to risk losing all my personal assets for
      a large potential reward.

3. I
   a. ☐ enjoy taking on difficult challenges.
   b. ☐ prefer to take a more organized approach.

4. In the face of failure, I
   a. ☐ am undeterred and pick myself back up to
      immediately try again.
   b. ☐ have difficulty starting over again.

5. I enjoy
   a. ☐ being fully immersed in a project and working
      long, odd hours to finish it.
   b. ☐ working in a structured environment with pre-
      dictable, steady hours.

6. If somebody disagrees with me, I tend to
   a. ☐ argue fiercely to convince them that I am right.
   b. ☐ move on, letting them think what they want.

7. When I encounter a problem, my first impulse is to
   a. ☐ come up with my own solution.
   b. ☐ find an existing solution that I can copy.

8. I am
   a. ☐ comfortable changing my style of behavior to
      achieve my goals.
   b. ☐ uncomfortable changing my style of behavior to
      achieve my goals.

9. Having employees or coworkers dependent on me for
   their livelihood
   a. ☐ motivates me.
   b. ☐ keeps me up all night worrying.

10. I
    a. ☐ thrive on competition.
    b. ☐ am not particularly competitive.

11. I am comfortable with new endeavors
    a. ☐ even if I don't know all I can about them.
    b. ☐ only if I know all I can about them.

12. For me, constantly working with new people in
    new situations
    a. ☐ is exciting and motivating.
    b. ☐ sometimes emotionally draining.

13. I feel
    a. ☐ comfortable sharing my ideas with others.
    b. ☐ uncomfortable sharing my ideas with others.

14. Generally, I would
    a. ☐ like to be actively involved in investing my
       retirement fund.
    b. ☐ not like to be actively involved in investing my
       retirement fund.

15. I would rather
    a. ☐ be at risk and paid for my exceptional
       performance.
    b. ☐ be paid a regular salary.

16. I tend to think that
    a. ☐ there is more than one way to solve a problem.
    b. ☐ there is usually only one way to solve a problem.

Scoring: Nine or more "b" answers, think about a corporate career; 12 or more "a" answers, seriously consider an
entrepreneurial track.

The ability to take a pass. Entrepreneurs know when to say "no." They walk away from deals that they perceive as too risky, from partners that lack sufficient experience or capital, or from lenders offering unacceptable financing terms.

Problem-solving ability. Entrepreneurs are creative problem-solvers. They analyze the problem, develop solutions, and move forward.

Communication skills. Entrepreneurs are highly skilled communicators. They are able to get their ideas across, and they know how to sell their ideas, listen to others, and negotiate effectively.

Networking skills. Entrepreneurs are highly effective at developing professional and personal relationships, building networks, and using networks to identify investment opportunities, access capital, and find partners.

Sense of responsibility. When entrepreneurs invest not only their own money, but also other people's money, they are cost-conscious, budget-focused, and time-sensitive. Good entrepreneurs know how to get the most value for their money, by, for example, hiring contractors best qualified to do the work at the most competitive prices rather than the contractor that submits the lowest bid.

Getting started as an entrepreneur is challenging. Some real estate entrepreneurs started down that road early in their careers, often with little or no capital or experience. They raised money from family, friends, and local investors and lenders, and started up their business by acquiring or developing one piece of property or providing consulting services to a few clients.

People today can still start their real estate careers as an entrepreneur, but it is much harder. Real estate has become a more complex and difficult business and would-be entrepreneurs face more competition in raising capital and finding investment opportunities. Starting-out entrepreneurs must have a high level of knowledge, experience, and sophistication. Some people who know they would like to be entrepreneurs work first for a large real estate organization that offers learning and entrepreneurial opportunities, as well as opportunities to develop professional and personal relationships. They then leverage their knowledge, experi-

ence, and connections to raise capital and start their own businesses.

You might take the same approach, working for a company first and then going out on your own. Whether you go out on your own early in your career or later on, you will likely go through a number of the same steps:

Begin, as do all entrepreneurs, with a vision. The simpler the vision, the better your chances of success. Start with a relatively low-risk, generic investment. For example, form a partnership with people you know and trust to buy a small apartment building and manage it, perhaps by contracting out to a reputable property management company. Later, you might work up to development or to the acquisition of more complicated properties, such as a large office building or a mixed-use development. The important thing is not to begin by attempting a project that's too big, complicated, or long term.

Look for investment opportunities. Where will you find your first acquisition opportunity? Begin with places that you know well in the city or neighborhood where you live. Drive around, walk around, and look at properties. Use your imagination and creativity to envision alternative uses for the neighborhood and specific sites that seem promising to you. Consider how you would add value to an acquired property. For example, if you bought and upgraded an apartment building, could you attract more tenants and increase rents? Get a feel for the local real estate market. Talk to brokers, developers, lenders, investors, city officials, and others who might provide leads on investment opportunities. Perhaps a proposed zoning change—to, for example, permit limited commercial uses in a residential neighborhood—will open up investment opportunities.

Perform due diligence. If you see an opportunity to acquire a property, prepare a market analysis on it, as well as a feasibility study, preliminary cash flow projections, and pro forma income and expense estimates. Define your market—for example, the companies, businesses, professionals, small businesses, or other organizations that would rent space in the property you're considering. How large is this tenant market? How will you attract tenants? What rents will you charge? What will it cost to acquire the property? If you acquire it, what improvements might be required to attract tenants and charge higher rents? Who are your competitors in this market?

Establish investment requirements. You also need to develop investment requirements for the property. What cash flow will potential investors expect? What returns on their investment? If you need assistance in addressing such questions, you might consider hiring professional consultants—or perhaps graduate students knowledgeable in market and financial analysis—to work out the numbers. Once you have all the necessary information, you can decide whether to spend the time and effort needed to find investors.

Raise capital. If you decide to go ahead, one of your biggest challenges will be to raise the necessary capital. Few lenders will risk financing development by an unknown, inexperienced, and unproven entrepreneur, even if the project is small. You will probably have to go through a long list of contacts and capital providers—including family, friends, business associates, property investors (individuals or institutions), brokers, development entrepreneurs and companies, and nonprofit organizations—in your efforts to find capital. You will have to think creatively about how you might attract investors.

Form a development partnership. Once you have found investors, you can form a partnership to buy or develop the property. To be sure, you could plunge ahead on your own, but the risks are high. A partnership allows you to share the risks, as well as draw on the talents, knowledge, and experience of other investors; access sources of equity capital; and obtain financing from lenders. Banks and other lenders will be more receptive to financing your property acquisition or development if you have experienced developers or investors as partners.

If you have little money to invest and can convince others of the value of your deal, you may be able to persuade partners to contribute capital in return for owning most or all of the interests in the partnership. You might even offer to accept a fee in lieu of an equity interest in the deal, which

would give your investors most of the profit. In such a deal structure, you would come away not with a lot of cash, but with the experience of having completed your first project, with the start of a track record. You can build on this to establish your credibility as an entrepreneur, look for other investment opportunities, attract other partners, and put together deals in which you have a larger equity stake. Then you can begin to accumulate capital and create wealth.

Prepare a formal business plan. At a minimum, your business plan should include the following:

- a description of the specific project; or, if a project has not been identified, a detailed description of the type of property or product that is being sought and its location;
- an analysis and evaluation of the market, including an economic overview and feasibility analysis of the project;
- a timetable of the entire program, from option or purchase to approvals, construction, and leasing/sale;
- your professional background and qualifications, and the qualifications of your team members, if there is a team;
- a financial analysis covering how much equity you and other investors are putting into the project, how much debt financing is required, the type of debt, various customary performance measures such as return on capital and IRR, and tax implications; and
- pictures of the site and drawings and plans if applicable/available.

The forgoing list is not intended to detail all the components of the business plan. Your objective in preparing a business plan is to demonstrate to the investor(s) that you are organized, disciplined, knowledgeable, and committed.

Establish a reporting methodology. Once you have secured your backers and started going ahead with the project, it is essential to establish a system of reporting that stresses frequent contact, full disclosure, and complete credibility. In your representations to investors, you need to take care that they understand the project. Avoid knowledge gaps, false assumptions on their part, and high expectations that are not deliverable. You're better off underestimating and overdelivering than you are underdelivering.

Q&A: Sam Zell

CEO of Equity Office Properties Trust, the largest publicly held office building owner and manager in the United States. Started real estate career as a college junior investing in apartment buildings.

"Real estate is a business with an unending scale of opportunity for anybody playing in it."

When did you become an entrepreneur?
In grammar school, I ran my own business—taking pictures at school parties. In high school, I took prom pictures. In college, I ran a business selling party favors. I started in the real estate business when I was a junior in college.

How did you get started?
The owner of the house in which I was visiting a friend had bought, with an associate, an adjacent house. He told us that they were going to tear them both down and build an apartment building for students. My friend and I knew a lot more about what students wanted than those two guys. So we put together a little brochure and pitched them. We said: "Look we're students, we understand what students want, we understand how to sell and how to manage buildings, and we'll end up doing it for you for less—and produce a better result." They bought it. That's how we started. We were so successful running the first building that they gave us another one to run. Then I had

an opportunity to buy a three-flat building. By the time I graduated from law school, we had 3,200 to 4,000 units on three different campuses.

What personal or professional qualities does it take to succeed in real estate?
To succeed, you need transactional acumen and an understanding of the business and the people in it. You must absorb a lot of knowledge, but real estate is a business with an unending scale of opportunity for anybody playing in it.

What do you look for in people who want to work for you?
Ambition, drive, motivation, analytical skills, and appetite for risk—for starters. And nobody can possibly grow a serious business today without personal leadership skills. The days of the tyrannical boss are long gone. The people who succeed are able to get others to follow them. I look for someone with high motivation and high energy, for someone who outworks, outthinks, outdoes, and outperforms.

—continued

Q&A: **Sam Zell**

continued

Where's the best place for a young person to get started? In a small or big company? As an entrepreneur?

First and foremost, get a grounding, develop a true understanding of how this business works. Understanding the business provides an intellectual base and tells you where in this business you may find a fit or where it makes sense for you to fit. I tell people to work for a bank, work for an opportunity fund, work as a number cruncher. A year or two of that kind of training is irreplaceable.

How do you see the industry evolving over the next decade?

Megacompanies will emerge, but their existence will not preclude entrepreneurial companies. That may sound contradictory, but I don't think it is. Huge specialized asset-rich companies—like Simon Properties, Equity Office, Equity Residential, or ProLogis—will always be part of the real estate format going forward. However, they will have to outsource the functions in which the entrepreneurial spirit is and always will be relevant—including the development of new properties and the assemblage of land.

Do you have to experience a down cycle to really mature as a real estate professional?

No question about that. Someone with a lot of gray hair—or in my case, no hair—learns over time that you need to attempt to understand what the exit or fire-sale value of a proposed investment might be. The greatest weakness in very bright people is that they don't understand that you have to figure out the downside.

How will tomorrow's industry differ from today's?

Real estate historically has been a mostly closed industry, very much a family business. In the future, it will be more like a professional business, exposed to a broader and deeper pool of talent.

Q&A: Isadore (Issy) Sharp

Chairman and CEO of Four Seasons, a Toronto-based, global hotel and resort management company, which he founded in 1960.

On the genesis of Four Seasons: "There really was no grand dream. I was just trying to put one deal together. I had an idea."

How did you get started?

When people ask me what was my vision for Four Seasons, I candidly tell them there really was no grand dream. I was just trying to put one deal together. I had an idea. Even though our businesses are different, I think it's probably the same with most real estate entrepreneurs.

What was the idea?

To build what I called a motor hotel in downtown Toronto. It would combine the best of a motel, such as convenience, with the best of a hotel, such as service. At the time (late 1950s), motels were located mainly along highways and hotels were located mainly in downtowns. It was an idea that went through a lot of changes from when I started until I finally got it built.

How did you get the idea?

I'm a builder by trade. While I was building a small motel for a friend, I got the idea. Actually, I couldn't see how my friend and his wife were going to make the motel work, but they succeeded by providing good service. I more or less stumbled into the motor hotel deal, rather than choosing to develop a hotel as opposed to offices, apartments, or a retail project. But the idea of a service business was more interesting to me than building apartments and houses.

How long did it take you to realize the concept?

It took me five years to convince people that my idea would work and persuade them to put up the money for the project. Working mainly at night—because during the day I had to earn a living—I showed people the (sort of) pro formas that I had put together and asked if they'd like to invest. I knocked on a lot of doors and got a lot of rejections.

What kept you going?

Having an idea that is clear in your own mind gives you the perseverance to stick with it despite the skepticism you may encounter. A clear idea keeps you going, even if its realization takes much longer than you had expected.

Was financing an obstacle?

Yes, because at the time I didn't have any knowledge, any experience. People would say they knew I could build something, but ask could I run it? My telling them that I'd hire somebody who knows how fell on a lot of deaf ears. I finally got help from the owner of a mortgage company that had loaned me money to build houses. I could raise half the money, he would lend me the other half.

How did you get up to speed on the hotel industry?

I learned simply from extensive reading and talking to many people—including a lender who knew a lot about hotels and motels. And I used common sense. I thought about what travelers might need, about what would make life on the road a little easier. As a result, we offered services and amenities that no other hotel company at the time was providing.

What does it take to be a successful entrepreneur?

No matter what business you're in, you have to have an idea that's so clear to you that all it will take to make it work is a little money, and you have to approach the realization of your vision like a fanatic. You must doggedly pursue your idea to the point that it gains credibility with others.

Do you have to be willing to take risks?

You're always aware of the risks, because people are quick to point them out. People told me that I didn't understand what could go wrong with my project. I would assure them that I did understand, but also show them how it could work. When you believe in your idea, you're able to answer the skeptics.

—continued

Q&A: Isadore (Issy) Sharp

continued

What advice would you give students in deciding on a career in real estate?

The first key to success in business is a great education. No matter what career you choose, get the best education you can afford. Nothing will serve your purposes more. The broader your education, the better. Study economics, psychology, philosophy, art, law—whatever rounds you out as a person and improves your ability to communicate well and think clearly. To succeed in your career, show people what you're capable of doing. If you see an opportunity that really appeals to you, take it. As a kid, you always did those things that you were passionate about. If you apply the same passion to your career, it will lead you to success.

What personal qualities are needed to succeed in real estate?

The key to Four Seasons's successful relationships with real estate developers around the world is their ability to deal with us in ways that build mutual trust and respect.

I strongly believe that success in the real estate business, as in the hotel management business, depends on trustworthiness. People starting out in their careers should never compromise their integrity for personal gain.

What type of people do you hire?

In the hotel management business, competitive advantage comes from the consistency and quality of customer service. We go to great lengths to hire people who really fit with our culture. Candidates go through at least four or five interviews, and a general manager conducts the last interview, regardless of whether the job is dishwasher or management executive.

What will make people tomorrow's leaders in the real estate industry?

Leaders have to demonstrate that they are trustworthy. By being trustworthy, they can earn respect, gain influence, and bring out the best in others. Leadership is not about the leader's accomplishments; it's about what the leader gets others to do.

Career Profile: **Francine Starks**

Francine Starks, founder of Terra Nova Consulting, a firm that provides consulting, research, and brokerage service to developers, applied skills she had developed as a consultant to high-tech firms to a startup real estate business.

Francine Starks left the high-tech industry to found a real estate firm.

A Career Switch

After earning an engineering degree at USC and a master's degree in electrical engineering and computer systems at Stanford, Starks worked for several years as an engineer. She then attended Harvard Business School, and after graduation worked in marketing and product management for such companies as Intel and Oracle. At Intel, she had an opportunity to work for a time in the corporate real estate department and enjoyed it so much that she began thinking of a career in real estate. But she decided instead to start a firm that provided strategic consulting services to high-tech companies.

Then a downturn in the technology industry caused her to think again about real estate. Her family had dabbled in real estate and she herself had had some success investing in real estate. Drawing on her experience in consulting, using capital from her property investments, and applying skills she had developed as a high-tech consultant, she started her own firm, Terra Nova Consulting.

Starks's client work has included negotiating the acquisition of a site for a 260-unit townhouse project; performing a market feasibility study for a four-acre residential development project; performing financial analysis for a five-block, 14-acre commercial strip; and serving as the interim project manager for a one-square-mile redevelopment project. She is a board member of the Ross Minority Program in Real Estate at USC, an initiative to help real estate and community development professionals refine development skills in areas that can benefit inner-city neighborhoods and minority areas (see page 102 for a description).

Career Lessons

"Some people in real estate seem to think you have to have specific real estate experience to be in this business," Starks notes. "They seem to have trouble understanding that general management skills, project management skills, and strategic thinking skills can translate to real estate."

What qualities does it take to succeed as an entrepreneur? One is a sharp eye for opportunities. "Opportunities are found by digging beneath the surface and looking at things other people aren't looking at," Starks says. "It also helps to have multidisciplinary experience, because with development you have to repurpose land and you never know what issues you will run into." Another essential quality is determination. "It is essential to be creative, to not see obstacles but rather to identify problems and find solutions," says Starks.

Career Profile: **Jon Hammer**

Jon Hammer, founder of Hammer Ventures, a San Diego–based condominium developer, decided to go into real estate when the dot-com bubble burst.

With an undergraduate degree in computer science, Jon Hammer began his career in the computer industry. Then the dot-com bubble burst, and he decided to go in to real estate.

Becoming an Entrepreneur

There was precedent in Hammer's family for a career in real estate. "My father and grandfather were both involved in development in North Carolina, mostly small projects done with back-of-the-envelope analysis." His first step was to return to school to earn a master's degree in real estate development (MRED) at USC. He worked as a financial analyst for Shea Properties, an owner and operator of commercial properties in California and Colorado and an autonomous business entity within the J. F. Shea Co. (see J. F. Shea Co. company profile on page 34), and then as an acquisition specialist for Fairfield Residential in San Diego.

In 2002, at the age of 26, he started Hammer Ventures to focus on multifamily acquisitions in San Diego. After a few core apartment acquisitions, he began to convert them to condominiums. Today, the company is in the business of converting rental apartments in California and elsewhere in the western United States to condominiums, building for-sale condominiums on infill sites, and providing entitlement services for its own projects and those of other developers. In the high-priced California housing market, condo conversions and new construction are a primary source of affordable housing for first-time buyers and other households.

As of 2004, Hammer had acquired more than $350 million of apartments for conversion and had 12 projects underway. "My long-term goal is to have our company evolve into a leading developer of attached housing in the western United States," Hammer says.

Hammer works 80-hour weeks, spending about one-quarter of his time seeking new deals, one-quarter seeking capital, and the rest managing his company, which has grown in size to more than 15 employees. "Although deal making is seen as the sexier part of the development business, a lot of my time is spent on managing the business," he reports. "It's just as important to manage our numerous projects as to pursue new projects.

When he started out, Hammer joined the local chapters of the Urban Land Institute and the Building Industry Association. He believes that "organizations such as these are great resources for a starting entrepreneur. He was among the first "Young Leaders" in San Diego, a ULI special membership category designed to foster interaction and education among real estate professionals under the age of 35. He has to date contributed four articles on the subject of entrepreneurship and development to ULI's *Urban Land* magazine.

Career Lessons

What advice does Hammer offer students who are thinking of becoming entrepreneurs? "First, have a clear vision of what you want to accomplish. And use every resource available—professors, family, friends, people in the industry, former employers can all help you to pursue your vision." Remember also, once a business is up and running, to "keep close watch on its health. It is very easy to get overextended. Remember that the company comes first, then the project."

Career Profile: **Vanessa Delgado**

The first attempt by Vanessa Delgado—director of entitlements for Primestor Development, a company that develops, owns, and manages a diversified portfolio of properties—to start her own development company was unsuccessful. But she hasn't given up on her dream.

Vanessa Delgado's development company startup was a humbling but educational experience, and she plans to try again.

In the Meantime

Delgado originally aspired to be a city manager. After earning an undergraduate degree in political science and Chicano studies at Stanford University and a master's of public administration at USC, she worked for a few years for a city planning department and then for a city agency that oversaw redevelopment. This work led her to decide that development was her true calling. She acted on this career decision by starting California Development Partners (CDP), a development company.

But when she experienced difficulty in getting her first project off the ground, she decided to temporarily put off starting a business, and she took a position as director of entitlements for Primestor Development. "It's a lot harder to be a developer than I anticipated, and than most students anticipate," Delgado says. Her biggest difficulty was obtaining financing. "Because of my lack of familiarity with the finance world, and lack of a track record in development, my access to capital was very limited."

In her position at Primestor, Delgado works on finding development opportunities and obtaining entitlements. The company has built or renovated numerous shopping centers in underserved Latino neighborhoods of Los Angeles, tenanted not only by mom-and-pop stores, but also by national retail chains. The company keeps most of the properties that it develops or acquires, and its portfolio now totals 1 million square feet of retail space under development and 1 million square feet under management. Among other projects, Primestor is developing La Alameda, a retail center in an unincorporated area of Los Angeles County near Huntington Park on an assembled 18-acre site; it is currently in the process of obtaining entitlements, preleasing national retailers, and planning construction on La Alameda. Primestor also is looking at development opportunities in other U.S. markets.

The developer carefully researches local markets in determining the best tenant mix for its properties. "We pay close attention to what communities want, and we know how to meet their needs," Delgado says. At first, Primestor found it challenging to convince national retailers to open stores in the underserved neighborhoods it targets, but the process has become less difficult because of the success of the tenants in the first retail centers.

Career Lessons

Delgado characterizes her attempt to start her own company as "a humbling but educational experience," and she still dreams of having her own development company one day. Meanwhile, as a young professional early in her career, she is making the most of her current position by learning all she can about working with local governments, building relationships with local communities, and financing projects. "I'm doing much of the same work now that I used to do on my own, and I'm getting more exposure to the development business," she notes. "Also, I have a very good understanding of the development needs of Latino communities in Los Angeles," adds this Los Angeles native. In short, she is learning from experience, and that is a key to a successful career.

Q&A: **Veronica Hackett**

Managing partner and cofounder of the Clarett Group, a New York–based developer of residential and mixed-use projects.

"I think successful development is less about having all of the expertise yourself and more about knowing how to bring experts to the team and how to effectively manage them."

What did you study in college?
I attended the College of Notre Dame of Maryland, where I had a classic liberal arts education and earned a bachelor's degree in history and economics. I went to New York University at night to get my MBA.

How did you get into real estate?
By happenstance. After working as an economic analyst for the CIA for a year, I joined a Wall Street firm as a financial analyst in its corporate finance department, but the firm went under during a recession. I needed a job and approached Citibank's Small Business Investment Company (SBIC), which made loans to small businesses. They weren't hiring, but Citibank offered me a position in its real estate lending department. I was their first woman employee in real estate.

Why do you think you were hired?
I was able to show that I had strong financial and analytical skills, based on my work on Wall Street and with the CIA. I was also about halfway through my MBA at the time. Also, the chairman of Citibank had made a strong commitment to expanding the roles of women at the bank.

What were your responsibilities?
I was the junior member of a team that provided construction loans to developers in the northeastern and mid-Atlantic regions.

What was your next job?
After about four years at Citibank, I was recruited by Chemical Bank, where I was eventually promoted to senior vice president, and managed the bank's international portfolio of owned real estate—including its corporate headquarters and regional offices—and its pension fund real estate business.

And then?
After about nine years at Chemical, I joined Park Tower Realty, one of the largest developers in the city, as executive vice president. There I had the opportunity to work on many high-profile office building projects.

And then you founded the Clarett Group?
Yes, in 1999 with Neil C. Klarfeld, the other executive vice president at Park Tower when I was there, my best friend as well as business partner. He died unexpectedly in 2004. While we were getting our residential development business underway, we provided development advisory services. One of our early clients was the New York Times Company, which we advised on the development of its new headquarters building in Times Square in the project's early days. We also advised the city and state of New York on plans to develop a 1 million-square-foot New York Stock Exchange building and tower. The scaffolding was about to go up when 9/11 struck, and the project was abandoned.

How were you able to get such prestigious clients early on?
Several reasons stand out. Over the course of our careers, Neil and I had been the key executives in the development of some high-profile projects, and we had earned reputations as people with strong financial and construction skills. Even though we had been corporate employees, we had established a name for ourselves by helping our employers to build a solid corporate image. Just as important as our experience and skills was the perception in the real estate industry that we were people who could be trusted. Also, many of our colleagues provided leads, recommended us to prospective clients, and were otherwise highly supportive. Finally, we were able to recruit highly talented and experienced professionals, beginning with Harold Jupiter, head of design and construction, who actually helped us to found Clarett.

Who are your equity partners?

Initially, we formed joint ventures with investors on a project-by-project basis. Our first partner was Fidelity, but its business model was deal-by-deal financing and we needed a larger, long-term commitment. That need led us to a multideal joint venture with Post Properties, whose founder, John Williams, I had known from my Chemical days. In 2002, we formed Clarett Capital, a partnership with Prudential Real Estate Investors, to develop a series of projects in New York. We now do everything through this Clarett/Prudential entity, bringing in third-party investors on a deal-by-deal basis. Two condominium projects by Clarett Capital are essentially sold out, two are under construction, and two are in the planning stage—all in New York. Thanks to our strong team, Clarett has made its mark on New York. We were recently ranked by a local paper as one of New York's top 15 developers. We have expanded geographically, too. For example, we have obtained a 99-year ground lease on seven acres on Hollywood Boulevard in Los Angeles, where we are planning to develop a 1 million-square-foot mixed-use project.

What does it take to succeed in the development business?

Development is all about managing a process. It requires a balance of strategic vision and attention to detail. It is critically important not to lose the forest for the trees. Success requires an ability to prioritize what needs to be done and to understand the interaction of all the decisions that have to be made. I think successful development is less about having all of the expertise yourself and more about knowing how to bring experts to the team and how to effectively manage them. Certain basic skills are important. Most successful developers are critical, strategic, analytical thinkers. Because the business is so capital intensive, you must have a basic understanding of finance and capital markets and be able to negotiate with the providers of capital. You can dream the world's most exciting project, but without capital it will never get built.

What do you look for in hiring people?

As a small company, we are limited in our ability to train people who are totally green. We tend to hire seasoned construction experts and MBAs, preferably those who have some real estate experience or relevant corporate finance experience. Our associates include people who have worked for a leasing broker, an architectural firm, and a construction company before going to business school. We have provided summer or part-time jobs to students during their two years in business school, and we have had great success in hiring them as full-time employees.

How can people just starting out in real estate get training?

Work hard to get into a large company with a great reputation, a company that has a training mechanism in place. When I worked at Citibank, you didn't get promoted until you trained someone as your replacement. I always strongly recommend participating in specific real estate educational programs and becoming involved in local and industrywide real estate organizations like ULI, local real estate groups, and university real estate organizations.

What are your long-term plans for the company, including your plan for succession?

We have a controlled-growth plan. We are committed to three geographic regions. We want to be seen as a strong, competent, boutique developer in our markets and we don't plan to be in 15 different cities. At some point, I would like to turn the company over to the next generation. It is traditional for New York real estate companies to be passed from one family member to the next. But Clarett is a "nonfamily" family. Our natural children have chosen different lives and careers, and personally I think children should not have to live in the shadow of a parent. So the future leaders and owners of Clarett will come from within the Clarett family.

Career Profile: Jeff Rouze

Jeff Rouze, partner in Historic Hollywood Hillview LLC, envisioned the restoration of Hollywood's historic Hillview Apartments and put together a partnership to accomplish it.

When he was a student at the University of Wisconsin at Madison, Jeff Rouze took to heart the the prediction of James Graaskamp, chairman of the department of real estate and urban land economics in the School of Business: "Sometime in your career, you will have the opportunity to do something wonderful and make a difference."

The Project

The dilapidated Hillview Apartments in Hollywood, a 1917 building with a glittering past, presented such an opportunity in Rouze's view. In 2002, he and others created a partnership with the Great Lakes Companies, a privately held developer of hotels, resorts, and seniors housing, to acquire the Hillview Apartments for $3.75 million. Since then they have invested in the building's substantial rehabilitation and restoration, financing the project with a combination of equity investment, public and private loans, and historic-preservation tax credits.

The Hillview was built in 1917 by movie moguls Jesse Lasky and Samuel Goldwyn to meet a need for housing for movie actors, who were not especially welcome in Hollywood's boarding houses, some of which posted "NO ACTORS, NO DOGS" signs.

Located on Hollywood Boulevard near Vine, the four-story, 54-unit Hillview became one of the most sought-after residences in Hollywood, home to Oliver Hardy and other movie stars of the era. Charlie Chaplin reportedly was a fixture in a basement speakeasy. For many decades thereafter, the Hillview continued to operate as an apartment building, but in the 1980s it lost tenants and income as downtown Hollywood declined. It suffered severe damage in the 1994 Northridge earthquake, and the city declared part of the structure unsafe. The building was vacant in early 2002, when arson destroyed much of the roof and part of the top floor. Its owner was considering demolition when Rouze and his partners bought the property.

A Monumental Challenge

Rouze has worked with the project's architect and contractor to preserve as many original features as possible. The external facade is being preserved as a condition for certification for the historic-preservation tax credits. The original mix of studio and one-, two-, and three-bedroom apartments—all equipped with modern amenities—and the lobby's historic detail are being retained. The basement, where movie stars once played pool, will house a CLUB 86 speakeasy that will target a young celebrity clientele, just as in days past.

"All in all, the project required very complicated structural engineering work to accommodate about 85 years of building code changes," Rouze notes. Although the restoration has presented complex engineering and construction challenges and taken longer than expected, the Hillview partnership is expected to complete the nearly $15 million project by year-end 2005.

Fulfilling his vision to restore the Hillview as a symbol of old Hollywood in a new age has been well worth the time and effort, according to Rouze. "A building that played such an instrumental part in film history needed to be preserved, returned to a productive use, and assured a healthy economic life. The time was long overdue to restore it to its former beauty."

Chapter 7
Education: The Foundation of a Successful Career

You're a high-school senior who has learned about real estate from your mother, a broker, and you think you might be interested in real estate as a career. What college should you attend? What courses should you take to help you decide whether real estate is a good career choice for you.

You're a sophomore at a small liberal arts college. You worked last summer and are still working part time during the school year for your roommate's father, a developer. From your job experience and talking with your friend's dad, you think you might be interested in development as a career. How can you learn more so that you can decide if this path is a good one for you?

You're a senior at a state university, majoring in economics. From working summers for a construction company, talking with people in real estate, and your own studying and reading, you know you want to go into real estate. Can

you get a job in the field with an undergraduate degree in economics? What type of job? Or should you go to graduate school?

You're a software engineer with a big technology firm. You've learned about real estate from investing with friends in a small apartment building. You've decided that you want to go into real estate full time, working for a real estate investment company or developer, and maybe someday start your own real estate business. How do you acquire the education to accomplish your goals?

These are challenging questions. This chapter on education—providing practical information and advice from both the professors and the graduates of a number of leading undergraduate and graduate real estate programs—offers some clues on how you can best go about planning your education for a real estate career.

Planning an Education

A number of colleges and universities in the United States, ranging from small to large, offer courses in real estate. Some schools offer undergraduate degrees in business administration, management, finance, or other disciplines with a major in or emphasis on real estate.

Only a few schools offer undergraduate degrees in real estate. Students in these schools benefit from a curriculum specifically designed around real estate. Undergraduate real estate programs offer students opportunities to acquire knowledge and develop skills that could increase their marketability with real estate companies, as well as resources aimed at helping them find real estate jobs.

Take a look at the online career center of NAIOP (National Association of Industrial and Office Properties), which provides links to the Web sites of schools offering undergraduate and graduate real estate degrees. (See NAIOP in appendix A for address.) Another source of information is the Urban Land Institute's *Directory of Real Estate Development and Related Education Programs*, 10th ed. It can be ordered from ULI, or your school library may have a copy. (See Urban Land Institute in appendix A for the online address providing links to the Web sites of real estate development and related education programs as well as ordering information for the directory.) The chart here called "A Sampling

A Sampling of U.S. Real Estate Degree Programs*

University	Degree Programs	Real Estate Center
Baruch College, City University of New York	■ BS in Real Estate and Metropolitan Development ■ BBA in Real Estate ■ MBA with real estate concentration	
University of California at Berkeley Haas School of Business	■ BA with real estate concentration ■ MBA with real estate concentration	Fisher Center for Real Estate and Urban Economics
Columbia University Graduate School of Business	■ MBA with real estate concentration	Paul Milstein Center for Real Estate
Columbia University Graduate School of Architecture, Planning, and Preservation	■ Master of Science in Real Estate Development (MSRED)	
Cornell University	■ Master of Professional Studies in Real Estate (MPS)	
Harvard University Graduate School of Design Advanced Studies Programs	■ Master in Design Studies (MDesS) with real estate and urban development concentration ■ Master of Urban Planning (MUP) with a concentration in real estate and urban development	
Massachusetts Institute of Technology	■ Master of Science in Real Estate Development (MSRED)	Center for Real Estate
University of North Carolina at Chapel Hill Kenan Flagler School of Business	■ MBA with real estate development specialization	Center for Real Estate Development
University of Pennsylvania Wharton School	■ BA with real estate major ■ MBA with real estate major	Samuel Zell and Robert Lurie Real Estate Center
University of Southern California School of Policy, Planning, and Development	■ Master of Real Estate Development (MRED)	Lusk Center for Real Estate
University of Southern California Marshall School of Business	■ BS in Business Administration with concentrations in real estate finance, real property development, and construction management ■ MBA with real estate concentration	Lusk Center for Real Estate
University of Texas at Austin McCombs School of Business	■ BBA with major in finance/real estate ■ MBA with concentration in finance/real estate	Real Estate Finance and Investment Center
University of Wisconsin at Madison School of Business	■ BBA with specialization in real estate ■ MBA with specialization in real estate	Center for Real Estate

*See appendix A for Web addresses.

of U.S. Real Estate Degree Programs" lists the graduate and undergraduate real estate and related programs at some of the leading U.S. universities.

As many of the career profiles in this book attest, you can succeed in real estate from many different kinds of backgrounds—an undergraduate degree from a small liberal arts college or an Ivy League university, with a major in accounting or English or any number of other disciplines. Many successful professionals in real estate started in entry-level positions in brokerage or in finance, working for a bank or investment company, for example. Whatever their backgrounds, they were able to demonstrate to prospective employers that they had the education, talents, and skills to work in entry-level positions in real estate. (See chapter 8 for a discussion of what employers look for.)

What this means is that you have many choices in selecting a college and a course of study. There are many educational paths to a job in real estate. Throughout your time in college— not just when graduation day is approaching—think carefully about your career choices, considering real estate only as one possibility. (Note, however, that if a real estate career occurs to you as a possibility only at the end of your college days or even at midcareer, it is not too late for you to get up to speed.)

Your career planning, of which education planning is an important part, should involve many of the following steps:

Explore the possibilities. Learn about various careers through reading and research. Make use of available school resources, such as a career center.

Narrow down the possibilities. Decide which kinds of career most interest you.

Decide if real estate is a possibility. If it is, conduct your own in-depth study of the industry. Much information is available in books, articles, and Web sites. (See appendix A for a list of sources of information on real estate.) Talk to some real estate professionals—brokers, property managers, developers, and others—about their jobs. Find out why they chose real estate as a career. Ask what it takes to succeed in real estate.

Enroll in appropriate courses. Take classes that will help you test your interest in real estate and also help you develop the knowledge and skills you will need to succeed in the industry. Finance, economics, accounting, and business administration are among the basics you will need. Introductory classes in architecture, design, or law can be valuable. You may also need classes in communications to hone your writing and speaking skills. Classes in government and politics can be useful for understanding the regulatory and political environment in which real estate developers and investors operate. A psychology class could help you learn how to understand and work with other people. And a class in philosophy or ethics could help you develop your critical thinking skills.

Do a self-assessment. What are your greatest strengths? What are your weaknesses? How do you overcome them? What interests you? What motivates you to excel? (See appendix C for a self-assessment questionnaire and appendix A for other self-assessment resources.) Do your interests match up with any of the various types of real estate career paths that have been described in the career profiles and elsewhere in this book? How do your strengths and interests match up with the job requirements of employers as described in chapter 8?

Get an internship. While you are in school, try to get an internship with a real estate company, or, if that is not possible, with a company outside real estate. You may be able to arrange an internship through your school. Alternatively, you can contact companies directly. Besides providing you with valuable experience in real estate and the business world and enhancing your résumé, an internship could lead to a job after graduation. Likewise, part-time or summer jobs—if you select them with a real estate career in mind— can provide useful experience.

Finally, decide if you are interested in a career in real estate. If so, begin to take steps to find employment after you graduate. Get to know people involved in real estate and business. Some suggestions:

- Attend the meetings of the local chapters of national real estate organizations, such as the Urban Land Institute. (See appendix A for a list of organizations.)
- Join local business or civic organizations that can help you make connections not only in real estate but in the

business world. Many corporations, businesses, and other organizations are clients of real estate companies.

- Attend on-campus career fairs and other events that connect you with companies and prospective employers. Talk to recruiters who visit the campus.
- Develop a database of people you meet, including their contact information. Over time, you can create a network of professionals, associates, friends, and mentors who will be able to steer you toward career and employment opportunities and provide career advice.

If you are diligent in your educational and career planning, by the time you graduate you should have what you need—the skills, the experience, and the network—to find an entry-level job in the real estate industry. Once you've started work, you will be in a position to learn more about the industry, validate your career choice, and consider the career options available within real estate.

Real Estate Degree Programs

After a few years in the working world, many real estate professionals return to school to study for a graduate degree in real estate, an MBA with a major in real estate, or another degree related to real estate. Real estate is an increasingly complex, highly competitive, fast-paced industry, and its practitioners are often finding that they need to further their knowledge and skills to advance. Professionals from other industries also are studying for advanced degrees in real estate in order to develop the depth of real estate knowledge and skills required to make a career change.

Jenny Lee graduated from Cornell University in 2000 with a BS degree in hotel administration and a concentration in financial management. After graduation, she worked for two years as an associate for Economics Research Associates, an international hospitality consulting firm, and then for approximately two years as an analyst for Jones Lang LaSalle Hotels, a global leader in hospitality investment banking. In 2005, she enrolled in a two-year MBA program at the University of Chicago, in order to strengthen her skill sets and develop her technical expertise in finance. After graduation, she expects to return to hospitality consulting or investment services.

There is a demand for highly educated real estate professionals. Employers in the industry increasingly seek job candidates with advanced degrees. A graduate degree can open doors to greater job and career opportunities and command a higher salary in the marketplace. To help you develop an understanding of the graduate and undergraduate real estate programs that are available, the following section takes an inside look at what some of the leading universities offer. The programs spotlighted are from USC's Lusk Center for Real Estate, Baruch College, Columbia University, Harvard Design School, Massachusetts Institute of Technology, UC Berkeley, and the Wharton School—in that order.

Lusk Center for Real Estate at the University of Southern California

Program in Brief
The Lusk Center for Real Estate is a co-venture of USC's Marshall School of Business and USC's School of Policy, Planning, and Development. The center's mission is to support the educational and career programs of real estate students at USC. The Lusk Center's student constituency works on degrees conferred by the Marshall School of Business; the School of Policy, Planning, and Development, which offers a Master of Real Estate Development (MRED) degree; the Law School; and the School of Engineering.

Q&A: Director of the Lusk Center and Director of the MRED Program
Stuart Gabriel is director of the USC Lusk Center and professor of finance and business economics, policy, planning, and development in the Marshall School of Business and School of Policy, Planning, and Development. **Raphael Bostic** is associate professor in the School of Policy, Planning, and Development and director of the MRED Program. Here they answer questions about Lusk Center programs and the students who take part in them.

What about real estate interests students?

Bostic: Many aspects of the industry interest them. First, it is dynamic. Developing land, building projects, acquiring and managing properties, raising and investing capital, and seeking new business opportunities are exciting activities. Second, it offers a variety of career choices. Third, it produces a physical asset. The results of your work—a development project or a building that you have acquired—are visible. Fourth, depending on your tolerance for risk, it offers opportunities to build wealth. And fifth, real estate can be a powerful force for change; it can create new communities or revitalize inner-city neighborhoods.

Gabriel: Another factor that attracts students is that real estate is a creative endeavor. It requires critical thinking and an ability to analyze problems and develop solutions.

What curriculum choices are available for USC undergraduates who are interested in real estate careers?

Gabriel: The Marshall School of Business offers a BS degree with a major in business administration and concentrations in finance, real property development, and construction management. The School of Public Policy, Planning, and Development offers a BS degree in public policy, management, and planning, which is designed for students interested in politics, government, leadership, law, and the design and preservation of the built environment.

What graduate programs does USC offer students interested in real estate?

Bostic: The School of Policy, Planning, and Development offers the MRED degree, which prepares graduates for key positions in real estate development. The MRED program integrates the three main elements of real estate development: design, finance, and policy.

Gabriel: The Marshall School of Business offers an MBA degree in real estate that focuses on the development and refinement of managerial and entrepreneurial skills. We also offer some dual degree programs, including an MBA/ MRED. The Department of Civil Engineering offers a master's of construction management degree.

How do the MBA in real estate and the MRED differ?

Gabriel: The MBA is a broader, two-year program. MBA students are more likely to go into the investment and finance side of real estate. The MRED is a one-year, real estate specific program. MRED students have decided on the development side of real estate.

What are the backgrounds of the faculty in the Lusk programs?

Gabriel: We have a solid core of Ph.D. faculty, assisted by visiting instructors with broad experience in development and homebuilding, finance, investment management, real estate law, accounting, and other fields.

What are the backgrounds of the students?

Bostic: Students come from many backgrounds including finance, architecture, construction, brokerage, and public sector work.

Are there opportunities for graduate students to travel overseas?

Bostic: The MRED program includes a ten-day trip abroad during which students meet with public officials, developers, and other professionals and learn about local markets. The destinations in recent years have included Sydney, Hong Kong, and Berlin.

Do you offer programs outside the classroom to further educate students about real estate?

Gabriel: We sponsor the Lusk Speaker Series that brings in industry leaders to talk about trends and other real estate topics. We host the Lusk Center Mentor program, which gives students the opportunity to learn about real estate from experienced professionals. Our MBA and MRED students compete in case study competitions with other schools around the country.

What resources do you provide for helping students find employment?

Gabriel: We sponsor an annual Real Estate Industry Night that brings together employers and students. At the 2005 event, which was held in February, 80 firms interviewed 160 students, making Industry Night one of the largest recruitment events of its kind in the country. We also sponsor an annual Real Estate Career Forum at which real estate professionals talk about the industry and career choices. We publish student résumés annually in our Résumé Book, which we make available to employers. And we publicize job openings.

What does it take to succeed in real estate?

Gabriel: Successful real estate people have a passion for the business as well as superb communication skills and powers of persuasion. They earn the trust of others. Success also requires a sustained commitment. Real estate is—like other industries—cyclical, and those who pursue it as a career must be prepared to work in difficult as well as good times.

Bostic: Perseverance is critical. You must have the mental toughness, the focus and the energy to work through the moments in every deal when things seem to come crashing down.

Q&A: Professor of Finance and Business Economics in the Marshall School of Business

Robert Bridges is an adjunct professor of finance and business economics in USC's Marshall School of Business. He talks here about the school's undergraduate real estate program and the career options for its students.

How is the Marshall School's undergraduate real estate program structured?

Students must select one of three concentrations to define their curriculum. The finance concentration prepares them for careers in real estate lending, securities, consulting, appraisal, and private equity, as well as entrepreneurial ventures and family businesses. The real property development concentration prepares students to work in the fields of real estate development and real estate investment. And the construction management concentration—a collaborative effort between Marshall and the Viterbi School of Engineering—prepares students to work in the world of construction, civil engineering, construction management, and development. Interestingly, the finance concentration attracts students from throughout the university majoring in a diversity of specialties, like cinema, biology, electrical engineering, dance, music, or philosophy. These students want to round out their studies with exposure to the world of real estate investing and finance.

How does the structure of the undergraduate program compare with the MBA program?

The curricular structure of the undergraduate program parallels our real estate MBA offerings, giving the undergraduates an academic experience roughly equivalent to that enjoyed by the MBA students. The Marshall School supports the undergrad program through clubs, recruiting events, industry mentoring and internships, and alumni groups open to current and past participants in the program. The undergrads participate in the Lusk Center's Industry Night and other recruiting events and are featured in the real estate Résumé Book managed by the Lusk Center.

Do other schools offer undergraduate programs for students planning real estate careers?

Several other colleges and universities offer undergraduate real estate programs, including UC Berkeley, the University of Texas at Austin, the University of Colorado, the University of Wisconsin, Cornell University, and the University of Pennsylvania. A growing interest in the field of real estate is bringing many academics to a new level of awareness about the importance of this type of training.

Does your undergraduate program include internships?

Mentorship and internship opportunities are cornerstones of the program. Most students intern during the summer of their junior year. A few find positions as sophomores. For a large number of students, these internships lead to job offers after graduation. Marshall and the Lusk Center have very aggressive and efficient placement mechanisms in place to help students find positions.

Are there opportunities for undergraduates to travel overseas?

In the spring of 2005, a group of Marshall School real estate undergraduates and I went to Hong Kong, where we met with investors, officials, developers, and others to learn about the local real estate market. It was the first overseas program that we have put together for our undergraduates, and it was highly popular with the students. We hope to schedule more.

What career areas attract graduates with a real estate bachelor's degree?

Our graduates boast highly productive and adaptable skills; compared with MBAs, their aptitude and the fact that they are just beginning their careers make them attractive to employers. Our undergraduate program has close ties with the real estate community and has forged a remarkable reputation separate from the reputation of the various graduate programs. Our alumni network is unequalled, and has evolved its own traditions and legacies. On the basis of the undergraduate program's reputation, its graduates find employment in the widest variety of positions imaginable. Quite a few go into a family business or entrepreneurial venture. Because we have a large number of international students, many graduates find employment overseas. The main categories of employment for our graduates are real estate consulting, commercial real estate brokerage, private equity and finance, and banking.

Who hires the program's graduates?

A variety of firms are interested in college graduates with real estate finance, development, and construction management backgrounds. Regional and national real estate recruiters depend heavily on our program for talent. Some larger banks and consulting firms annually stage well-organized recruitment efforts that result in quite a few hires. Many other firms reach students via our e-mail network and regular events to which we invite firms interested in hiring. Consulting firms, banks, fund managers, and other companies look for graduates with the finance concentration. Development firms and brokerage companies look for students with the real property management concentration. And construction firms—including international companies involved with very large projects—are frequently interested in our construction management graduates.

Q&A: Director of Alumni and Student Services at the Lusk Center

Sonia Savoulian is the Lusk Center's director of alumni and student services. She talks about employer expectations and student expectations.

You know a lot of employers. What do they think is the value of a real estate program?

Real estate is not a profession that a student can simply step into. Fundamental skills are required, beginning with finance. Graduates going into development must have an understanding of the entitlement process and real estate law. And a general knowledge of the real estate process is necessary. Students transitioning from another industry into real estate need to play catch up. Many who have worked, for example, for a high-tech company in managing projects or crunching numbers feel that the skills they developed in those jobs can make them marketable to real estate firms. That's true, but they also need to arrive at a solid understanding of what makes real estate work.

What are the expectations of employers in hiring?

Employers value certain personal characteristics. Integrity is a must. An outgoing personality is key, especially in brokerage or development jobs. A willingness to take on challenges and to engage in creative problem solving is also high on the list.

What classes, programs, or events do graduates say have been the most important?

The finance courses are always cited as the most important. For MRED graduates, the course in entitlements is key. Graduates regularly use the content from this class and the real estate law class in their jobs. Some MRED students grumble about the need for so many design classes in a development program, but we consistently hear from our alumni that those architectural classes have provided much added value to them on the job. The most popular classes in the MRED program are its series of elective classes that focus on the development of a specific product type, taught by practitioners who manage companies that build these products.

What's the value to students of the Lusk alumni network?

Because the Lusk Center spans all disciplines across the USC campus, we are able to attract the interest of a large number of employers from all sectors. We also connect with a large pool of alumni working in all aspects of real estate. For students, these connections represent a tremendous benefit. One of our alums said it best: "When I came to USC, I knew I would creating a golden Rolodex. I did not realize that it would actually be platinum."

What sectors of real estate interest students?

MBA real estate students focus on the finance side. They are very interested in the actual deal making, working for real estate investment banks or other capital providers, and playing an active role in determining portfolio acquisitions or creating financing packages. The MRED students are driven toward development. Over the past four or five years, residential development has been the strongest sector for employment for MRED graduates. Many students are interested in urban infill markets. The retail and hotel sectors also have been strong draws. MRED graduates tend to be entrepreneurial. About 25 percent of the people in each graduating class will either go out on their own or work for a family business.

And what careers attract undergraduate students?

They typically launch their careers in either finance or brokerage. Both these fields represent an excellent training ground for people beginning on a career path in real estate.

What are the starting salaries of your graduates?

We publish an annual employment report that tracks the placements of graduates. In our 2004 report, the latest available, we looked at placements for that year's graduates. For undergraduates, placements were predominantly in real estate finance, consulting, and brokerage—with salaries averaging $40,000. For MRED and MBA in real estate graduates, placements tended to be in development or finance—with salaries plus bonus averaging $107,000.

CAREER PROFILE: **USC Graduate; Advisory Board Member, Ross Minority Program in Real Estate; Commercial Broker and Developer**

Gabriel Guerrero dropped out of USC to support his young daughter, returned to earn his undergraduate degree in business management, and went on to start a successful commercial real estate business. In 2003, he completed the Ross Minority Program in Real Estate at USC (see sidebar below) and now sits on the program's advisory board, where he is in charge of fundraising. Here the role that his education at USC has played in his career is spotlighted.

In 1985, Guerrero left USC after his sophomore year because he needed to make a living and support his young daughter, Christina. He returned to USC in 1987 and graduated in 1989 with a degree in business management. He tried a number of pursuits in the corporate sector, including starting a marketing business, but was unfulfilled: "I knew I didn't want a nine-to-five job in a corporation for the rest of my life, but I wanted to be sure my hard work would allow me to get paid for my efforts and have time to spend with my daughter. She was my inspiration."

ROSS MINORITY PROGRAM IN REAL ESTATE

Stan Ross

Located within USC's Lusk Center for Real Estate, the Ross Minority Program in Real Estate is an intensive, comprehensive educational program that is designed to provide developers in inner-city neighborhoods with the technical expertise and access to resources that are needed to develop significant real estate projects in their communities.

PROGRAM HISTORY

In 1992, following the civil unrest in Los Angeles that had been provoked by the Rodney King verdict, a group of government, business, and community leaders—including Barbara Harris, Linda King Wright, and Richard Benbow, met with David Dale-Johnson, director of USC's Program in Real Estate and a faculty member of the Marshall School of Business, to discuss how to encourage more minority students and professionals to pursue careers in real estate and to apply their talents and energy to the revitalization of inner-city neighborhoods. Dale-Johnson spoke with Stuart Gabriel, then an associate professor in the business school (see his bio in Q&A on page 96). Those discussions led to the creation of the Summer Program in Real Estate (the original name of what is now known as the Ross Minority Program in Real Estate) within the Lusk Center. Dale-Johnson served as director of the Summer Program and later the Ross Program, until he retired in 2004 after 25 years at USC.

When my wife Marilyn and I became associated with USC, we further endowed the program to help it to expand and provide greater scholarship opportunities for deserving students. We were motivated by a combination of factors, including the need for more diversity in the real estate industry, the lack of sufficient opportunities for minorities, the lack of short and intensive educational programs for real estate professionals that would enable them to continue working full time, and the opportunity to offer professionals more training and hands-on exposure to real estate development. We asked only that the professionals who participate in the

When a friend, Dario Franceschi, suggested that Guerrero should apply his talents and energy in the real estate business, Guerrero joined his business. With Franceschi as his mentor, he learned the commercial real estate business firsthand. In 1995, he took a position as a broker with a leading brokerage firm and became one of its top producers.

Guerrero began talking with friends, clients, people in the real estate business, and USC alumni—he had been president of the Latino Business Students Association while at USC—about starting his own business, and received strong support for the idea. "I wanted to succeed like my clients had, and at the same time create opportunities for others," he says. But his firm restricted its brokers from investing in client transactions. Guerrero asked his clients: If I went out on my own, would you use my brokerage services in new business deals? He had created good relationships with them, and they all said "yes."

In 2000, he launched Southern California Commercial Real Estate Inc. He didn't have to look far for a business model: "I wasn't trying to reinvent the wheel. I was simply trying to do what other successful real estate people had done." The company started in brokerage and grew into development and investment. It aggressively buys and sells properties for clients and also develops rental or for-sale multifamily and commercial properties, mostly in southern California. It employs 17 people, many of them USC graduates.

Guerrero on starting a company: "I had to take what I knew, create my vision for the company, and try to create an organization and corporate culture around that. I had a passion and an ability to work with and motivate people with

program use their talents to benefit inner-city neighborhoods and minority areas that are underserved in terms of rental and for-sale housing, as well as retail and other real estate product.

PROGRAM DETAILS

The Ross program is offered in two formats: a two-week summer program and an eight-day winter program extending over six weeks. The participants are real estate and community development professionals who aspire to refine their skills in areas such as real estate investment and development, urban revitalization, non-profit community development, economic development, affordable housing, or public sector planning and development. In the program, students acquire technical expertise, gain an understanding of the development process and development team, and learn how to leverage resources, build networks, and work in teams. The program is strongly supported by local governmental agencies, financial institutions, nonprofit and community-based organizations, educational institutions, and the corporate community. More than 450 professionals have been through it, many of whom have since played key roles in significant commercial, mixed-use, and housing developments throughout the nation.

The summer 2005 program attracted 36 professionals from as far away as Israel and Italy, as well as from Indianapolis, Atlanta, Houston, and southern California. Exposed to the basics of real estate development and finance, the fundamentals of market analysis, highest-and-best-use analysis, and team learning, the students in this session developed technical expertise and learned how to leverage resources and build networks. They worked in teams to apply their classroom lessons to a case study in which they had to determine the highest and best use of an urban property involving complicated development issues. They also participated in various networking and educational dinners outside of the classroom, including a reception that allowed them to interact with alumni and Lusk Center supporters and industry partners, among whom were some of the most influential leaders in the real estate industry.

different personalities. It's been fun." In just a few years, Southern California Commercial has become a serious competitor against larger real estate firms. "I love going up against them," Guerrero says. He has won some business by cold-calling property owners and asking them to contact him when they planned their next sale, saying he could get a higher price than competing brokers. Among other transactions, his company has brokered the $42 million sale of an apartment building in a Los Angeles suburb; the sale of two $42 million apartment complexes in Las Vegas; and the $18 million sale of a retail center in Monterey Park.

One early development venture—a completed 42-unit condominium building with ground-floor retail on a site in Chinatown near a new (Gold Line) rail-transit stop that is attracting new development—involved Guerrero's partnership with veteran developer and investor Jim Osterling, currently a principal of Bridge Residential Advisors LLC, to develop projects in downtown Los Angeles. Guerrero worked on the project's design and construction plans, approvals (with the help of Ed Reyes, a life-long friend and a city councilman whose district includes Chinatown), and financing (with the help of Stan Ross).

Also of note is that Guerrero's company has optioned five acres in east Los Angeles where he grew up. He is thinking of building 38 two- and three-bedroom townhouses of up to 1,800 square feet, which would sell for around $400,000— considered affordable in southern California. "You're in business to make money, but you also have to try and give back by building affordable projects that meet the community's needs," Guerrero comments.

To hone his development skills, Guerrero completed the 2003 summer Ross Minority program. He values the opportunity that this gave him to network with other real estate professionals and community activists, learn about their

Career Profile: Nicole McAllister

Nonprofit planning and development work for economic and housing development corporations prepared Nicole McAllister for an academic position at USC's Lusk Center for Real Estate, where she is executive director of development and external affairs.

After earning a bachelor's degree in urban studies and planning from the University of California at San Diego, Nicole McAllister entered the Graduate School of Architecture and Urban Planning at UCLA. She was determined to put her education and talents to use in helping others. "I wanted to make a difference," she says.

Dunbar EDC

The opportunity came at a UCLA career fair, where McAllister learned from Anthony Scott, then the executive director of the Dunbar Economic Development Corporation (EDC), about Dunbar EDC, a nonprofit organization seeking to promote affordable housing, economic development, and community enrichment in South Central, an urban neighborhood immediately south of downtown Los Angeles. As a graduate school student, she interned with Dunbar EDC. Later, with a master's degree in urban planning in hand, she joined the organization as a project manager.

Her first job was to assist with the conversion of a historic hotel (originally called the Somerville) into 23 units of low-income housing for large families. Somerville Place is still owned and operated by Dunbar EDC.

On her second project—the conversion of an old Craftsman style house into five low-income rental units— McAllister was on her own as project manager. "I shudder to think of how they let me loose. I didn't know anything, but I somehow figured it out—and it turned out to be a beautiful project." The conversion process taught her a lot about the challenges of a rehab project. As it turned out, the Dunbar EDC had to go back to the Los Angeles Housing Department, one of the project's investors, for more financing to cover unexpectedly high costs—resulting, for example, from the need to remove lead-based paint and bring the plumbing up to code. "It was a relatively small amount of money, about $160,000, but we could not have completed the project without it," McAllister recalls.

Another project at Dunbar CDC involved "scattered sites" housing. She called brokers, poured over tax delinquency reports, and drove around the South Central area experiences in real estate development or community work, and get feedback on his project plans. "I was too busy to go back to school full time. This gave me a crash course in only a few weeks," Guerrero says. He came away with new ideas for developing projects: "Now that I'm more experienced, I'm more confident about doing my own development deals." Guerrero is giving back here as well: Having been appointed to the Ross program's advisory board in 2003, he is now in charge of fundraising. "I see this program as a vital component to my success in development, and I want to help assure that others will have the opportunity to participate in it."

Guerrero thinks that recruitment and training are critical factors in his company's success, and that his experience in brokerage has helped him recruit and train. "I like to find talented people and help them to succeed in this business," he says. Prospective hires are initially interviewed by other staff members. Guerrero conducts the final interview and makes the hiring decision. Some recent success stories: An employee in her 20s who learned how to develop leads and help close sales received a $100,000 check for helping to get an $18.5 million deal under contract. And, after only four months, an employee with an undergraduate degree in communications applied Guerrero's training in making calls and building relationships to earn $200,000 in commissions. Camaraderie and mutual support are encouraged in the work environment. For example, each salesperson is assigned an exclusive territory in which to develop business, in contrast with the traditional practice of having multiple brokers compete in the same market.

Guerrero's advice to students who are interested in pursuing a real estate career? "Carpe diem (seize the day). Don't be a creature of circumstance. Be the creator of your own circumstances. Find a way to jump in and get started in real estate. Make your own opportunities."

to find single-family houses that could be rehabbed and purchased by first-time, low-income buyers. The effort identified about a dozen suitable houses, and McAllister and a colleague worked with a local lender and Fannie Mae to find and qualify low-income buyers for these units.

Hollywood Community Housing Corporation

McAllister moved on to the Hollywood Community Housing Corporation (HCHC), an organization created in 1989 to help address a severe shortage of affordable housing in that city. Here she was responsible for major acquisitions as well as the syndication of multifamily-housing tax credit projects.

One of her first projects was to help obtain low-income housing tax credits for a 30-unit apartment building that included units set aside for special-needs residents. She also worked on the acquisition, demolition, and conversion of a run-down, city-owned apartment building into 18 units of bungalow style apartments. One of her biggest challenges was the community. "We were providing housing for people living with HIV/AIDS and I was surprised by the vehement opposition from supposedly progressive residents," she says.

Lusk Center for Real Estate

While working at the Dunbar CDC, McAllister had participated in the Summer Program in Real Estate (now the Ross Minority Program; see page 100) at USC's Lusk Center. That led to her being hired as the center's director of development in 1999, where she was put in charge of restructuring the center's development efforts, including annual giving, major gifts, board development, corporate and foundation relations, and communications and public relations. In that capacity, McAllister has presided over the increase of the Lusk Center's endowment from $4 million to $20 million and an increase in annual giving from $183,000 to $1.4 million.

Career Lessons

Looking back, McAllister feels that her work in the nonprofit sector provided her with more responsibility and more freedom than she might have been given in the private sector. While her academic education gave her a theoretical foundation, her work with nonprofit organizations gave her the management experience that she has applied in managing the operational, budgetary, development, and external affairs of the Lusk Center.

Baruch College

Program in Brief

The Baruch College of the City University of New York offers a BS degree in real estate and metropolitan development, with courses offered both by the School of Public Affairs and the Zicklin School of Business. This program started in 1997. In the fall of 2005, Baruch established a Department of Real Estate under the direction of Professor Ko Wang. It offers a BBA major in real estate, a BBA minor in real estate, and an MBA program with a concentration in real estate under the auspices of the Zicklin School of Business. These programs along with a certificate program in real estate offered under the joint auspices of the Steven L. Newman Real Estate Institute and Baruch College's Division of Continuing and Professional Studies are part of what is known as the Newman programs in real estate.

Q&A: Director of the Bachelor of Science in Real Estate Program

John Goering is a professor with Baruch College and the director of its BS degree in real estate program.

What about real estate interests students?

They have learned about real estate from their family and friends, or the media, or other sources. By the time they come here, most of them are certain that a career in real estate is the right thing for them. They know what they want to do: to create wealth, have a satisfying career, contribute to the social good, or achieve other goals. Baruch is one of America's most diverse colleges and the students in the BS program come from a variety of backgrounds.

What curriculum choices are available for undergraduates who are interested in real estate careers?

We provide a fairly scripted curriculum for students in their junior and senior years. It includes courses in finance; valuation and appraisal; real estate analysis, including spreadsheet software; property management; real estate law; and the dynamics of metropolitan growth and development. Our students identify developable sites and prepare full business proposals for them that include market analysis, risk analysis, and financing—and they pitch their proposals to professional real estate investors. This learning technique is not new at the graduate level, but it is new for undergraduates. Subject to my approval, students can take related elective courses—for example, an architecture and design course from another college. A real estate adviser who works for me assists our students with curriculum planning, career path decisions, identifying job opportunities, preparing for job interviews, and so on.

What resources do you provide for helping students find employment?

We have an internship program that places students with local employers. A full-time internship coordinator works with employers on placing students in internships as well as in permanent real estate jobs. We seek internships that will be valuable learning experiences for the students, not just grunt-work jobs. We organize a job fair for internships and permanent positions that is a hand-tailored event for real estate majors separate from other such events on campus. A number of local real estate companies, banks, and other employers participate and the event has been well received by students. We have roughly seven scholarships available for qualified students and the best graduating real estate majors receive an award that is supported by the developer Joseph Moinian. William Newman, chair of the New Plan Excel REIT and one of our most notable resources, has been a major donor to the college and the Newman programs in real estate. The Newman Real Estate Institute organizes periodic conferences of relevance to both students and the real estate industry.

What suggestions do you get from employers about structuring your academic program?

Our board of directors and alumni provide feedback from the industry side. We also seek advice from organizations such as the Real Estate Board of New York and ULI, as well as from other academic real estate programs. Courses cannot be too narrow, otherwise they would be like trade school courses. Employers value students who have taken real estate accounting and finance courses. Often, they expect entry-level employees to be proficient in ARGUS. Baruch has a well-known strength in accountancy and finance, so it's natural for us to build on these courses. At the graduate level, we have introduced an MBA program with a minor in real estate to meet increasing demand in the industry for real estate–oriented MBAs. We also think about what kind of research at the MBA or doctoral level might be of value to the industry and about developing proprietary research products that might be useful to both the industry and graduate and doctoral students.

What can be done to promote careers in real estate?

There is a perception in the industry that a real estate degree has no more value than, say, a degree in marketing. One of the biggest challenges for schools offering such degrees is to change that perception. I meet with as many real estate companies and REITs as I can and try to make them aware that Baruch not only has a business school, but also a degree program in real estate. However, this is an issue that is bigger than any individual or any single school can address. A number of schools—for example, Columbia, New York University, and Baruch—have good real estate programs. Such schools need to work together and with organizations such as the American Real Estate Society (ARES) to demonstrate the value of a real estate degree and to develop sound relationships with employers that will result in more internships and job opportunities for real estate program students and graduates. We also have to encourage companies to think more creatively in hiring, to think past hiring based on family relationships or small networks, and to recognize that job candidates with real estate degrees offer employers very valuable skill sets.

CAREER PROFILE: 2001 Graduate of Baruch's Real Estate and Metropolitan Development Program; Loan Officer with CapitalSource Mortgage

Colleen Rainford planned to study mathematics and switched to business. A course in real estate law led her to pursue a BS in real estate and metropolitan development and, after graduation, a career in real estate.

In high school, Rainford wondered what she would do with her life after graduation. A native of Jamaica, she had moved to the United States with her family when she was ten years old. She applied to several colleges, and was accepted by Baruch College. She had planned to study mathematics, but then switched to business studies. She was particularly interested in finance, an interest that dated back to her elementary-school years. "Once a week, our class would learn how to invest in stocks using play money," she recalls.

Her business studies included a course in real estate law, and she experienced "sort of an epiphany" while taking that course, in that she realized real estate was the career for her. She enrolled in the school's real estate and metropolitan development program, taking courses in business, public policy, and real estate. As an undergraduate, Rainford spent a lot of time in the field conducting research projects in New York City.

"We learned not only about real estate finance and economics, but also about the effects of the political and social environment on real estate," Rainford says. For one of her research studies, she lived in a city neighborhood to investigate why some people rent and others buy homes and to study the relationships between race, housing affordability, and homebuying opportunities. She interned with New Plan Realty Trust, a shopping center REIT, and with the Steven L. Newman Real Estate Institute, a nonprofit organization that offers educational resources, conferences, and research for real estate professionals.

As an intern at the Newman Institute, Rainford worked on two large development proposals for nonprofit organizations. For one, a $200 million retail and residential development in Queens, she helped prepare the project's pro formas and put a financing package together. For the other development project, she worked on the early planning aspects, helping to prepare floor sketches and plans and determine the number of units.

Before graduating with honors from Baruch, Rainford wasn't sure where she wanted to work, "but finance seemed like a good fit." Her degree, internship experience, and knowledge of real estate and finance helped her to land interviews with investment banks, brokerage firms, mortgage companies, and other prospective employers. "I knew I had much to learn, but I understood how to put together multimillion dollar development deals, finance property investments, and speak the language of real estate, and this was very attractive to employers." She networked with family, friends, and professional contacts, and by following up a job tip from the friend of a relative, she interviewed with CapitalSource, a New York mortgage broker that arranges financing for individuals and small investors. She accepted a position as a loan officer with CapitalSource, where she has been working since graduation.

Rainford continues to plan for the future. "Within five years I'd like to have my own mortgage company, and eventually go into for-profit development in the international market," she says. "You don't need a lot of money to get started on your own in real estate. If you have a vision, a team, and a network, you can raise the capital and succeed in this business." She also wants to apply her education, experience, and talent in helping others. Currently, she is working with CapitalSource to promote homeownership in New York City by providing free workshops for people who want to learn about buying coops or condominiums. Long term, she would like to help provide housing for people around the globe.

Rainford has achieved the confidence to pursue a career in real estate. "My education has made real estate tangible. Real estate isn't just something for the Donald Trumps of the world. My education has put me on a professional level with people who grew up in real estate."

Columbia University

Program in Brief

Columbia University offers a Master of Science in Real Estate Development (MSRED) degree. Begun in 1991, the MSRED program emphasizes the practical core competencies (real estate finance, enterprise management, and product implementation) and the theoretical framework (public policy and market research methodologies) needed to prepare students for careers in development.

Q&A: Director of Columbia's MSRED Program

Michael Buckley is director of the MSRED program. In the following interview he talks about careers in real estate, the value of a graduate education, and what the industry can do to encourage more students to pursue real estate careers.

What about real estate interests students?

At Columbia's MSRED program we have identified three career drivers. First, many candidates have a family connection through their parents or other relatives in real estate. Second, many MSRED students are mid-career changeovers from allied professions such as architecture, construction, or law. Third, most have a deliberate financial incentive; they

intend to sit on the "check-writing side of the table," to instigate and deliver projects and to create value.

What influences their impression of career opportunities in real estate?

Increasingly, their peers, notably those who are ambitious and want to create new environments. Less so, the senior people in real estate. Also, the popular media coverage of projects that have transformed urban areas and people who have made it big in real estate. Students recognize that developers both earn money and exercise influence over lifestyles.

How do people interested in a real estate career learn about Columbia's program?

About two-thirds are expert Web surfers, and have searched our Web site.

What does it take to succeed in development?

At Columbia, we believe that the next-generation developer requires four skill sets, and we focus our curriculum in these core areas. First, the next-generation developer must have a thorough knowledge of finance, understand how to analyze the financial and market feasibility of projects and be comfortable accessing the capital markets. Second, he or she must be able to manage the enterprise. A development organization requires talent, processes, and resources. One of the challenges for a young developer is to manage professional talent—for example, a contractor, a lawyer, and a leasing agent—and direct complex processes.

Third, the next-generation developer must manage the product design process. Rather than ask an architect to design the product, a good developer starts with imaginative ideas for product design and challenges the architect to interpret them. It is the developer's role to identify the performance parameters for new product and then manage the development team to arrive at a consensus on the development idea: What product should be built or renovated? Who should be targeted? How does the product respond to demographics, preferences, and lifestyle changes? It's the developer's role to identify the performance parameters for new product.

Finally, the next-generation developer must manage public expectations on quality-of-life issues and community integrity. This mandates a new focus on cooperation between the developer and the public sector, both financially and in the regulatory process, to secure a consensus for approvals and to realize benefits from development for a wide range of stakeholders. For example, a city might—for a project like a mixed-use residential and retail center in an underserved neighborhood that will provide economic development benefits to the community—acquire land and create a tax-increment financing district to provide infrastructure, stabilize and assist in the renovation of older structures, or remediate brownfields. Public/private partnerships have proven that if the project does well, the community benefits. Without public/private initiatives, development will go elsewhere. At Columbia, we believe in the value-capture potential of using public investment to leverage private investment.

Can students do more than work on specific skills to prepare for careers in development?

Many of our students have an appetite for more than skill building. They are interested in engaging in more intellectual debate and direct research. Hence, we have established the Center for High Density Development, through which our students can explore critical success factors and performance measurements for high-density development. This more intensively academic pursuit gives students a new language framework for discussing the policy impacts; social, cultural, and innovation benefits; and financial value creation of higher-density development.

What classes are most important to students?

Real estate analysis with an emphasis on real estate finance and feasibility is clearly a core skill. For nonfinance people, its concepts—for example present value or capitalization rate—provide a whole new way of thinking. However, we recognize that if students wanted to learn only about finance, they could—and should—enroll in a business school program. We believe a well-rounded grounding in development includes courses in product design, public/private partnerships, enterprise management, and marketing, among others. We are not a "B for business" school. We're a "D for development" school.

What is the value of internships to students?

Our students are typically mature—26 to 28 years old—and committed to a career in real estate. They have work experience, but not always in real estate. We think diversity in experience is a powerful factor in the accelerated teaching environ-ment and in the classroom. We offer internships at development companies in our spring semester to help selected students overcome the terror of entering a new discipline. More than half of the 82 students in the class of 2005 took internships with real estate companies involved in residential, office, and urban retail development; opportunity fund investors; and pension fund advisers. Some students took intern positions in the economic development arms of public agencies and some foreign students worked with associations, such as the Royal Institution of Chartered Surveyors.

What is the value of a graduate degree for students going into real estate?

Some of our graduate students will be better than others at acquiring skills, but the Columbia MSRED program will equip all of them with the tools they need to pursue a career in real estate. More importantly, many—at least 40 to 50 out of 85 in the program—will be changed fundamentally. We have patiently promoted the intensive and focused training that the program provides, so that now developers and financial institutions recognize that it has a transformative effect on students. Thus, the degree has real economic value. That value may not be apparent for students in their first or second year out of school, when they usually earn marginally more than before they started the program. But by the third year, everyone is doing quite well. Based on feedback from employers—and graduates themselves—our alumni match up very well against MBAs in competing for significant development positions.

What resources do you provide for helping students find employment?

Believing that the graduate degree itself should be good enough for a student to find a job, many graduate programs do not believe in dedicated career placement. We, however, focus on career development and we help students find jobs. We invite executive recruiters, employers, and new alumni to campus—and the students pay close attention to them. Because being able to present ideas effectively is a hugely valued skill in real estate development, we make use of videotaping and other team-building tools to help students improve their presentation skills. Finally, our alumni are a great resource for students seeking employment; more than 30 percent of our referrals are from recent graduates and many alumni hire MSRED students as associates to work on their teams.

What can be done to promote careers in real estate

The real estate industry could influence an entire generation in a very short time by providing more internships, supporting more undergraduate scholarships—say 100 annual scholarships awarded through ULI instead of only a few—and supporting 500 annual real estate development scholarships at the graduate level, particularly scholarships for minority and foreign students, based on need. The industry should also sponsor a fellowship program. It would be powerful if private real estate companies were to underwrite a one-year, think-tank style study program for, say, 45 selected graduates in a university/developer environment. Surely half of the 45 would derive so much benefit from the selection process and the university/developer collaboration that they would emerge as future leaders of the industry. The industry's current leadership could take the initiative in organizing, overseeing, and guiding such a program and selecting fellows. We in university real estate programs could help by providing teaching roles and research opportunities. This is a great and potent mixture.

Real estate development is an interdisciplinary enterprise, and we should make sure that students are exposed to its most important disciplines. We need more cross-teaching that involves faculty and professionals in architecture, urban design, planning, preservation—all present in Columbia's MSRED program—and other fields, such as law and construction.

More development industry involvement in community enrichment would also help promote real estate as a career. The public perception that developers are rich and greedy and have no concern for communities is persistent. The community-minded motivation of many of our MSRED students, who want to use their new skills to transform the urban environment and save significant buildings, should be better publicized.

Q&A: Columbia MSRED Graduate; Development Project Manager with the Athena Group

Kenya Smith has an undergraduate degree in architecture from Howard University and a master's of science in real estate development degree from Columbia University. He is a project manager with the Athena Group, a private real estate development, operating, and investment company headquartered in New York, and eventually would like to have his own design and development firm focused on inner-city redevelopment and revitalization. Smith talks here about his career choice and the value of the MSRED degree in attaining his goals.

Describe your job with Athena.

I work in the development group. I help to do feasibility studies to determine what the market wants and what can be built, and I work with government officials, neighborhood groups, nonprofit organizations, and other organizations to obtain regulatory approval of projects and build community support. I work with architects, engineers, contractors, and others on design and construction plans and on the pro forma assumptions—timing, costs, et cetera.

How did you get interested in architecture?

I always liked buildings and building models. In high school I took some classes related to design and architecture, and from there studying architecture as a college undergraduate was a natural progression for me. By my third year in college, I realized that I eventually wanted to be on the development side, because it is the developer rather than the architect who controls the design; the decision of what design elements are included in a development project is ultimately in the hands of the owner; it is the owner's budget constraints and taste that rule.

What about development interested you?

I learned how architecture and development can shape the urban environment and improve the lives of people. I was inspired by John Portman, the founder of John Portman & Associates, an architectural and engineering firm that operates worldwide; Portman is a pioneer of the architect as developer role. I believe that if you want to control your design and projects, you need to be the developer.

How did you decide on Columbia?

I always wanted to go there. It offers an environment of excellence. Its MSRED program strikes a good balance between design and development. Attending Columbia gave me a deep understanding and appreciation of the power of development in New York City.

What were some of the most valuable courses you took?

Real estate repositioning; some finance courses; a class in real estate entrepreneurship, which was very helpful because my long-term goal is to go out on my own as a developer.

Any courses you wish you had taken?

I would like to have learned a little more about real estate capital markets.

What was the value of the MSRED degree in helping you to get a job?

Like a movie producer, a developer manages the process of producing a project—the land acquisition, the planning and design, the entitlements, and the construction. The MSRED program helped me to learn how to ask the right questions in deciding whether to develop a project—where to develop, what to develop, what makes economic sense but also is right for the community. It also helped me to shape and focus my architectural and construction experience. This experience coupled with my understanding of finance gives me a marketable job skill and the edge I will need to become a successful developer. To gain more experience, I wanted to work for a smaller, specialty company. My job with the Athena Group came about through the help of the MSRED program and its director, Michael Buckley. By virtue of the type of projects it develops, Athena is a boutique firm. The best part of my job is that it gives me exposure to most every aspect of development, including finance, design, construction, marketing, and tenant and community relations.

What are your long-term career goals?

I would like to establish my own design and development firm, focused mainly on inner-city redevelopment and the revitalization of declining neighborhoods in places like Detroit or Camden, New Jersey—and maybe New Orleans. Eventually, I would like to go into overseas development; one possibility is luxury resort and residential development in the Middle East or other markets.

What does it take to succeed in development?

An open mind, a lot of patience, and the personality to be able to work with people from many different backgrounds. You must have a lot of perseverance, because all projects have their own level of complexity. You need good problem-solving

skills, because nothing ever goes the way you think it will and obstacles constantly crop up. Many things go on simultaneously when a project is under development, and you have to stay focused and prioritize your tasks.

Q&A: MA in Real Estate Finance from Columbia; Senior Managing Director of Eastern Consolidated Properties

Eric Michael Anton, senior managing director of Eastern Consolidated Properties, a full-service commercial real estate investment banking firm with clients worldwide, received his master's degree in real estate finance from Columbia University. Since joining Eastern Consolidated in 1998, Anton has completed more than $1.5 billion of real estate transactions in New York and nationally, and in 1999 he was named Most Promising Commercial Broker by the Real Estate Board of New York, an award that recognizes the achievement of a broker with less than five years experience in the metropolitan New York market. Formerly, Anton was an executive of Starrett Corporation, a manager of mixed-use projects for the Port Authority of New York/New Jersey and the City of New York, and the associate director of marketing for Bovis Lend Lease, a construction services company. Anton is a graduate of Brown University, where he majored in European history and political science. He talks here about his career, his education, and his goals.

What is your current job?

I represent owners of real estate who want to sell their properties or investors who want to buy all types of property. I also arrange financing for these clients. I spend about 75 percent of my time on investment sales and 25 percent on financing. I'm always working on new projects with new clients. Our company is the third largest investment sales firm in the New York market. This is an extremely competitive market, and it can be a rough business because the financial stakes are so high. But if you're clever, you can make a lot of money, and you get to work with a lot of creative people and see all types of different real estate deals in their formative stages.

How did you get interested in a career in real estate?

I had originally planned to be a lawyer, but I lost interest. I had always loved buildings and architecture. My father was an architect, and my college roommate's father was a big-time developer. Through this connection, I landed a union job as mason tender on the ABC Capital Cities project in midtown Manhattan, carrying bricks and shoveling cement. This experience certainly gave me a valuable insight into how buildings are constructed. I also took some classes in urban development. I was especially interested in Jane Jacobs's *Life and Death of American Cities*, which helped spark my interest in real estate.

What was your first job after you graduated from Brown?

I knew I didn't want to work for a bank. So I applied and was accepted into an executive training program at Saks Fifth Avenue, which I completed in six months. The training was great, but the retail business was not for me. I started looking at other industries, and was fortunate to land a position with Bovis Lend Lease, an international construction company. I spent four years there, and the experience was terrific. However, I learned that I wanted to be on the real estate side of the business.

Why did you decide to attend Columbia?

I wanted to stay in New York. I applied to New York University and Columbia, and went with Columbia because I felt the program had more of a development focus, that I could get a better understanding of the theories behind the development business.

What courses did you find most valuable?

My finance courses were critical, because I didn't have an undergrad background in finance. A class taught by Michael Buckley, the director of Columbia's MSRED program, on the relationship of design and development was very helpful. I currently work on many adaptive use projects, and this class helped me to ask the right questions about development projects.

Are there any courses you wish you had taken?

Possibly another class in law. For example, a class in contracts would have been very useful. I did take a very good zoning class.

What are your long-term goals?

I'd like to stay in New York, remain in the brokerage business, and start a small development business. I'm currently looking at some development deals to do on the side. I don't see myself working for a big company.

What does it take to succeed in brokerage?

You have to have a thick skin. If you get beaten down working on a deal for a client, you have to be able to dust yourself off and continue to fight the deal to the finish. It's easy to almost do a deal for a client, but you only get compensated if you successfully complete the transaction.

Harvard Graduate School of Design

Program in Brief

Harvard's Graduate School of Design offers two paths to a graduate real estate degree: a Master in Design Studies (MDesS) degree with a concentration in real estate and urban development and a Master of Urban Planning (MUP) degree with a concentration in real estate and urban development. The MDesS program is aimed at midcareer professionals. The MUP program is for students who have less experience in the real estate industry. Both programs prepare graduates for careers in real estate development and finance or in urban development in the public or private sector.

Q&A: Professor of Real Estate Development at the Graduate School of Design

Richard B. Peiser has been the Michael D. Spear Professor of Real Estate Development at the Harvard Graduate School of Design since 1998. In 1986, he founded the USC Lusk Center's Master of Real Estate Development program, and from 1986 to 1998 he was on the faculty at the University of Southern California as associate professor of urban planning and development, director of the Lusk Center for Real Estate, and academic director of the MRED program. In the following interview, he discusses the interest of students in real estate careers, the educational choices available to undergraduate and graduate students, the requirements of employers, and other career topics.

What about real estate interests students?

Students are interested in a wide variety of careers in real estate, but, over the years I have taught, probably 90 percent have wanted to be developers and owners. Recently, this focus on development has abated somewhat as students see opportunities in investment banking, fund management, and REITs. Still, most want to be entrepreneurs.

How do students learn about career opportunities in real estate?

At first, many of our students do not know much about the full range of disciplines involved in real estate. They learn from their contacts in the industry. Special programs—such as the speaker series I initiated at USC and that we now have at Harvard—are needed to widen their knowledge of the different paths into real estate.

What does it take to succeed in real estate?

In my opinion, there are six critical success factors: integrity, perseverance, skills in interpersonal relationships (salesmanship), analytical skills, creativity, and the self-confidence to say "no."

How is the real estate education program at Harvard structured?

Courses are offered at three schools—the Kennedy School of Government, the Graduate School of Design, and the Harvard Business School. The key classes break down into three main areas: finance and deal structuring, physical planning and design, and urban context. Within the finance and deal structuring area, classes are available in real estate finance, capital markets, and public/private development. Classes in the physical planning and design area include building typologies, site planning, and urban design. And those within the urban context area include market analysis, political approvals, ethics, negotiation, law, urban economics, and public finance.

What's the value of part-time and summer work in helping students find permanent employment?

Part-time and summer jobs are critical. A job in brokerage, mortgage banking, and even property management can help a student gain an initial understanding of the industry. And these are the fields where they will find entry-level jobs after graduation. Internships are also valuable, especially in allowing foreign students to get working experience in an American context.

What experience do students need to prepare for careers as entrepreneurs?

I strongly recommend that they spend time in several aspects of the industry—from on-the-job-site construction work to sales to finance. In order to be an entrepreneurial developer, you must have the self-confidence to manage all aspects of a deal, from acquisition, approvals, design, and finance to construction, leasing, management, and disposition.

What suggestions do you get from employers about structuring your academic program?

We constantly get input from employers, and in many cases we follow their advice. They want students with excellent finance backgrounds, project management exposure, legal understanding, and—depending on the job—an understanding of design and construction. Of course, the specifics depend on the job. Employers typically want to train their new hires in the details of their own business niche.

What resources do you provide for helping students find employment?

Most notably, opportunities to network with high-level industry people. Students attend one or two networking events at all of our board meetings. We also bring in many industry speakers. The key to getting a real estate job is to ask 30 to 50 people for career advice—not for a job. Eventually, you will find someone who either likes you enough to hire you (which is always the unstated agenda of an interview) or knows someone who is looking to hire someone like you immediately.

What is the value of a graduate degree for students going into real estate?

The value of such a degree is growing, especially for jobs in investment banking, fund management, and REITs; or for a career as an entrepreneur. You can still get to the top of an organization by working your way up, and you can still do deals successfully. Doing deals requires capital and self-confidence, but not a graduate degree. However, for getting a first job with a larger firm, the graduate degree helps a lot.

What can be done to promote careers in real estate?

In my experience, many people in the industry want to help students, but they need a framework for doing so. I don't think that universities should provide this framework alone. They should work through industry groups like ULI, NAHB (National Association of Home Builders), NAIOP (National Association of Industrial and Office Properties), ICSC (International Council of Shopping Centers), and other organizations. The Urban Land Institute has been a very important resource for students who know how to take advantage of its network. In addition, every school has its own network of alumni and friends who provide the key links between the school, the real estate students, and the industry. USC is probably the leader in promoting contacts between students and industry. The involvement of USC alumni in southern California with students probably makes the USC experience a model for the rest of the country, what every university strives for. The Harvard culture, as well, fosters lifetime involvement by alumni, who are eager for opportunities to interact with students.

Q&A: Alumna of Harvard Graduate School of Design; Entrepreneur; GSD Teacher

Bing Wang, founder and managing partner of HyperBina, a Boston-based design and planning firm, and a cofounder and principal of China Real Estate Investment Company (China REI), earned a master's of architecture degree in urban design and a Ph.D. degree in design from the Harvard Graduate School of Design. She now teaches design and development courses at the school. Her career focus has been on large-scale real estate projects in China. She has been involved in the planning and design of a residential complex in Beijing, Beijing University's new library, an indoor stadium for the Rochester Institute of Technology, and single-family houses in Weston, Massachusetts. While a doctoral student at Harvard, Wang worked for Lehman Brothers as an investment consultant. She earned her undergraduate degree in architecture and design from Tsinghua University in Beijing. She talks here about her career path.

Why did you choose to study design as an undergraduate ?

Because of my outstanding performance in high school, I was privileged to be admitted to Tsinghua University without having gone through China's national college entrance tests. I was looking for direction in choosing a course of study when the professor who interviewed me—a tenured professor at the university's school of architecture, though I didn't know that at the time—suggested architecture because it combined science and artistic expression (I had loved drawing from a very early age).

What interested you in attending the Harvard Graduate School of Design?

While in college, I worked for a development company connected with the university. By the time I had graduated, I realized that to have an impact on the physical environment I needed to do more than just design forms. Thus, I decided to attend graduate school. It had been a childhood dream of mine to study at Harvard. My grandfather had gone to Japan and the United States for his graduate studies. We were very close, and he greatly influenced my thoughts and dreams.

What sparked your interest in development while you were at Harvard?

It was more the overall structure of the curriculum than it was any single class. I realized that to have an impact on the built environment, I would have to understand various aspects of the urban environment from the physical layout of cities to the political decisions that influence the development process. Harvard's urban design and planning program offered a range of courses, including urban politics and urban planning and economics, that could further my understanding. Also, GSD's hiring in 1998 of Richard Peiser as the first tenured real estate professor emphasized the importance the school gave to the impact of development on the physical environment.

How did you come to work as a consultant for Lehman Brothers?

When I was at Harvard, I got to know through the school's many events some of the firm's investment bankers who worked in real estate. Their interest in research I had done on nonperforming loans in China led to my working at Lehman during the summers and over school holidays. My primary assignment was to write a report on investment strategy in China for the firm's Tokyo office. My value was that I understood the culture and the opportunities in China's real estate market. I then worked with Stephen A. Roth, chairman emeritus of Secured Capital Corp., director of Secured Capital Japan Co., and director of STAM Europe, to establish China Real Estate Investment Company (China REI) and its Shanghai-based investment management arm, KaiLong REI. China REI and KaiLong REI are among the first real estate investment and investment management companies to provide a bridge between western capital and the real estate market in China.

How do you spend your time?

I spend most of my time in Boston, teaching part-time at Harvard, doing research, and working for both HyperBina and China REI. My design firm, HyperBina, has been commissioned to master plan and design a 460-acre urban project in the Qingpu district of Shanghai. The project is a mixed-used development located on the bank of the largest lake in the Shanghai metropolitan area. I visit Asia roughly every other month to work on investment opportunities for China REI, including joint ventures with the leading developers in Asia.

What are your long-term goals?

I plan to continue my practice both with the design firm and China REI. I also want to continue academic research and teaching because the intellectual understanding of what I do is important to me. My book, *Architectural Profession and Modernity in China*, based on my doctoral dissertation at Harvard, will be published by the end of 2005 by China International Publisher (formerly Foreign Language Press), the most authoritative publisher of English texts in China.

MIT Center for Real Estate

Program in Brief

In 1983 the Massachusetts Institute of Technology established the MIT Center for Real Estate with a mission to improve the quality of the built environment and to promote more informed professional practice in the real estate industry. The center created the first one-year master's of science in real estate development (MSRED) degree, and in 1984 enrolled the first students in the MSRED program.

Q&A: Managing Director of the MIT Center for Real Estate

Marion O. Cunningham is the managing director of the MIT Center for Real Estate. In the following interview, she discusses the center's MSRED program and opportunities for students in pursuing careers in real estate.

Why did MIT create the MSRED program?

The cofounders—Hank Spaulding, a developer and industry leader, and MIT professor Lawrence Bacow—realized that the real estate business had become more complex and more international in scope, and that traditional MBA programs did not adequately cover the territory. They established the MSRED program to bring together the various disciplines—including architecture and design, urban economics, construction, law, and finance—that are integral to development.

What are the backgrounds of the MSRED students?

We encourage candidates to acquire experience in real estate before applying for admission to the program. Many of our students have worked as brokers, construction managers, planners, architects, commercial loan officers, consultants, financial analysts, and engineers. Many students have graduate degrees when they come to the Center for Real Estate. These degrees tend to be in business, law, architecture, civil engineering, management, and planning. About a third of our students come from other countries, which reflects the globalization of real estate.

How is the MSRED curriculum structured?

When the program started, students were required to take eight courses. There was no room for electives unless the student was able to establish that he or she had already taken the class. Now, the number of core subjects has been reduced to six, giving students a chance to take at least two electives. Students today also are exposed to a more robust offering of subjects. For example, they can take courses throughout MIT or at Harvard through a joint MIT/Harvard program.

Are there opportunities for students to study abroad?

We are adding opportunities to study internationally and learn about the dynamics of development in other countries. For example, some students recently went to the United Kingdom and Germany to study real estate projects in those countries. We also are trying to partner with foreign academic institutions to create study programs for students in our respective institutions.

What resources do you provide for helping students pursue real estate careers?

Our career services are predicated not on finding jobs for students, but on giving them the skills, information, and opportunity to achieve their career goals. To that end, we help students connect with real estate professionals who can provide career guidance, job leads, or jobs. Among other initiatives, we host seminars at which industry leaders discuss trends in real estate and other topics; we sponsor informal networking meetings and alumni events attended by students, alumni, and other real estate professionals; and we offer skill-building workshops on writing résumés, interviewing, and networking. We also post job offerings from employers on our Web site.

What careers do your graduates choose?

Some graduates continue in the same line of work and type of business they were in before earning their MSRED. Others go off on another career path, for example, an accountant becomes a housing developer, or a planner becomes a project manager. Based on responses to an online survey on our Web site's career page, about half our graduates go into development or project management. Other popular areas are advisory services, consulting, finance, and investment management. Our students are showing more interest in the nonprofit sector, for example, in working for nonprofit organizations that build or own affordable housing. Five or six graduates in each class have a very strong entrepreneurial drive and start their own businesses. Our students are fulfilling the vision of the founders of MIT's MSRED program. They are building the future.

University of California at Berkeley

Program in Brief

The Haas Real Estate Group is a research-based academic unit within the Haas School of Business at UC Berkeley. The group offers undergraduate, MBA, and Ph.D. degree programs. The real estate program of the business school includes the associated Fisher Center for Real Estate and Urban Economics, which serves as a research and education center, a forum, and a career resource for students. Berkeley's Institute for Business and Economic Research administers a program, the Berkeley Program on Housing and Urban Policy, that supports research and teaching on housing and urban development and is associated with the Fisher Center.

Q&A: Professor of Real Estate Development at the Haas Real Estate Group

Robert Edelstein is a professor of real estate development in UC Berkeley's Haas Real Estate Group and a member of the Fisher Center for Real Estate and Urban Economics. In the following interview, he answers questions about real estate education at Berkeley and real estate as a career.

What about real estate interests students?

Let me address that question from my perspective of having been a professor for the last 35 years, first at Wharton and now at Haas. Although students are drawn to real estate for many reasons, two of its attributes seem to be central to most of them. First, they see real estate as an area in which they can, if successful, earn great rewards—although they also recognize that it is risky. Therefore, real estate attracts students who have an entrepreneurial drive and spirit and are willing to take risks. The second attribute of real estate that interests students is that it offers many avenues to success. Furthermore, students perceive that success can occur when you are independent and your own boss, which is, however, a perception that may not be fully consistent with reality.

What does it take to succeed in real estate?

Real estate careers can cover a wide spectrum of activities, from rocket science to the nitty-gritty, with Wall Street securitization types on one end and hard-nosed property and asset managers and hands-on builders on the other. Typically, the most successful people are entrepreneurial, well organized, and well trained in the aspects of real estate with which they deal, and they understand how their specialty fits into the multidisciplinary business of real estate. This ability to see the whole picture or to understand how your part of the real estate business affects the other players is the key, I believe, to a successful career. For example, the most successful architects frequently understand the financial implications of their aesthetic decisions and the most successful developers understand financial analysis while they also appreciate what people find attractive and functional in buildings.

What classes are most important to students?

Students who are seeking a real estate career are best served by having a real estate major or concentration within a degree program, such as an MBA program, which can provide a context for addressing the relationships among the multidisciplinary aspects of real estate. I recommend students take a broad core of basic business courses, and then specialize in the real estate courses offered in the program. At the universities where I have been involved, real estate students are able to take business-related courses along with courses in architecture, city planning, law, and engineering, subject to their capabilities and penchants. Students should work to acquire a broad view that will enable them to make adjustments as the world of real estate changes.

What is the value of part-time and summer work to students?

We feel that a summer internship or participation in an intercollegiate real estate team competition—such as the NAIOP Challenge, the Bank of America Low-Income Housing Challenge, or the University of Texas at Austin's National Real Estate Challenge—is an integral part of the student training. These contests require students to use their general academic skills in approaching real-world problems. The integration of academic insights and skills into the practitioner world makes for success. An internship or a real estate team challenge leads students to interactions with real-world practitioners and gives them an understanding of the requirements of specific types of jobs. Internships are sometimes followed by job offers.

What resources do you provide for helping students find employment?

We use our board members as well as outside speakers and lecturers in our program, in order to bring professional practitioner experience to the classroom at an early stage in the students' careers. We work through our policy advisory board, whose members come from firms involved in virtually every aspect of real estate, to match students with jobs. We devote considerable time and resources to promoting student interactions with professional practitioners—through, for example, "firm nights," internships, and our real estate job placement service. We also encourage and support the Berkeley Real Estate Club, which is made up of alumni and current students. Such activities assist our students in finding jobs and employers in finding appropriate hires.

What is the value of a graduate degree for students going into real estate?

I believe that our program gives students the analytic tools as well as practical know-how they need to enter the most sophisticated parts of the real estate job market. Of course, at Berkeley (as well as Wharton), the students themselves are quite energetic, enthusiastic, and motivated—we offer a program that creates value-added, but we are working with very

good raw material. Students have told me that the Berkeley degree (as well as the Wharton degree) is a useful "identifier" for getting them in the door for job interviews. In essence, we have created brand recognition for graduates of our real estate program. Students also report that the large network of Berkeley alumni out there in the real estate world can be helpful; alumni quite often mentor new graduates.

How can the academic world and the real estate industry work together to promote careers in real estate?

In addition to existing programs and initiatives, there is always more that can be done. I suspect that it is mostly up to the universities to embrace the practitioners in real estate who may want to become involved in academic programs. Generating more practitioner involvement in academic programs can be done individual-by-individual and firm-by-firm, as well as through practitioner organizations such as ULI, NAIOP, and CoreNet Global. The key to the expansion of practitioner/academic interaction, quite frankly, is resources. Personally, I have more opportunities to chat up outside nonacademic professionals for our program than I have time. I believe this is true of most academics. This indicates to me that we need more resources in the form of additional faculty or staff. To accomplish this, it would be useful to have an endowment that is dedicated to the purpose of encouraging the interplay between industry and academe.

CAREER PROFILE: UC Berkeley Civil Engineering Major; Cofounder and Co-CEO of Divco West Properties

Stuart Shiff, cofounder and co-CEO of Divco West Properties, always loved buildings, studied civil engineering at the University of California at Berkeley, and worked at a real estate firm headed by his uncle before setting off on his own at the age of 28. Divco West is a growing real estate investment and management company and fund sponsor headquartered in San Francisco. Shiff's path from engineering student to real estate CEO is traced in the following career profile.

When Shiff was in high school, he worked as a volunteer in a hospital emergency room, and his father, a doctor, was encouraging him to go into medicine. But the teenage Shiff had other interests. Driving around the Silicon Valley, where his family had moved from his native Montreal, "I'd spend as much time looking at all the new buildings as I would checking out the girls," he says.

His interest in buildings took him to UC Berkeley, where he majored in civil engineering. During the summers, he returned to Montreal to work for his uncle, Sam Aberman, head of Divco Ltd., a real estate company. His uncle didn't cut him any slack: "I started at the bottom, operating a jack hammer and doing odd jobs." In his senior year, Shiff took a real estate class taught by Kenneth Rosen, professor of real estate and urban economics in the Haas School of Business. "It changed the way I looked at real estate," Shiff says. "I loved tangible assets, and I realized I could add more value to real estate through financial engineering than civil engineering."

After graduation, Shiff went to work for Divco Ltd. as a development officer responsible for land entitlement, development, and leasing. One day, Shiff's grandfather, who had an interest in the company, asked him if he should approach Sam Aberman about his taking Shiff on as a partner. After some reflection, Shiff decided that his career interests lay elsewhere.

Then Shiff happened to meet David Taran, a tax attorney whose family was in the manufacturing and retailing business. The Taran family had been long-time investors in Divco, although Shiff hadn't known any of them personally. With financial help from their families, Shiff and Taran started buying small office buildings and industrial complexes around Montreal. They then moved to the Silicon Valley, and in 1993, when Shiff was 28 years old, they cofounded Divco West Properties, which has become a fully integrated real estate investment and management company and fund sponsor.

From the start, they decided to focus on specific geographic markets. "With an illiquid asset like real estate, you have to have a thorough understanding of the asset's position in the marketplace and the risks in market cycles," Shiff notes. With a loan from an institutional investor, they started acquiring industrial buildings—a relatively safe product that doesn't require extensive tenant improvements"—in Silicon Valley. In 1995, Divco West began to diversify into office properties. Taking a somewhat contrarian approach, the company looked for inefficiencies in the market that would enable it to acquire properties at attractive prices, add value, and sell them

for substantial gains. "At one point, we were buying retail buildings when nobody wanted them," Shiff recalls. One office property that Divco West bought for $40 a square foot later sold for $170 a square foot.

When signs of a dot-com slowdown appeared, Divco West started to sell its Silicon Valley properties. "We managed to sell about 80 percent of our properties before it got really bad," Shiff says, adding that "it's hard to time the market perfectly." The dot-com slump also delayed the development of a 6.6 million-square-foot campus for Cisco Systems on 700 acres of land owned by Divco West.

The slump slowed but has not stopped Divco West's growth. Since its inception, the company has acquired, managed, and leased more than 14 million square feet of commercial space and disposed of more than 9 million square feet of commercial properties in various markets, including Silicon Valley, San Francisco, Los Angeles, Denver, and Phoenix. Its $290 million Page Mill Properties real estate equity fund focuses on acquiring commercial real estate assets in northern California and other high-tech markets.

The Wharton School of the University of Pennsylvania

Program in Brief
The Wharton School of the University of Pennsylvania has offered a real estate concentration for MBA students and undergraduates since 1985. The concentration consists of three required courses in the real estate department and two electives. Wharton's real estate department is closely involved with the Sam Zell and Robert Lurie Real Estate Center, which was established in 1983 to promote excellence in real estate education and research. The Zell/Lurie center helps develop curriculum for the real estate department.

Q&A: Professor of Real Estate at Wharton
Peter Linneman is Albert Sussman Professor of Real Estate and a professor of finance and business and public policy in the Wharton School. He also is principal of Linneman Associates, a consulting firm that provides strategic and M&A (mergers and acquisitions) analysis, market studies, and feasibility analysis to a number of leading U.S. and international companies.

How do students learn about career opportunities in real estate?

For our undergrads, the discovery of real estate as a career generally comes through taking real estate department courses. About 55 to 60 percent of Wharton undergrads take at least one real estate course; and those undergrads who go on to a career in real estate were usually turned on by a course. Among our MBAs, about 60 percent take one or more real estate courses and about half of Wharton MBAs who go on to a career in real estate were turned on to such a possibility by a first course. The other half of MBAs who pursue a career in real estate came to Wharton already focused on real estate. None of the courses in the real estate department are required of Wharton students, but they have a good reputation—and the Samuel Zell and Robert Lurie Real Estate Center has a high profile among students.

What does it take to succeed in real estate?

The criteria for a successful career have changed. In particular, as real estate has become more mainstream, the need for entrepreneurial talents has diminished. Other than basic intelligence, the keys to a successful career are people skills, numeracy skills, and a passion for real estate. A small subset of Wharton graduates with a real estate concentration will become entrepreneurs, but not most. This is definitely progress: For years, real estate held little attraction for nonentrepreneurs, who make up the bulk of all business talent.

What's the value of part-time and summer work in helping students find permanent employment?

For most students, I think, part-time experience is of limited use for anything but the money earned, which is a necessity for many students. The work that they usually perform in part-time jobs consists of small and compartmentalized tasks that teach them little that they will find useful later. However, summer jobs can be valuable if they show students what goes on in a real estate job other than just rows and columns on a spreadsheet.

What suggestions do you get from employers about structuring your academic program?

Over the past 20 years, the Zell/Lurie center has worked regularly with Wharton's industry support base to develop, evaluate, and improve our curriculum. Every one of our courses as currently constituted evolved out of industry input. In addition, a typical course brings in four industry leaders to lecture on course topics. Also, we write up about seven new cases a year with the help of industry leaders. The main problem that both we and employers see is the inability of students to clearly write up or articulate their research results and ideas.

What resources do you provide for helping students find employment?

Each student has an industry mentor. In addition, the Zell/Lurie center sponsors two career panels a year and hosts a job fair attended by about 60 firms. We also sponsor a Ballard industry luncheon about every other week at which about 15 students meet with industry leaders over lunch followed by two or three hours of one-on-one meetings. Of course, we provide a lot of individualized counseling and networking help.

What is the value of a graduate degree for students going into real estate?

The main value of our degree—an MBA with a concentration in real estate—is the knowledge the graduate comes away with as well as his or her better appreciation of what they don't know. But our mission is to help all Wharton MBA graduates better understand the role of real estate in their careers, most which will not be in real estate. I feel, by the way, that our equal commitment to real estate majors and nonmajors is what distinguishes our program from most others. Furthermore, the key to our real estate program is at the undergrad level, not the MBA degree.

Why focus on undergraduates?

The educational mission of the Wharton real estate department is to produce sophisticated, skilled real estate professionals, and if we want to get the best and brightest turned on to real estate, our best bet is to plant the seeds in the minds of juniors and seniors, who are at a stage in their education when it's easier to stimulate talent. Real estate programs should commit to developing courses that non–real estate students might want to take as juniors and seniors, but most such programs ignore this mission. Real estate education needs to focus less on teaching students who have already chosen real estate as a career, and much more on showing young non–real estate students how exciting and diverse a career in real estate can be. Wharton's program is unusual in its focus on non–real estate students and undergraduates. By the way, because we serve such a broad base, we have the depth of student demand needed to economically justify having nine to ten full-time faculty. If we focused only on real estate students, we could support perhaps one to three full-time faculty, which is not a critical mass for intellectual give and take. I feel that this is the fatal flaw of almost all current university real estate programs.

Q&A: Director of Finance at the University of Pennsylvania; Instigator of a CREW Pilot Mentoring Program at Penn

Pamela Arms, 2005 president of the Philadelphia chapter of the CREW (Commercial Real Estate Women) Network, left a position in banking to join the University of Pennsylvania as director of finance in September 2004. Members of CREW Philadelphia had been talking for some time about starting a mentoring program for young women in college, and the idea gained traction when Arms joined the University of Pennsylvania. In the following interview, she talks about this pilot program for mentoring female students in real estate and about the growth potential for CREW Network's university program.

After you joined the university, what steps did you and CREW Philadelphia take to get a program going?

In the fall of 2004, Nina Shallcross, CREW Philadelphia's membership chair, and I met with Janice Leberman, coordinator of the Samuel Zell and Robert Lurie Real Estate Center of the Wharton School, to discuss how CREW could build relationships with the university and, in the process, begin to develop a mentoring program. One result of that discussion was that we participated in a Wharton real estate job fair in January 2005. Ten CREW members staffed a table that was visited by more than 75 students, primarily women, as well as representatives from many of the companies in attendance. It was our first opportunity to educate the Wharton community about CREW Philadelphia.

What other steps did you take to build relationships with the university?

We went to one of our long-time (male) CREW members, Asuka Nakahara, associate director of the Zell/Lurie center, for help in procuring speakers from the university for our 2005 programs. We were delighted to make a connection with

Joseph Gyourko, director of the Zell/Lurie center, who was the guest speaker at our April 2005 luncheon. I also utilized my working relationship with Penn's facilities department to organize a behind-the-scenes tour of the new studios of WXPN, the University of Pennsylvania radio station, and the World Café, a music performance venue that is home to World Café Live, a nationally syndicated program. The radio station and music venue are located in a former industrial building controlled by Penn that has been rehabbed by a local developer in conjunction with the university. The tour was part of a joint meeting with Meyers Associates, a local architectural firm, that featured an all-Penn speaker panel.

What about the CREW Philadelphia mentoring program at Wharton?

For the 2005–2006 school year, CREW Philadelphia is working with the Zell/Lurie center on a pilot mentoring program. Many of the more senior members of CREW, myself included, are experienced mentors. We're in the process of matching up ten CREW members with ten women students—undergraduate and graduate. The mentors will be available to meet with the students in person at least once a semester. Contact is to be initiated by the students, not the mentors. Our goal is to help these women bridge the transition from student to job market (or graduate school). Our mentors will be a resource for students who want to know about life in the workplace or who want guidance in making important decisions about career choices, jobs, or the pursuit of an advanced degree. After the students graduate and the formal mentoring period ends, the mentoring relationships may continue on an informal basis.

What's next?

We will evaluate the pilot program and decide whether to expand it. There is a need for mentors not only in Wharton, but also in related schools on campus, including PennDesign, Penn Law, and Penn Engineering. Beyond this, national CREW will be looking at the pilot program to see if it might serve as a prototype for a national program. To encourage students to join CREW, the national organization has put together a discount membership plan for students and non-profits. If our local membership votes "yes" on this plan, the Philadelphia CREW will sign on in 2007. Our current membership dues are $110 paid to the local chapter and $140 paid to national CREW, but under the discount plan, if CREW Philadelphia were to offer a discounted student rate of $55, for example, national CREW would charge only $70.

Does CREW Network's university program have real growth potential?

CREW Network has approximately 6,500 members in 57 chapters in the United States and Canada—and the vast majority are college graduates and hold advanced degrees as well. Informal inquiries reveal that a few of these members, though not many, are teaching real estate courses or are or working on university campuses. Four of CREW Philadelphia's members work at the University of Pennsylvania. However, we do know that many of our members have strong ties to their alma maters or excellent business relationships with universities. CREW Network's university task force is exploring the feasibility of conducting a survey to determine not only where our members attended school, but also the schools with which they have extensive relationships. On the basis of this information, we can build a network of mentoring relationships with universities in markets with CREW chapters—and possibly as well with schools in markets with exceptional university real estate programs but no local CREW chapters. Our members represent a tremendous resource. And they want to be there for the young women in universities today, just as the pioneering women in real estate were there for us when we were entering the business.

Q&A: Wharton MBA; Associate Director for MetLife Real Estate Investments

Kelley Brasfield, shortly after earning a BA degree in English from Miami University (in Oxford, Ohio), met Peter Linneman, Albert Sussman Professor of Real Estate at the Wharton School, through a mutual friend; went to work at Linneman Associates, a strategic advisory and consulting firm, as a research analyst; learned on the job; found herself drawn to real estate; and, after four years at Linneman Associates, enrolled at Wharton, where she earned an MBA with a major in finance and a concentration in real estate. She is currently an associate director for MetLife Real Estate Investments, which maintains a portfolio of $35 billion invested in real estate products, including equities and commercial mortgages. In the following inter-

view, she talks about her course of study at Wharton and her career to date.

Why did you choose Wharton?

While working for Peter Linneman, I met a lot of people in the industry, talked to people about graduate programs, and did my own research. Wharton was my first choice because of the caliber of its students and the quality of its business and real estate programs.

Which courses did you find most valuable?

Real estate finance, accounting, and real estate law helped me to learn the basics and prepare for the real world of real estate. A class in negotiations was not real estate–specific, but it was helpful in teaching me how to communicate and get what I want in an artful manner. I also took a private-equity finance class, which was very useful in teaching me to think creatively about financing. One of my favorite classes was in real estate development, taught by a senior executive from Trammell Crow; in the first half of the class, we went over cases and, in the second half, participants from the companies involved in the cases came in and spoke to us.

What was the value of the Wharton degree in finding a job?

For someone with an undergraduate major in English, the value of the MBA was immense. It gave me the knowledge, the contacts, and the resources to feel comfortable in going out into the job market.

How did you find your first job out of school?

While I was in graduate school, I interned for a summer with Roseland Property Company, a leading redeveloper of luxury apartments and homes in the northeastern United States. It was a smaller company where everyone would pitch in, and it was very entrepreneurial. At the end of the summer, Roseland offered me a position. I knew that when I graduated I didn't want to go into investment banking or consulting. I decided to try development, and my next decision was whether to work for a larger or smaller shop. I decided on a smaller shop, so I could get more involved in the development process. My decision was to say "yes" to Roseland.

—continued on page 122

Q&A: A Program to Interest Girls in Real Estate Careers

The CREW (Commercial Real Estate Women) Network started life in the 1980s and has grown into a national network—representing nearly every real estate discipline—that focuses on advancing the success of women in commercial real estate. The CREW Foundation which was founded in 1998 as the philanthropic arm of the CREW Network, supports programs that assist women and girls to achieve economic self-sufficiency and promote the entry of women into commercial real estate. To date, the CREW Foundation has awarded more than $500,000 in grants. Complementing the CREW Foundation's national efforts, local CREW chapters annually raise approximately $1 million for charitable organizations and programs in their own communities. CREW Careers: Building Opportunities™ is a CREW Foundation program that is designed to interest girls in commercial real estate careers.

In the following interview, Irene L. Hosford, 2005 chair of the CREW Foundation, and Anne DeVoe Lawler, 2006 chair, discuss the CREW Careers™ program.

Irene L. Hosford, *managing partner of Hosford & Creasey, a Dallas law firm.*

Anne DeVoe Lawler, *partner at Jameson Babbitt Stites & Lombard, a Seattle law firm.*

Why did CREW start the Careers program?

Hosford: We believe that with proper education, mentoring, and help, women of diverse backgrounds can succeed and that commercial real estate is a great platform for success. Reflecting this philosophy, the foundation's program helps girls to learn about commercial real estate and to realize that they can have exciting and rewarding careers in this industry.

What is the program's value to CREW?

Lawler: It helps us realize our goals of achieving parity and increasing gender and ethnic diversity in the area of commercial real estate. It also affords our members opportunities to organize and lead local-chapter programs and to mentor girls—to inspire them and help them realize real estate career aspirations. For CREW's senior members, many of whom were given a helping hand when they first came into the industry, this is a chance to return the favor by helping the next generation.

How is the program structured?

Hosford: It's a trademarked program initially directed at teenage girls. The CREW Foundation provides direction to participating CREW chapters, along with a curriculum guide and teaching plans. Activities include an interactive presentation of a project from land acquisition to development to lease up, a hard-hat tour of a local development project, and tips on preparing for a job interview. The foundation also assists local chapters with developing a budget, finding sponsors, and publicizing the event and it provides tools to help chapters evaluate the success of the program. The local chapters apply their imagination and creativity in organizing and producing programs, either a one-day program or a multiweek program.

How did the program start?

Hosford: The Dallas CREW chapter developed a pilot program, on the basis of which the CREW Foundation developed a national prototype. We tested it with ten chapters in March and April of 2005.

How many people participated?

Lawler: In all, 267 girls, mainly from Girl Scouts and Girls Inc.—along with 328 CREW volunteers and local representatives of Cushman & Wakefield, Key Bank Real Estate Capital, and Starbucks Coffee Company, which had contributed donations.

What were the results?

Lawler: The girls enjoyed meeting and talking with women in commercial real estate careers, and they actively participated in the site selection, construction, and lease up for the model retail project. The girls were intrigued by the idea of a career in commercial real estate, and most look forward to participating in CREW Careers: Building Opportunities™ again. We look forward to keeping a number of them engaged as they proceed through school.

What's the next step in rolling out the program?

Lawler: We are analyzing and refining the curriculum, and expanding the participation. In 2006, 20 chapters, including the original ten, will participate. Ultimately, we think that most local CREW chapters will produce the program year after year.

Hosford: We are also expanding our base of corporate supporters. One of the drivers of this initiative is the increasing number of commercial real estate companies that see the business advantages of encouraging diversity. They understand that encouraging diversity is a long-term value proposition; that starting young, following through, and making opportunities available to women will eventually bring about a change for the better in their business culture and performance.

What are your goals beyond the Careers program?

Lawler: CREW Careers™ is simply a first step in a series of initiatives we are planning to interest girls and women in careers in commercial real estate and to help them to succeed in their careers. We plan to engage in a more formal mentoring program. For example, we might invite girls to sit in on a broker's negotiation of a transaction or to observe what a lawyer does in the course of a day. We expect to eventually expand to include college-student participants. We hope to interest more companies and organizations in providing support, from helping to fund the CREW Careers™ program to providing scholarships, internships, and jobs. We would like to make the transition between young women first learning about commercial real estate to their finding satisfying and rewarding careers in the industry a seamless one.

Will you follow up with the girls who have gone through the program?

Hosford: We expect some of the girls to eventually go into commercial real estate. No matter the educational level attained—high school, a community college, or a four-year university program—women can find satisfying careers and make a comfortable living in commercial real estate. We will survey or otherwise track the participants in each year's program to find out what career choices they make, to follow the progress of their careers, and to provide support along the way.

continued from page 119

What is your current job?

I'm an associate director for Metropolitan Life's real estate investments group. MetLife makes debt and equity investments. I work on the debt side, making loans on commercial properties in the United States, Canada, Mexico, and the United Kingdom. I analyze the direction and risk of the commercial real estate portfolio as well as the pricing of loans.

What are your long-term career goals?

I had always fancied myself as an entrepreneur or developer, but came to realize that it wasn't for me. I learned after working for Roseland that I prefer working for a larger company doing my part in helping the company achieve its goals. I found my place with MetLife in my current niche, and I want to move up to a more senior role and oversee more of the portfolio.

What does it take to succeed in real estate?

You not only have to know real estate, but you also have to understand business. Also, you must have exceptional people skills. Whether you're applying to city hall for a building permit or to a bank or other lender for a loan, you need to be extremely articulate.

Q&A: Wharton BS Degree; Property Investments Underwriter at Lubert-Adler

Jared Prushansky is responsible for underwriting new investments for Lubert-Adler, a Philadelphia-based real estate private equity firm specializing in redevelopment through joint ventures with local operating partners throughout North America. He earned a bachelor's of science degree in economics with concentrations in finance, real estate, and accounting from the Wharton School. In the following interview, he talks about how his interest in real estate developed.

What do you do at Lubert-Adler?

Every week is different, but one recent week may be seen as a microcosm of the range of my responsibilities. At the beginning of the week, I traveled to Chicago to close the sale of 32 Mervyn's stores to Developers Diversified for $320 million and two days later I was back in Philadelphia working on a 120-page PowerPoint presentation for Mervyn's refinancing. The beauty of Lubert-Adler is that you get as much responsibility as you can handle.

When did you first know you wanted to pursue an undergraduate business education?

When I was in high school, I took an economics class—actually, it was more about stock market investing, which I thought was fun and exciting. That's when I decided I wanted to study business in college, and Wharton was my first choice.

How did you get interested in real estate?

When I was still in high school, I had the opportunity to learn some aspects of real estate from a local owner and operator of strip shopping centers. When I got to Wharton, I took Professor Peter Linneman's "Introduction to Real Estate Finance and Investment" course. He tried to take us out of our textbooks and computers, and into the real world of real estate. He also invited real-world practitioners to come and talk to us.

Are there any courses you wished you had taken?

Architecture and design. The more I learn about real estate, the more I appreciate the importance of architecture in creating successful projects.

How did you find your first job after graduation?

While I was at Wharton, companies were recruiting on campus and I was offered a summer job at Morgan Stanley. This led to a full-time job with the firm's real estate group after I graduated. I worked on both investment banking and private equity projects for Morgan Stanley.

What are your long-term goals?

For now, I want to stay where I am. Lubert-Adler offers a great learning opportunity and an ideal environment for me to continue to grow. If I stop learning and no longer enjoy the work as much as I do today, then I will figure it out.

What does it take to succeed in real estate?

This is very much a relationship business. People skills are the most important part. If you can't communicate with, connect to, or read the people you interact with, you can't succeed.

Chapter 8
What Do Employers Want?

In 2002, ULI convened a meeting of real estate executives on the subject of human capital in the real estate industry. The meeting took the form of a discussion of a report by Equinox Partners, an executive search firm, based on a human capital survey of more than 500 real estate executives, managers, and employees that was sponsored by companies in the real estate business. The ULI/Equinox report (available on ULI's Web site; see appendix A for URL; search on "Equinox") was designed to help real estate companies recruit and retain the kind of talented, energetic, and dedicated employees that every company values.

At this meeting, a number of key issues were hot topics: How can real estate organizations find the best-qualified managers and employees? How can they do a better job of training people and helping them to advance in their careers? And, equally important, how can they promote cultural diversity in the industry (and in individual companies)?

In some other industries, it has long been routine to focus on human capital issues. But the Equinox human capital survey was something of a seminal event for the real estate industry. Although people have been buying and selling real estate since the earliest days of the Republic, the modern U.S. real estate industry has developed only in the last 30 years or so. And only in the past few years has the industry's leadership begun to pay as much attention to human capital as to finding investment opportunities, completing projects, and closing deals.

Throughout the real estate industry today, companies are aware of the need to focus resources on finding, recruiting, training, supporting, mentoring, incentivizing, and advancing the careers of professional-level employees. If some predictions of a looming U.S. labor shortage prove out, competition among companies in real estate and other industries to attract workers could intensify in coming years. Many companies have undertaken to broaden their recruiting efforts,

start up or improve training programs, and institute better career planning and advancement programs. To be sure, such efforts vary across the industry. Some companies are proactive in addressing human capital issues, while others are moving more slowly.

Differences in recruitment, training, and career advancement practices are more a reflection of the organization's leadership than of its size. The principals of the smallest businesses can be just as diligent in recruiting, hiring, and mentoring as the executives of the biggest companies. Of course, smaller organizations usually have fewer resources to work with. Whereas they may combine a number of executive and managerial functions —chief executive officer, chief financial officer, chief administrative officer, human resources director, and director of sales and marketing— into one or two positions, large organizations usually have a human resources director and human resource departments that may also contract with outside firms for human resource services; as well as structured recruiting, hiring, and career advancement programs.

No matter their size and resources, real estate companies seek to find and hire the best people available. Whom do they look for? Essentially, they want people who can add value to the organization. Can a candidate help the company increase its revenue and profits, reduce costs, operate more efficiently, win new business, increase its market share, or achieve other business goals? Most real estate companies invest a substantial amount of time and money in finding, recruiting, hiring, training, mentoring, promoting, and managing people—and they want to know whether they will get a return on their investment. Will the candidate learn and grow on the job? Will she or he be able to move up to positions of more authority and responsibility, perform at a higher level, and thus increase her or his value to the organization?

GENERAL GROWTH PROPERTIES: FOCUS ON MAXIMIZING TALENT

The practices that General Growth Properties—a Chicago-based REIT that owns, develops, operates, and manages shopping malls across the United States—has put into place for finding and retaining talent are fairly commonplace in other industries, but relatively leading edge in the real estate industry. For Judy Herbst, senior vice president for human capital, and her 45-person team at General Growth, the mission is clear-cut: "Our focus is strictly on how we maximize the talent in our organization."

That means recruiting, retaining, and developing the very best people. The company has about 5,200 employees and owns about 200 properties. Take benefits. "We are building a benefits strategy that supports people at different points in their careers and in their lives," Herbst says. Traditionally, real estate companies have not offered the same level of benefit incentives that companies in other industries offer.

General Growth has a bonus program for which every full-time employee is eligible. The bonus kicks in once the company's annual economic goals are met. The program is tailored to metrics that specifically measure the company's success in its real estate business. There is, for example, a cash value-added incentive that takes into consideration factors such as how much the company pays for land or its cost of capital. The bonus is paid out over a several years, a "banking" feature that is an added retention incentive. "We're always looking at what keeps people here," Herbst notes.

For the human capital department, retention begins with ensuring that people who join the company are in the right position—for themselves and for the company. An assessment program developed by the Gallup Organization helps identify the talents of current employees and future needs for talent. "It helps us apply people's talents in work they enjoy doing for the company," Herbst says, adding that "it's a win for our employees and for us."

What are the evaluation factors for job applicants at General Growth? The applicant's cultural fit is key. "We're a high-achieving culture," Herbst says. Another factor is the applicant's sense of urgency in accomplishing goals. It's not only a matter of speed, but also of how well a job can be done or a goal achieved. "We're often delighted, but seldom satisfied" is a company mantra, according to Herbst. Other top evaluation factors include an applicant's tolerance for risk and willingness to assume responsibility.

FINDING TALENT

The human capital department has its own recruiters, known as "talent consultants." "They provide the framework that helps our leaders bring in the best talent," says Herbst. Company employees are brought into the talent hunt through a referral bonus program for employees who recommend people who are hired by General Growth.

Finding talent, both inside and outside the firm, is a collaborative effort of human capital and the company's managers. "We provide support, but the bottom line is that it's the manager's responsibility to find good talent. We place that responsibility on every manager," says Herbst, who has been in HR her entire career, including eight years with General Growth.

The company looks first for needed talent within its own ranks. "We are very focused on internal promotions and helping people to advance their careers in our organization," says Herbst. It also recruits on college campuses and at industry conferences and other venues. Available positions are posted on its Web site. On occasion, General Growth may use a search firm to fill a specific need.

A growing portfolio of properties has created a current need for asset and leasing managers and people with accounting skills. The company offers training programs for new employees such as assistant general managers and assistant marketing managers— people who do not necessarily have real estate experience, but who have a degree and are interested in working in the industry. They are assigned to a smaller property where they work under the direction of the property manager. "They get hands-on experience and, if they perform well, they advance to higher management positions or larger centers," Herbst says.

In addition to helping with recruitment, human capital works closely with the company's managers on training and development, compensation, performance evaluations, employee fulfillment, and other HR issues. "We see ourselves as business partners with our operating people," Herbst says.

INTERNSHIPS

A nationwide internship program, known as General Growth Prodigies, has as of spring 2005 provided internships to more than 400 college students. An intern typically works ten to 15 hours a week at one of the company's properties, learning about marketing, leasing, accounting, and management under the direction of the property manager. Some interns are paid; others are not, but they receive college credit. "The internship program initially met with some skepticism within the company, but it has been highly successful and more than 100 of our properties are now participating," Herbst says. (More information on the Prodigies program and career opportunities in general can be found on the company's Web site.)

MENTORING

General Growth lacks a formal mentoring program, but new hires are encouraged to find mentors inside and outside the organization. Saying that "it's still a challenge for women to move up the ladder in the real estate industry," Herbst herself mentors women who work for the company and other companies throughout the Chicago area. "We have a high promotion rate for women, and more women are in senior management positions than when I got here eight years ago," Herbst notes. The company focuses on the recruitment of minority employees as well, through its internship program and other initiatives.

STARTING OUT AT GENERAL GROWTH

Students who may be interested in working for General Growth after graduation should try to get an internship, advises Herbst. Her advice for anyone currently interested in working for the company is to do your homework on the company and find someone in the organization who can connect you with hiring managers. In preparing for an interview, she says, "do an honest self-assessment to determine the value you would bring to our organization, and be able to communicate what you have to offer. Show that you are positive, enthusiastic, and flexible."

As concerns a career at General Growth, according to Herbst: "To move up the ladder, you must have a real passion for our business, and stamina. We expect 110 percent from our people. You must have a sense of urgency. We have a lot to get done, and to get done quickly. And you must be very aware how you interact and work with other people. Interpersonal skills are the biggest challenge as you move up the ladder. Generally, we hire people with the ability to do the job. But are they sufficiently self-aware to be able to maneuver the political waters?" At General Growth "everyone is the CEO of their career," Herbst says. "We can provide the tools and resources, but then it's up to you."

Evaluation Factors

An analysis of hiring practices in the industry and the interviews of real estate professionals conducted for this book reveal that nearly every company and business in real estate evaluates prospective job candidates first on their core skills; second on certain innate qualities they demonstrate; third on how likely they are to fit into the corporate culture; and finally on how their education, experience, and skills relate to the job being filled.

Core Skills

The core skills valued by typical employers in the real estate industry include the following:

Analytical ability. Employers look for candidates who are able to understand the whole through an analysis of its components and how they fit together; who can see relationships in apparently unrelated data; and who have the ability to interpret complex information.

Communication skills. Candidates should be able to use words effectively to impart information or ideas; listen carefully in order to understand what other people are saying; and understand how others perceive what they are saying.

Financial skills. Job candidates should demonstrate that they know the basics of money and finance; that they are aware of the relationship between finance and real estate; and that they have an understanding of the financial structure of the hiring organization.

Interpersonal skills. Employers look for candidates who have a genuine interest in other people; get along with people of diverse backgrounds; and are able to work effectively with others at every level of an organization.

Leadership. Employers value candidates who are self-aware as well as aware of the feelings and concerns of other people; who can solve problems, provide clear direction, and motivate other people to follow a course of action; and who take risks and act decisively.

Learning skills. Candidates should demonstrate that they are inquisitive, open to learning, and eager to learn; that they have the ability to acquire and apply knowledge; and that they learn from experience and learn from others.

Collaboration skills. Employers look for candidates who can work well in teams; who understand the division of roles and responsibilities; who will share credit for jobs accomplished and put the group's priorities before their own; who know when to lead and when to follow; and who are sensitive to the interests of other people.

You may object, as many real estate students have: "But those skills aren't unique to real estate. Every company in every industry requires them." True enough. The core skills are transferable skills. They are the foundation of a career in any industry, in any profession—which is one reason why some people who began in teaching, computer technology, banking, medicine, engineering, aviation, or other professions have been able to make a successful career change into real estate.

Having the core skills to do a job is not enough. You also must be able to demonstrate to prospective employers that you have these skills. Some (usually large) companies may test you for particular skills. At organizations with no formal testing program, you can show your skills through the job application process. For example, you can demonstrate your communication skills in your cover letter, résumé, and other written submissions and in job interviews. You can demonstrate your analytical skills and financial sense by familiarizing yourself with the company—its organization, management, markets, competition, business challenges, and financial structure—and inserting relevant comments, observations, and questions into your job interviews and other conversations with company managers. You can also bring attention to any of your past undertakings and activities that you think bear on your interpersonal and collaboration skills.

Leadership skills may not be a requirement for the entry-level position for which you are applying, but the company still will want to know if you have leadership potential. How can you demonstrate that you do? If you have served in a leadership capacity in any organization or activity—a student group, a professional organization, a charitable or volunteer organization—include that experience in your résumé and bring it up in interviews. If you have never been a leader, start thinking about acquiring leadership experience. Join a school or community organization and work your way up to a leadership position. Taking on leadership roles will help you to develop your interpersonal, communication, collaborative, and other core skills as well.

Your academic performance in school and the specific courses you have taken that are related to real estate can demonstrate your learning skills to prospective employers. A professional license or designation—broker, appraiser, property manager, or other designation—shows employers that you are proactive about acquiring knowledge. Equally important, you need to show your eagerness to keep learning. As has been emphasized throughout this book, you should become well informed about the real estate industry, industry trends and issues, and the business world. Then make sure in job interviews to show that you are well informed. Before specific job interviews, you should spend time finding out what you can about the company's business and organization, so that you can impress your interlocutors with your interest and knowledge.

Innate Qualities

The innate personal qualities valued by typical employers in the real estate industry include the following:

Capability. Employers look for an aptitude or capacity for real estate, basic know-how and competence, the ability to perform specific jobs or tasks, indications that the job candidate is an efficient person.

Drive. Employers try to determine if the candidate will be likely to take decisive action to achieve a goal, solve a problem, or seize an opportunity.

Enthusiasm. Energy and enthusiasm—an intense desire to accomplish goals—accompanied by a can-do attitude, motivation, and a commitment to hard work are perhaps the top-ranking personal qualities sought by most employers.

Integrity. The recent spate of corporate financial scandals has put ethics high on the list of concerns of real estate companies. Companies are looking for job candidates who will behave in accordance with agreed codes of conduct; who are honest, trustworthy, and dependable; and who respect other people.

Flexibility. The ability to adapt easily and quickly to changing situations and circumstances is crucial in many real estate jobs, and employers seek to identify that quality in prospective employees.

Focus. Many employers value the ability of candidates to concentrate their attention on their work. They look for people who demonstrate purposefulness, concentration, tenacity, intentness, and centeredness.

Resourcefulness. Real estate companies want people who are able to act effectively and imaginatively, especially in difficult situations. They look for mental adroitness in their job applicants, and evidence that they will be a self-starters who can work independently.

For real estate companies, as noted, enthusiasm trumps other personal qualities in hiring decisions. One manager explains why some candidates stand out: "They are professional, they are very dynamic, and you can see that they would be flexible and will be able to work in an ever-changing environment—but mostly, they've got this positive energy and enthusiasm." Another points out that for her company "experience is not critical in hiring for an entry-level position, but a demonstrated enthusiasm is essential." Adam Smith, a land acquisition manager for John Laing Homes,

Forest City Enterprises: Attracting Aspiring Professionals

Forest City Enterprises is a Cleveland-based, diversified real estate company that acquires, develops, owns, and manages commercial and residential properties across the United States. When Jim Talton joined the company in 2003 as executive vice president of human resources, he knew from his own experience in senior HR positions at leading retail, chemical, and pharmaceutical companies that real estate had relatively low visibility among students looking at career options. Since then, the number of inquiries he has fielded about career opportunities in real estate generally and at Forest City in particular has grown significantly.

Students in real estate and other academic programs and young professionals in real estate companies as well as in architecture, accounting, finance, engineering, law, and other disciplines are increasingly looking at real estate as a career. "More professionals who have been working in banking, insurance, and other businesses are talking about going back to school to study real estate," Talton notes. "Depending on their education, skills and experience, there are many areas in the real estate business where they can be very successful."

Training and Recruitment

Forest City has created a small in-house training program that gives selected employees hands-on experience in the development business. "One of our trainees is a graduate of Harvard's real estate program who was working in finance, and now she's studying to be a developer," Talton reports.

Participants in the training program start out in research, where they learn how to identify and evaluate markets for development, find properties, and consider possible uses for properties—and, in the learning process, they sharpen their analytical skills. They then move on to a position in which they assist a Forest City project manager to develop a property. If they perform well there, they are given the opportunity to develop a property themselves, beginning with a small commercial project. Once they have gained development experience, they can move on to developing larger projects.

A development track may be of particular interest to aspiring professionals, but as a large and diverse company, Forest City offers opportunities for professionals to work in accounting, law, finance, technology, property acquisition and management, and many other areas as well.

To recruit and retain talented people, the company offers on-the-job training and mentoring programs that help them learn, grow professionally, assume more responsibility, and advance in the company. The company is committed to expanding the diversity of its workforce.

Forest City recruits for a range of positions, from entry-level analysts to senior managers. One recruit who distinguished himself working in a city's manager's office was hired as a special assistant to the company chairman to provide advice in the company's relations with local governments and communities.

Forest City has recruited at some colleges and is developing a strategic recruiting program to reach more campuses. The company interviews students during the school year for jobs as paid interns the following summer. Each year, it tries to identify 35 or 40 potential candidates to work in various departments and in different cities. Interns work with key people in each department under the direction of the department manager. "It gives them a chance to learn about the company and gives us the opportunity to look at their skills," Talton observes. "We hope to hire as many of our interns as possible after they graduate, at least 50 percent or more."

LEADERSHIP DEVELOPMENT

The company has received board approval to start a leadership development program known as Forest City University that will enable selected employees to take time off from their regular jobs to spend a couple of weeks a year studying, learning, and sharing ideas and experiences in order to refine their core competencies and learn new skills. The faculty will include company managers as well as outside professionals. "We are providing additional training in management competencies that we consider important to the success of Forest City," Talton says. "If we are going to stay competitive, we have to identify, train, and grow the people who will be leading this company in 15 or 20 years."

When Talton was recruited by Forest City, his first question was: What are the company's growth prospects? Today, he says, the company's growth has given it a higher profile not only within but also outside the real estate industry. "It's been something of a sell to attract people to real estate, but that's changing as companies like ours continue to grow."

one of the largest U.S. homebuilders, says: "I've always had a passion for real estate, for both the social aspect—the opportunity to meet people—and the creative side." It's a trait that helped him land his current position.

Some people are naturally open, gregarious, outgoing, and enthusiastic. Job applicants who are comparatively reserved can demonstrate their enthusiasm quietly—by doing their homework, learning about the company, asking thoughtful questions, and communicating clearly. The important thing is to come across as sincere in your interest in real estate, in the company, and in the position. Hiring managers are quick to discern feigned enthusiasm. In fact, if you are not enthusiastic about getting the job, then maybe you should be looking at other job opportunities with other organizations instead.

Innate capability is another key personal quality. Employers want to know if you are capable of doing the job. Be prepared to explain your accomplishments in previous jobs, in internships, at organizations where you were a volunteer. "Past performance, regardless of what it is, is the strongest indicator of future success," notes a hiring manager. By demonstrating your capabilities, you can show that you have what it takes to succeed in the company to which you are applying. You can also draw on your past work and volunteer experience to demonstrate your drive, resourcefulness, flexibility, focus, and other personal qualities.

Cultural Fit

Organizations are defined by their culture, which comprises the assumptions, values, and beliefs that are predominant within the organization. A company's culture shapes its mission statement, business strategy, organization, operations, and human resources policies. Employees within an organization tend to think, act, and speak in like-minded ways based on the organization's culture. The culture generally informs many daily decisions—how to dress for work, how to talk to managers and peers, what to say in meetings, how late to work, and when to speak up or hold one's tongue. The culture is evident in the organization's perquisites, from who gets preferred parking to who gets stock options.

One of the most difficult things for newcomers to an organization is fitting into its culture. What are the right ways of speaking and acting? Which behaviors are rewarded, which are punished? Will they be told by their boss whether or not they are doing the job that is expected of them? Or will they learn how their performance has been judged in more subtle ways, such as being included in (or excluded from) an important meeting?

Because corporate fit can be such a challenge, company executives try to determine through interviews and informal conversations whether job candidates will be able to adapt to the organization's culture. Candidates may have the requisite skills and talents, but can they become part of the corporate family?

FOCUS ON INTEGRITY

A number of well-publicized corporate financial scandals in recent years have brought the behavior of companies and their senior executives, managers, and employees under intense public scrutiny. The Sarbanes-Oxley Act of 2002 (SOX) requires publicly traded companies to establish an internal audit function that must be certified by external auditors; to submit annual reports attesting to the existence and reliability of their internal controls related to financial reporting; and to include CEO and CFO certification in their financial reports. SOX applies only to public companies, but many private companies, including real estate companies, have adopted SOX practices on their own initiative or at the behest of investors and lenders.

Corporate ethics is a concern of many companies. It goes beyond what the law requires; ethical behavior is about maintaining the company's reputation and its relationships with investors, lenders, clients and customers, suppliers, regulators, and the markets where it does business. Companies running the gamut from Fortune 500 corporations to private real estate partnerships have adopted and promulgated their own ethical governance policies.

This means that companies are concerned with hiring people who are not only the best qualified, but who also subscribe to the company's values. Many review résumés, conduct interviews, and perhaps even test job candidates from the perspective of weeding out prospects who may be dishonest or unscrupulous.

The bottom line for jobseekers in all this is: Be truthful and honest in your résumé and in your conversations with prospective employers. Obtain the company's statement of values. (If it is not available in a company publication or on its Web site, ask for it. And if the company doesn't have a values statement, ask why.) And read it and take it to heart. Finally, if you are hired, live up to the company's values—and help the company to do the same.

How do you learn about a company's culture? You could start by doing some reading up on the company—check out its Web site; see if you can find blogs in which it is featured; and review recent news stories and other published materials. Talk to its employees (and clients and contractors) at all levels, and to outsiders knowledgeable about the company. Visit the company's job sites.

On the basis of this "cultural" research, you can decide if you're right for the company and if it is right for you. If your decision is to approach the company about a job, prepare to present yourself as someone who would be a great fit in the organization. Think about how to act, what to say, how to dress. Be prepared to discuss accomplishments, hobbies, and interests that would communicate to hiring managers that you understand the culture and would fit in. If, for example, the organization of the company is formal and hierarchical, you might want to bring up your military experience; and if the company values resourcefulness very highly, you might bring up your service in the Peace Corps.

Job-Specific Qualifications

Finally, companies evaluate prospective employees on their specific education, experience, and skills for the job. The job in question, for example, may involve writing skills, but not at the level of a professional journalist. For a real estate organization, the requirement that the applicant be able to write well usually applies to writing reports, letters, memorandums, e-mails, and similar communications. Different jobs require different levels of specific skills.

When you are looking at job listings or talking with a prospective employer about a job, you should organize the job requirements by category: core skills, personal qualities (including cultural fit), and job-specific qualifications. Such an exercise can help you match your skills and characteris-

Q&A: The Irvine Company: Employment Policies

Bruce Endsley, *senior vice president for human resources at the Irvine Company, a privately held company best known for the new communities it has developed on The Irvine Ranch in Orange County, California, (see company profile on page 4), describes the company's employment policies in the following Q&A.*

What are your responsibilities as HR director?

My primary responsibility is talent management. I help the Irvine Company attract and retain the highest-quality staff, and I work with the company's leaders to develop and implement programs that support the achievement of the company's goals.

Do you outsource recruiting?

We complete a vast majority of our recruiting efforts with our own HR staff.

What skills does the Irvine Company value?

We look at both IQ and EQ (emotional quotient) skills. Two group presidents—Clarence Barker, Investment Properties Group, and Joseph Davis, Irvine Community Development Company—queried on this question say that in terms of IQ-related skills, analytical/critical thinking and strategic thinking are much in demand. Managers must have the ability to analyze problems and opportunities and evaluate various options, and they must have the ability to plan a course of action and to execute. These skills are essential in a dynamic, ever-changing industry that requires excellent development and investment timing. EQ or interpersonal skills are as important as IQ skills. Barker and Davis consider the following EQ skills and personal characteristics to be most in demand: 1) the ability to work in teams (of both employees and nonemployees); 2) the ability to communicate well; 3) a strong motivation and work ethic; 4) dependability in meeting deadlines; 5) a professional demeanor, which is important in a highly visible company like the Irvine Company; and 6) leadership.

How do you find candidates to fill positions in your company?

We use seven main sources: 1) the Irvine Company's résumé database; 2) internal job postings; 3) employee referrals; 4) referrals from business associates; 5) the company's Web site; 6) external job postings with professional associations, schools, and so forth; and 7) search firms.

How should a professional approach your company about employment?

The best way is to develop a contact with a respected member of our organization or to obtain an exceptional referral. An applicant can also submit a résumé to the HR department. Résumés should be impressive, with an emphasis on accomplishments.

Do you do informational or courtesy interviews when no position is currently available?

Rarely.

What are examples of the professional skills you look for in an applicant?

Financial analysis. It's the easiest entry and offers the most career options. Other skills we look for include construction, architecture, and land planning.

How should a professional prepare for a job interview with your company?

Be prepared to respond to three basic questions: 1) Can you do the job? We are looking for skills and experience. Tell us how you can add value to the company. 2) Will you do the job? Here we are looking at your motivation. Provide us with examples of your work ethic, how you have juggled multiple projects, other achievements. 3) Will you fit in? We want to know if you will be comfortable within the company culture and a business environment. You are off to a good start if you present a polished, professional appearance.

—continued

Q&A: The Irvine Company: Employment Policies

continued

In your evaluation of applicants for entry-level professional positions in your company, who makes the cut, and why?

Our focus is on the following nine factors: 1) real estate education and experience; 2) analytical skills; 3) understanding of our business; 4) commitment to excellence; 5) willingness to work long hours; 6) flexibility; 7) cultural fit; 8) an error-free, accomplishments-oriented résumé; and 9) professional manner and appearance.

What entry-level professional positions are available to recent graduates? What are some possible career paths within the company?

Very few entry-level positions exist. Most positions require a minimum of two years of experience. On the asset management side, the office division hires entry-level property assistants, who must have an undergraduate degree. The typical career path for an entry-level property management person is property assistant, to property coordinator, to assistant property manager, to general manager, to portfolio manager. And the apartments division hires entry-level leasing consultants and community administrators. Either of these positions can advance to assistant property manager, to community manager, to regional manager, to vice president for property management. On the development side, a typical career path is entry-level financial analyst, to senior financial analyst, to finance manager or project manager, to director of development, to senior director of development, to vice president for development. People stay in jobs at least one to two years before earning promotions and two to three years is more the norm; once they reach director level, they typically stay in their jobs three to four years before being promoted.

How much value do you give a person's education?

We require a degree for most entry-level professional positions, except in the apartments division. The quality of the school is important. A degree in real estate, business, finance, urban planning, or architecture is valuable. An MBA or a master's in real estate degree is valuable. Experience is critical, even if it is only summer or volunteer work. We think that working while in school shows that an applicant can juggle multiple priorities. Other factors we look at include grade point average, membership in real estate or other relevant clubs, and leadership experience in, for example, school, charities, or a church.

What in-house training programs do you offer professionals joining your company? Do you offer a mentoring program?

Until recently, we generally offered only external "training" in the form of attendance at conferences and seminars as well as executive coaching. Having grown from 400 to 2,300 employees, we have a greater opportunity to grow our own talent and so we are now offering more in-house training. We are currently considering establishing a program to use our own executives as mentors for other employees.

What does it take to move up the ladder to a senior management position in your company?

EQ-related skills become more critical to success as you move up the ladder. Clarence Barker and Joseph Davis list core competence combined with a generalist/broad understanding of business, critical thinking, ability to achieve results, and attention to detail as the key IQ-related skills for advancement. They see the key EQ-related skills for advancement as the ability to relate to people (interpersonal relations), flexibility and openness to change, and leadership.

THE IMPORTANCE OF FIRST IMPRESSIONS

Stan Ross

During my years as managing partner of Kenneth Leventhal & Company, a national accounting firm specializing in real estate, our process for hiring people for various positions was thorough. After conducting the initial interviews for a job, we often found that two or more people were equally qualified. To decide who was the best person for the position, we asked selected partners and managers, including some who had not been involved in the initial screening process, to conduct further interviews and evaluate the candidates.

When candidates had essentially the same technical qualifications, we focused on their core skills and innate qualities, including their ability to work with teams, their people skills, their communication skills, and their work ethic. We asked: "What is the most challenging assignment you have had?" or "What is the biggest failure you have experienced?" We tested their judgment with questions like: "We recently had a situation where we disagreed with a client's presentation of its financial statements. How would you communicate this difference of opinion to the client?"

Particularly for accounting positions, we focused on the knowledge, quality of work, and integrity of the candidates. We might have asked: "If you were reading a report from our company that was ready to be delivered just in time to meet the client's deadline, and you found an incorrect or inappropriate conclusion, what would you do?"

Over the years, I learned that the company's thorough review process often validated my initial impressions of a candidate. First impressions matter, a point stressed by Malcolm Gladwell in his best seller *Blink*. This cannot be emphasized enough: From the moment your job interview starts, what you say, how you look, and how you act will be key evaluation factors.

tics to what is required—and thus help you to narrow your job search and to sell an employer on your ability to do a job for which you are well suited. No employer expects a new hire to get up to speed on the first day on the job; they expect you to go through a learning curve. What they try to ascertain in reviewing your experience and talking to you is whether you have the skills and personal characteristics that equip you to learn quickly on the job and reach the performance level required of the position.

What job-specific skills and experience are necessary for entry-level positions? Let's look first at the typical organization of large companies that develop or own real estate, highlighting entry-level positions. Then we'll look at how companies—first developers and owners and then real estate services providers—define specific entry-level jobs in their recruitment material and job listings.

Functional Divisions and Job Titles

Here's a look at how a large company that develops, owns, or manages commercial properties typically is organized. Many of the job descriptions provided here are adapted from a list provided by NAIOP (National Association of Industrial and Office Properties) on the real estate careers section of its Web page (see appendix A for URL). Entry-level positions on the following list of job titles and in the accompanying chart are underlined.

ORGANIZATIONAL CHART FOR A TYPICAL LARGE REAL ESTATE COMPANY

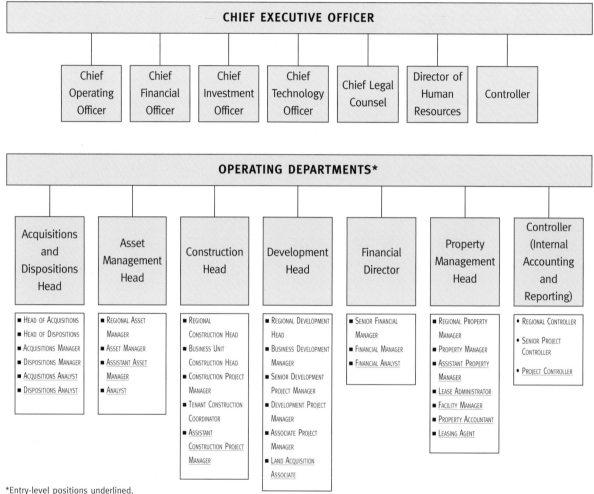

*Entry-level positions underlined.

Senior Management

At the senior management level, a large real estate development company is much like any other large corporation, with a chief executive officer, chief operating officer and so on:

Chief executive officer (CEO). Directs all company operations and activities to maximize profitability; establishes objectives, plans, policies and standards; reports to—and may be a member of—the company's board of directors.

Chief operating officer (COO). Assists CEO in overall direction of company; establishes and implements operating procedures; plans and directs daily operations of company; evaluates operating results for CEO review; reports to CEO.

Chief financial officer (CFO). Manages company's financial plans, policies, and practices; plans and directs treasury, budgeting, and forecasting functions; directs auditing, tax planning and reporting, and accounting functions; maintains relationships with financing sources; develops financing for development projects; reports to CEO or COO.

Chief investment officer (CIO). Coordinates the focus and objectives of the company's development, leasing, asset management, and property management departments; reports to CEO or COO.

Chief technology officer (CTO). Plans and manages the company's IT operations, including strategic planning, application/systems, computer operations, and vendor relationships; reports to CEO or COO.

Chief legal counsel. Establishes standards for and reviews the legal aspects of the company's financial documents and contracts; assures compliance with legal requirements in locations where company is operating; acts as liaison with outside counsel; usually reports to CEO.

Director of human resources. Develops, implements, and evaluates personnel policies and programs; oversees recruitment, training and development, employee and labor relations, compensation and benefits, and performance management.

Controller. Manages company's accounting practices, preparation of financial reports, and maintenance of financial records; oversees budgeting, forecasting, financial analysis, and financial control systems; usually reports to CFO.

Operating Management

At the operating (management) level, the positions in a typical large development company are specific to the real estate business.

Acquisitions and Dispositions. Typical positions relating to the company's acquisitions and dispositions function include:

Acquisitions and dispositions head. Manages overall acquisitions and dispositions; supervises head of acquisitions and head of dispositions.

Acquisitions head. Identifies and analyzes acquisition opportunities; negotiates acquisitions.

Acquisitions manager. Assists head of acquisitions in identifying opportunities to acquire properties, possibly within a designated geographic region.

Acquisitions analyst (a.k.a. site acquisitions specialist). Assists in the sourcing and acquisition of property for development; conducts market research; contacts brokers and owners about property acquisition opportunities; assists in negotiations with sellers and other parties.

Dispositions head. Identifies and analyzes disposition opportunities; negotiates dispositions.

Dispositions manager. Assists head of dispositions in identifying opportunities to dispose of properties, possibly within a designated geographic region.

Dispositions analyst (a.k.a. site dispositions specialist). Assists in the disposition of property; conducts market research to determine the value of properties; contacts brokers and potential buyers; assists in structuring sales transactions and negotiations with buyers.

Asset Management. Typical positions relating to the company's asset management function include:

Asset management head. Oversees the company's portfolio of real estate assets (which are owned and managed) through acquisitions, dispositions, and day-to-day operations, including management of revenue and expense items; works to maximize the portfolio's performance; supervises regional asset managers and asset managers.

Regional asset management head. Provides strategic oversight of existing and potential real estate assets within a designated geographic area.

Asset manager. Manages business plans and budgets for properties in a designated portfolio of properties.

Assistant asset manager (a.k.a. asset management associate). Assists asset manager with business planning and budgets.

Analyst. Reviews the condition and maintenance of assigned properties; manages their bookkeeping and cash flow accounting; handles rent reconciliation; prepares property financial reports and annual budget forecasts.

Construction. Typical positions relating to the company's construction function include:

Construction head. Establishes and enforces company's engineering and construction standards; ensures that construction work meets or exceeds standards within cost estimates; monitors quality of work in progress; supervises regional construction heads.

Regional construction head. Enforces construction standards and ensures project quality in within a designated geographic area.

Business unit construction head. Ensures that construction work in a particular product line, such as office buildings, meets or exceeds standards within cost estimates; provides technical input on the feasibility of proposed projects; monitors quality of construction work.

Construction project manager. Provides overall direction on assigned construction projects; reviews and makes recommendations on planning and design of projects; negotiates contracts or participates in contract negotiations; monitors day-to-day progress and activities on project construction sites.

Assistant construction project manager. Assists project manager with construction project management, on-site monitoring, and contract negotiations.

Tenant construction coordinator. Coordinates construction of tenant space in assigned facilities; supervises construction to ensure that it meets the owner's expectations; reviews plans; estimates costs; obtains bids; inspects and approves completed project.

Development. Typical positions relating to the company's development function include:

Development head. Provides oversight for all the company's development activities; establishes development strategies and evaluates development opportunities; conducts market evaluations; acquires sites; analyzes the financial feasibility of proposed projects; negotiates construction loans with prospective lenders.

Regional or divisional development head. Evaluates development opportunities within a designated geographic area or for a specific division; conducts market evaluations; acquires sites; analyzes the financial feasibility of proposed projects; negotiates construction loans.

Business development manager. Identifies development opportunities; follows up on development leads and contacts; participates in the structuring and financing of projects; assures the completion of development projects.

Senior development project manager. For specific—and usually the company's more complex—projects, oversees the entitlement and development process from site selection to construction; secures development permits; meets and negotiates with government agencies; manages project budgets; monitors the construction process.

Development project manager. For specific—and usually the company's smaller, less complex—projects, oversees the entitlement and development process from site selection to construction; secures development permits; meets and negotiates with government agencies; manages project budgets; monitors the construction process.

Associate development manager. Assists development project managers with the management of smaller projects.

Land acquisition associate. Finds and qualifies land for development based on company's land requirements; maintains a land search database; initiates discussions with property owners about the possible sale of property.

Financial. Typical positions relating to the company's financial function include:

Financial director. Manages the company's accounting practices, records maintenance, and financial reports; supervises financial managers.

Financial manager. Within a designated geographic or functional area, manages accounting practices, records maintenance, and financial reports; supervises financial analysts.

Senior financial analyst. Provides managers with financial analyses, development budgets, and accounting reports; analyzes financial feasibility for the most complex proposed projects; conducts market research to forecast trends and business conditions.

Financial analyst. Provides managers with financial analyses, development budgets, and accounting reports; helps maintain and update asset valuation models for the company's investment portfolio; analyzes financial feasibility for moderately complex proposed projects; conducts market research to forecast trends and business conditions.

Property Management. Typical positions relating to the company's property management function include:

Property management head. Oversees the management of all physical facilities owned and managed by the company; establishes and monitors budgets; monitors operational efficiencies; maintains and renovates facilities; supervises contracted services; maintains good relationships with tenants; supervises regional property managers.

Regional property management head. Oversees the management of facilities within a designated geographic area.

Property manager. Manages one or more properties, which generally are assigned by size category, for example, properties over 1 million square feet or properties under 500,000 square feet; collects rents; maintains tenant relations; prepares annual budgets; may have leasing responsibilities; generally works on the site.

Assistant property manager. Assists property managers with the day-to-day operations of one or more properties.

Lease administrator. Provides analysis and support for property management, facility planning, lease administration, and financial reporting; tracks lease information, property values, capital expenditures, and rental rates; may assist with lease negotiations.

Facility manager. Directs the operations of designated properties on a day-to-day basis; supervises contract maintenance and operations workers—including janitors, electricians, and mechanical engineers. Non–real estate corporations with a large number of facilities to operate as well as large real estate owners and developers employ facility managers.

Property accountant. Performs cash management, general ledger accounting, and financial reporting for one or more properties.

Leasing agent. Markets space; finds tenants; participates in lease negotiations; may require a broker license. (Note: some large development companies employ their own leasing agents, while others hire outside brokerage firms to lease space in their buildings.)

Internal Accounting and Reporting. Typical positions relating to the company's internal accounting and reporting functions include:

Regional controller. Oversees financial budgeting and reporting within a designated geographic area; directs budgeting and forecasting activities, auditing, tax planning and reporting, and accounting.

Senior project controller. Oversees financial and accounting activities relating to one or more designated projects; supervises project controllers.

Project controller. Participates in assigned accounting activities, audits, tax reporting, and tax payment work for one or more designated projects.

Entry-Level Jobs at Development/Investment Companies

Analyst is a common entry-level position. An analyst's job requirements will vary depending on the company and the position itself, but the job usually involves a variety of work and working for different people. Associate is another common entry-level job title, but an associate's job usually requires a higher educational level (for example, a master's degree) and a higher level of skill than an analyst's position.

Starting Out with a Large Developer/Owner

Large companies usually rotate their analysts and associates through several operating units. One might start, for example, in the development division, move to property management, and then to asset management before starting to move up the ladder. This kind of rotation gives new hires a good grounding in the company's operations and helps them to better understand its way of doing business and the real estate business in general.

If you cannot meet the experience requirements of a job that is available, but are interested in working for the company, see if there is another job in the organization for which you might qualify. And then take advantage of on-the-job training and new hire rotation policies to decide if you want to move up the career path in a particular operation, such as development or property management. Some of the largest companies also provide formal on-the-job training through company "universities"—such as the Trammell Crow University (see appendix A for URL).

For example, you might start out as an assistant property manager or property manager of a small building, advance to managing a larger building, and then move up to managing all the properties in one of the company's regions. Or you might start in property management and decide later that you want to switch to a development track. Just remember that if you start with a large, full-service company in a different position than you had planned, you usually will still have the opportunity to pursue the career path you want.

To help you become familiar with what kinds of entry-level positions are available at large development companies, there follow edited summaries of and comments on some actual recent job listings. The names of the companies and any identifying information have been omitted.

Analyst (1). The following listing for an analyst comes from the Web site of a company that invests in existing properties and the projects of third-party developers.

Wanted: analyst to provide financial analysis and underwriting of investments for projects involving a wide variety of property types and investment structures. Looking for a highly qualified and motivated player to work on research for and financial modeling of the company's investments. Candidate must be able to work independently, complete due diligence of investments in a timely manner, and effectively prioritize and manage multiple due-diligence assignments.

Among the responsibilities listed for the analyst (1) job:

- perform property and portfolio financial analyses, for example, appraisals, internal valuations, and portfolio return forecasts;
- review or create detailed financial pro formas using ARGUS and Excel software;
- participate in drafting acquisition submittals to the company's Investment Committee;
- conduct risk and sensitivity analyses—including hold-or-sell analyses—on current portfolio properties and prospective additions to the portfolio;
- conduct property inspections and assessments of competitive products;
- review leases, abstracts, and contracts;
- coordinate requests for and receipt of due-diligence reports and information;
- keep acquisition project files current;
- reconcile company's pro formas with third-party pro formas; and
- underwrite and document all pro forma assumptions.

Among the requirements listed for the analyst (1) job:

- a BA or BS degree;
- excellent analytical skills and reasoning abilities;
- proficiency with Excel and ARGUS software;
- demonstrated ability to be a strong team player;
- effective communications skills;

- initiative (must be a self-starter);
- a strong work ethic; and
- familiarity with an entrepreneurial environment.

The analyst (1) job listing begins with a general description of the position and of the key skills and qualities that the employer is seeking. A specific knowledge of financial analysis and underwriting of property investments, a high degree of motivation, and the ability to work independently and on multiple projects simultaneously appear to be the most important qualifications.

The listing describes the specific job functions in a "responsibilities" section and gives details on required skills and characteristics in a "requirements" section. Note that many of the core skills and other common evaluation factors discussed earlier in this chapter are included in this job description—for example, strong analytical, communications, and team-playing skills; as well as initiative and a strong work ethic.

The listing asks for two specific credentials—an undergraduate degree and proficiency in the named software applications. College students usually develop some degree of proficiency in these and other computer software application programs. The question is whether they have the level of proficiency required for specific jobs with such requirements. Unlike many other job listings, this one does not require a degree in a particular area of study. Neither does it require experience. Translation: If you have a college degree, you may land a job like this one—if you can demonstrate to a prospective employer that you have the necessary skills and personal characteristics.

Analyst (2). Compared with the previous listing, the following listing for an entry-level analyst position from a regional developer/owner/investor describes a different job with similar skill requirements.

Wanted: an entrepreneurial, self-motivated individual to perform analysis and underwriting for the company's property acquisitions and asset management functions, and to assist with the development of business plans, debt underwriting, the preparation of debt and equity packages related to new acquisitions and existing assets, and the coordination of due-diligence items. Good writing and analytical skills are critical to excelling in the position.

Among the responsibilities listed for the analyst (2) position:

- underwrite property acquisitions;
- perform analysis on portfolio properties;
- assist in the preparation of business plans;
- assist in the preparation of debt and equity packages related to new acquisitions and portfolio properties; and
- assist in the coordination of third-party reports, market analysis, site tours, and other due-diligence items.

Among the requirements listed for the analyst (2) job:
- ability to enjoy working in a team environment;
- ability to take direction from others;
- ability to multitask;
- ability to meet deadlines;
- good writing skills;
- good analytical/financial analysis skills;
- working knowledge of Excel and other Microsoft Office applications; and
- knowledge of ARGUS software a plus.

The job listing does not state that an undergraduate degree is required, but the job description and skill requirements suggest that it is—or at least that it would be preferred. Note that "assist" is used a number of times in the description of job responsibilities and in different areas— business plans, equity, debt, and due diligence. This suggests that in assisting individuals or teams, analyst (2) would get broad exposure to development financing, which is very useful in starting a real estate career.

Development Associate (1). The following listing for a development associate comes from a multifamily developer looking for recent graduates of MBA or master of real estate programs.

Wanted: a development associate to work with a development director to find new development opportunities; prepare financial analyses; work with consultants on the design of projects; finance development; navigate the entitlement process; monitor construction progress; interact with financial partners; manage risk; monitor lease-up or unit sales; and sell assets. The associate will be involved in all aspects of the development process. A strong quantitative/financial background is important to this position and multifamily and/or construction experience is a plus, but not a requirement.

This listing mentions only one required skill, "a strong quantitative/financial background." However, it is evident from the job description and educational requirement—a master's degree in business or real estate—that a very high level of skill is required. No experience is necessary, but an applicant with experience in multifamily properties or construction presumably would have an edge in competing for this position.

Development Associate (2). This listing for a development associate is from a developer and manager of sports, entertainment, and commercial projects.

Wanted: development associate for work on all aspects of sports and entertainment–oriented project development.

Among the requirements listed for the development associate (2) job:

- proven professional talent and experience in feasibility analysis, real estate finance, investment analysis, project leasing and marketing, development planning, project management and administration, and public and regulatory approvals;
- strong communication, analytical, and organizational skills;
- demonstrated leadership abilities;
- desire to become involved in an entrepreneurial environment;
- bachelor's degree in business, construction administration, architecture, engineering, or equivalent;
- master's degree in business administration, real estate, or finance; and
- prior work experience in the real estate or construction industries a plus.

Unlike some listings, this one does not require a certain number of years of experience. But the job candidate must "prove" his or her experience across a range of disciplines. The development associate (2) position requires the same communication, analytical, and organizational skills that are required for every professional job in real estate companies. These core skills are the foundation for higher-level or more technical skills, such as project management and administration.

Property Manager. The following listing from a national REIT is for a property manager for one of the buildings in the company's portfolio.

Wanted: experienced property manager to maintain day-to-day relationships with customer contacts and oversee the daily operations of assigned buildings.

The job responsibilities are listed in 22 bullet points along the lines of the following example of one: Anticipate and respond to customer needs/requests.

The job requirements, provided in a single paragraph, are as follows:

- college degree in business administration, real estate finance, or related field;
- one to three years experience in property operations and customer relations;
- effective written and verbal communication skills;
- strong customer-service skills;
- ability to multitask and prioritize; and
- proficiency with Microsoft Office software.

This listing requires not only a college education, but also a specific degree. It also requires specific experience. If you don't have the requisite experience, how could you qualify for a job like this? The time to start thinking about this question is while you are still in school. If you think that you might be interested in property management, try to get a summer job or internship with a property management firm or with the property management group of a large real estate company. Employers usually count summer jobs and internships as relevant experience.

Assistant Project Manager. The following listing for an assistant construction project manager comes from a provider of brokerage, management, development, and other real estate services.

Wanted: a construction manager to assist in the implementation of new construction, renovation, and rehabilitation projects.

Among the requirements for the assistant project manager position:

- strong communication and interpersonal skills;
- strong computer application skills;

- working knowledge of AIA (American Institute of Architects) documents;
- knowledge of construction accounting procedures;
- bachelor's degree in construction management, architecture, engineering, business, or equivalent;
- zero to three years experience in construction/project management; or
- any similar combination of education and experience.

The "similar combination" line shows that this employer will be flexible in considering the experience requirement. For example, your education may help to compensate for your lack of experience in construction management, provided you can meet the other requirements—core skills, specific knowledge requirements—for the position. You could acquire the specific knowledge required through college courses or other educational programs.

Land Acquisition Specialist. If you are interested in working for a developer or homebuilder, starting out as a land acquisition or land search specialist would literally give you from-the-ground-up experience in the development process. And you would acquire a skill—finding land—that is becoming more valuable as the supply of developable land across the nation shrinks. This listing for a land acquisition specialist comes from a residential developer and homebuilder.

Wanted: a land search specialist to help define the company's land needs and identify and qualify vacant land based on these needs.

Among the responsibilities listed for this position:

- locate and document available land using county Web sites, Internet searches, aerial photos, and property databases;
- create and maintain a land search database;
- confirm land's physical status by site visits;
- contact property owners; and
- initiate discussions leading to the eventual purchase of selected properties.

Among the requirements listed for the land search specialist job:

- high level of comfort with technology;
- ability to learn new technology applications and software;

- experience with GIS (geographic information systems) a very strong plus;
- strong Internet and Web searching skills; and
- excellent verbal and written skills.

Starting Out with a Small Developer/Owner

Small developers and owners may not advertise available positions, neither on their Web sites or elsewhere. The only ways to learn about openings are through networking or contacting the company directly. Jobs may not be as well defined as in large companies, and the jobholder's responsibilities may extend beyond the specific job. For example, someone hired as an assistant project manager might also be called on to assist with financial analysis, construction work, land acquisition, administrative work, and other assignments. In short, the typical employee might do a bit of everything.

If you start out with a small developer, you will be working in a fast-paced environment. You will be assigned multiple tasks, and will have to prioritize, work quickly, and make good decisions under pressure. The company may lack a formal training program. But you can learn on the job, and you probably will be learning multiple jobs simultaneously.

What do small developers look for in a candidate? One small developer says he prefers to hire people with architectural or construction management degrees and construction experience, but he considers candidates without the necessary qualifications who show a passion for the construction business: "I like to talk to people who want to understand how a building goes together, people who have a curiosity about the construction business and an appreciation for its complexities."

Starting Out with a Homebuilder

In the United States, a small number of companies build thousands of houses a year nationwide and command the largest share of the market. And thousands of medium-size and small companies construct a few hundred or a few dozen homes a year—in a single region or a single metropolitan area. The biggest homebuilders are structured like large development companies with a CEO, a CFO, and so on. They are involved in the entire homebuilding cycle, from the acquisition and development of land to the construction and sale of housing units. A small homebuilder, on the other hand, usually is not involved in the development business. Such a company typically builds on land it buys that has already been developed.

Like large commercial developers, large homebuilders provide new hires with opportunities to rotate through the organization to learn about the company and the homebuilding business. Some builders offer positions that provide training. Small homebuilders, like small developers, are generally loosely structured. New hires are assigned a variety of tasks and are expected to work well without much supervision in a high-pressure environment.

The following listing comes from one of the biggest homebuilders in the country.

Wanted: assistant project managers whose background clearly demonstrates an ability to successfully direct all business and development facets in a production homebuilding company.

Among the responsibilities listed for the assistant project manager position:

- gradually assume profit and loss responsibility;
- participate in overseeing new home construction; and
- participate in managing land acquisition, the approval process, and sales and marketing operations at the company's communities.

Among the requirements listed for this job:

- a graduate degree, or a bachelor's degree in real estate, construction management, or a related field;
- a highly developed business sense; and
- sales experience a plus.

Entry-Level Jobs at Real Estate Services Providers

As is the case for large development companies, large real estate services companies usually offer multiple career paths. You might start out as a sales agent, then obtain your license and go out on your own as a broker. Or you might decide to move into another area of the company, such as property management, investment management, or research.

Starting Out with a Commercial Broker

Commercial brokers include firms, such as CB Richard Ellis and Jones Lang LaSalle, that operate worldwide, employ thousands of people, and offer a range of integrated real estate services—including sales and leasing, property management, facilities management, and investment advisory services. At the other end of the spectrum are smaller firms that operate in a single region or city, employ a few to a few hundred people, and focus on particular services, such as sales and leasing. The biggest firms are organized much like large development companies, with a board of directors, a CEO, and executives in charge of geographic markets or service lines. Large commercial brokers offer entry-level positions in sales and other specialties.

Sales Professional. The following job listing comes from a large, multifaceted real estate services firm.

Wanted: sales professional to negotiate the leasing, selling, and investing of commercial real estate for clients.

Among the requirements listed for the sales professional position:

- zero to two years experience in administration, marketing, or sales; and
- degree in business administration or marketing or other degree.

Director of Brokerage Services. The following listing from a real estate services firm offers a similar entry-level opportunity, but in a different type of job.

Wanted: director of brokerage services to oversee the day-to-day business/clients of a team of brokers.

Among the requirements listed for this job:

- zero to two years experience in financial accounting or sales; and
- bachelor's degree in business administration.

Starting Out with a Property Manager

Rather than work in the property management division of a large development, investment, or real estate services firm, you might choose to start with an independent property management firm that provides services to owners and other clients. Many such firms hire and train novices in property management, including customer relations, vendor relations, budgeting, maintenance, and other property management tasks.

Starting Out at a Commercial Bank

Commercial banks provide real estate developers and investors with construction loans; income property financing; structured financing, such as acquisition financing; and specialized financing, such as financing of foreclosed property purchases. Large commercial banks hire college graduates with bachelor's degrees or MBAs for full-time training in their various business lines, including real estate finance. New trainees are exposed to and have an opportunity to learn about different financing documents.

One bank recruits financial analysts for its business units—including its wholesale banking group, which encompasses real estate finance—and provides them with a 24-month training program. Following this training, analysts may be considered for a position with wholesale banking or another business unit.

During a series of interviews, candidates for this program are evaluated for their knowledge of accounting and finance, interpersonal skills, and other skills.

Among the requirements for participation in the training program:

- an undergraduate degree, preferably in business, finance, marketing, or accounting; or equivalent work experience;
- business experience through internships, part-time work, or full-time work;
- proven leadership qualities;
- strong potential in sales, marketing, and customer service; and
- solid verbal and written communication skills.

Participation in such a training program would provide opportunities to learn about real estate finance—including how to value collateral, how to assess risk, and how to evaluate the financial feasibility of development projects. You might decide to pursue a career with a large bank—and to focus on real estate. Or you could go to work for a developer, where your banking skills would be highly valued. Alternatively, you might work in real estate lending for a smaller bank that lacks a formal training program but can provide on-the-job experience.

Starting Out at a Commercial Real Estate Lender

A number of companies specialize in offering loans to developers, owners, and other real estate businesses. They may provide financing directly, or they may act as intermediaries in providing financing from other sources, such as life insurance companies, pension funds, and agencies like Fannie Mae and Freddie Mac. The largest financing companies typically offer a range of loan products, including construction loans, bridge loans, conduit loans, and tax-exempt financing. Some may also provide equity capital in return for an equity position in development projects.

Starting out in an entry-level job at a commercial lender can be a good route to learning real estate finance. The following listing for a real estate analyst is from a commercial lender.

Wanted: real estate analyst to provide property analyses.

Among the responsibilities listed for this analyst job:

- review and analyze current and historical income and expenses for properties;
- determine terms and conditions for loans under application;
- prepare loan submission for lender review;
- order and review third-party reports, including appraisals, environmental inspections, property condition inspections, and seismic reports;
- conduct on-site property inspections;
- assist in loan closings; and
- compile market data and maintain information database.

Among the requirements listed for this job:

- bachelor's degree;
- zero to two years professional experience;
- excellent computer skills;
- excellent communication skills;
- excellent analytical, quantitative, and problem-solving skills;

- detail oriented; and
- ability to multitask and to work independently with minimum supervision.

Starting Out at an Investment Bank

Investment banks serve clients in a variety of industries and businesses including real estate. Some investment banks specialize in real estate, providing equity, debt and advisory services to developers, owners, and other clients.

Competition for investment banking jobs is intense, and the selection process is rigorous. In a 1997 book on the subject, *Fast Track: The Insider's Guide to Winning Jobs in Management Consulting, Investment Banking, and Securities Trading*, Mariam Naficy reports that investment bankers and recruiters look for specific skills in prospective job candidates—analytical skills, communication skills, interpersonal skills, quantitative skills, integrity, leadership skills, collaboration (team playing) skills—as well as motivation and energy. But having these skills is only a start in trying to secure a position with an investment bank.

An entry-level investment banking position in a service line or function outside of real estate can provide a way in, and leave open the opportunity to move laterally into real estate at a later point. Alternatively, you could seek a position with an investment bank that specializes in real estate.

Starting Out at an Investment Advisory Firm

Investment advisory firms provide investment management and related services to clients, and many of the largest firms provide services to a range of clients, including real estate owners and investors. Some investment advisers specialize in real estate.

The largest firms offer on-the-job analyst training programs for new hires with undergraduate degrees and associate training programs for new hires with advanced degrees. Their training programs cover various investment modes and concerns, including equity and fixed-income structuring and research, institutional equity, investment banking, investment management, and private wealth management. Real estate research, investment, and management are areas that are usually included in these training programs.

Investment advisory firms are interested in job applicants who, regardless of their degree majors, demonstrate a strong interest in business and finance. They seek energetic, creative, well-rounded, outgoing, and self-motivated individuals. The work environment is dynamic and high pressure, and to thrive in it you need to be a quick learner and to have strong quantitative and analytical skills.

Starting Out with Other Services Firms

An internship, a part-time job, or a entry-level job in a firm that provides professional services—such as design, market analysis, accounting, or legal services—to real estate clients can be a good start to a career in real estate. At an accounting firm, for example, you could develop your skills in financial analysis, forecasting, computer modeling, and due diligence; at an architecture firm, you could learn about building design; and at a law firm, you could become familiar with real estate law. Of course, there is always the possibility that taking such a route could lead you into a career in accounting, architecture, or law rather than a career in real estate.

Q&A: Hines: Career Opportunities

David LeVrier, *senior vice president and chief administrative officer of Hines—a privately owned company involved in developing, acquiring, leasing, and managing real estate as well as in providing investment management and advisory services worldwide—is the company's senior human resources officer. He joined the company in 1977 after graduating from the University of Houston with a BS degree in law. LeVrier describes employment policies at Hines in the following Q&A.*

What professional skills and experience are most in demand in the real estate industry in general and at Hines specifically?

Companies in the United States and around the world, and in every industry including real estate, are grappling with the question of how to find and develop the next generation of leaders. At Hines, we have intensified our efforts to find the future leaders of our company. Real estate organizations such as Hines are doing business in an increasingly complex business, financial, regulatory, and real estate environment—and the organizations themselves have grown larger and more complex. Hines now operates throughout the United States and in 11 other countries. We have about 2,900 employees, compared with 1,000 when I joined the company. Managing such an organization requires exceptional leadership abilities.

How do you identify tomorrow's leaders?

It's admittedly a subjective process. There are no fixed guidelines. We're having a lot of internal discussions as to how to identify potential leaders early in their careers, or even while they are still in college. Identifying future leaders in the undergraduate population is an interesting challenge.

What are the qualities of a leader?

Hines has an entrepreneurial culture and history, and our top people are outstanding deal makers. They also have developed strong management skills. In my opinion, some organizations have leaders who are excellent rainmakers—people who know how to bring in the business—but who may not necessarily understand what's required to be an effective manager.

What are the career opportunities for someone interested in joining Hines?

An employee could focus his or her career in one of four areas: 1) project development, which involves identifying opportunities to develop projects for clients, contracting for services, and completing projects; 2) finance and accounting, which increasingly involves managing the process of buying, selling, and trading real estate for clients; 3) property management, an area accounting for much of our U.S. employee base; and 4) support services, involving such functions as human resources, communications, and risk management.

Where do people start out at Hines?

People out of college or with a few years of experience usually start as trainees and work their way up. A trainee in property management, for example, might be assigned to work under a property manager at a site. A professional with a degree in accounting and a few years of experience with an accounting firm, for example, might start as a project accountant handling the accounting activities for a Hines property or entity.

What does it take to advance in the company?

In an entry-level position, you don't have anyone reporting to you. But as you rise in the organization, you will assume management responsibilities and you must have the skills to get things done through other people. Sometimes even MBAs who are stellar at analyzing and solving business problems must learn on the job how to manage others. You have to demonstrate outstanding leadership skills to advance to senior management positions in our company—or any other company.

How do you recruit people?

We visit college campuses to meet with undergraduates to identify potential candidates to join our firm when they graduate. We recruit at the top business schools for the best MBA graduates for our development business. We make frequent use of the Internet, targeting general job boards and professional organizations, to recruit for all levels of positions within the organization. Candidates also contact us directly through our Web site.

—continued

Q&A: **Hines: Career Opportunities**

continued

Do you recruit from other companies?

As we grow, we sometimes have a need for an experienced professional for a management position. We may try to recruit someone at another organization who we have met in a business situation and consider a strong candidate, but we do not recruit from competitors. We may also find property managers at buildings we acquire. But we generally prefer to recruit people out of school or with only a few years of experience—and then help them learn and grow within our organization.

How should people contact your company?

Access the careers page of our Web site. Contact our HR department in Houston directly. Talk to people in our company they may know personally or through an introduction. If they decide they may be interested in working for Hines, they can submit a résumé and application online.

Do you list available jobs on your Web site?

Yes. Anyone with Internet access can see what positions are available in our company worldwide and read a description of each position and the skills required. Interested candidates can apply online. HR partners with our managers to coordinate and/or manage their recruiting needs and shares résumés with them. As is true for many companies, the Web is an increasingly important recruiting tool for us.

Do you recruit in the United States for positions overseas?

We are a decentralized organization. Our HR department and our U.S.-based leadership recruit for positions in the United States, while our leadership in Europe, Asia, or Latin America recruits for positions in those respective regions. Decentralization does not preclude someone from the United States being recruited for a development position in France, for example, but this would be rare.

What do you look for in a candidate?

As I said earlie.r, it's a subjective process. We don't open a playbook and look for specific skills. We look at how truly interested people are in joining Hines. What is their passion for what we do? In some people, this jumps out. We look to our people to help generate business. Can we put this person in front of anyone? Beyond these questions, we look at a person's schooling, the organizations they've been involved with, their work experience and its relevance, and other factors.

How does the interview process work at Hines?

For entry-level positions, candidates generally interview with HR and the hiring manager. Candidates interviewing for management positions meet with HR, the hiring manager, and other members of the management team. MBA candidates interviewing for development positions meet with several members of the management team, including one of our regional executive vice presidents, and Jeff Hines, our president. Our senior managers are the people who build and run this company, and they play a key role in making the final hiring decision.

How should someone prepare for an interview at Hines?

Come prepared to demonstrate that you have studied the company thoroughly. Ask questions. If you do not ask questions, we assume you are not as interested as we would like you to be. We will ask you about your job experience. If you are a recent college graduate or have not been in the workforce for long and do not have extensive job experience, the important thing is to be prepared to talk in detail, with examples, about what you have accomplished to date.

Chapter 9
Finding That First Job

You've done a lot a research and thinking, and real estate feels like a good career choice to you. Now, how do you find the job that's right for you?

You could plunge right in and search job ads on the Internet, find those that match your interests and skills, send in your résumés, and hope for replies. Companies are increasingly advertising jobs on the Internet. You can find job listings on the Web sites of real estate companies as well on the Web sites of job listing services and professional organizations like ULI and NAIOP (see appendix A for a list of real estate professional organizations, including URLs).

In real estate, the leading job listing service is Select-Leaders, which lists jobs in every sector of the industry and in a number of job categories. (See appendix A for URLs of this and other job listing services mentioned here.) SelectLeaders also has a job listing network through which the jobs it lists are simultaneously listed on the Web sites of nine professional organizations, including ULI, as well as on GlobeSt.com, an online real estate news service. Other real estate listing services include:

- RealEstateJobStore.com;
- Real-Jobs;
- iHireRealEstate; and
- RealEstateJobs.com.

Some universities that offer real estate and related programs have job listings on their Web sites. A number of general job search engines and listing services also post jobs in real estate, including:

- Monster;
- CareerBuilder.com;
- Business.com;
- Yahoo! HotJobs; and
- Indeed.com.

While the Internet is a powerful tool for connecting employers and job hunters, it does have its limits. Employers list many types of jobs, not just the entry-level jobs that are available for people starting out in real estate. You may not find a suitable job offer that also excites you. If one does spark your interest, your e-mailed résumé probably will be competing with many others. Some employers do not post jobs online, because, among other reasons, they want to avoid a flood of résumés.

An online job search may not lead to your finding a job, but even then it is not a waste of time. In the process of searching, you will deepen your understanding of real estate and of the kinds of jobs available within the industry.

A Focused Job Search

There is another way to job-search. Many of the young professionals who were interviewed for this book obtained their first real estate job by using variations of the more focused approach to job hunting suggested by Richard N. Bowles in his classic book on the subject, *What Color Is Your Parachute?* (2004):

- assess your skills;
- decide where you want to use your skills;
- find the company that interests you the most, whether or not it has a job opening; and
- obtain an interview—through developing contacts—with a manager who makes hiring decisions.

ABOUT RECRUITERS

Recruiters are consultants who work for clients to fill jobs. There are two types of search firms—retained and contingency. Retained search firms are paid to find, qualify, and recommend candidates, regardless of whether the candidates are hired. They usually have exclusive assignments to find candidates. The largest retained firms generally focus on the recruitment of senior executives to fill positions paying $100,000 or more. Among these are Equinox Partners, which focuses exclusively on real estate; Ferguson Partners, which serves the real estate and financial services industries; Heidrick & Struggles, Korn/Ferry International, Spencer Stuart, and Russell Reynolds Associates, all of which serve all industries, including real estate. Usually, clients retain contingency firms to find candidates for mid-level and junior positions, and contingency recruiters usually are paid only when the candidates they recommend are hired.

Should you try contacting recruiters? Executives at the large retained firms usually won't reply to your phone calls or e-mails unless you have been recommended by someone they know. Unsolicited résumés go into a very large database of prospective candidates, and the chances of your résumé matching up with a position for which the firm is recruiting are low. That being said, efforts made to connect with recruiters while you are in school could pay off later. If your school invites recruiters to the campus for career days or other events, make a point of meeting them. And as you meet people in the real estate industry, find out if they can introduce you to recruiters.

Skills Assessment

Begin your focused job search with a skills assessment. Suppose you had 30 seconds on an elevator to describe your professional skills to a momentarily captive audience: your fellow passengers. What would you say? You may feel comfortable talking about your skills, but if you're in need of a skills check, a number of self-assessment tools are available. CareerJournal.com, the "executive career" Web site of the *Wall Street Journal*, contains articles, discussions, links, and resource lists on various aspects of making career decisions and looking for jobs. Some of the resources listed under "Career Planning, Careers, and Job Hunting" in appendix A provide guidance on how to assess your skills, and the "Is Real Estate for You?" questionnaire in appendix C can help you assess your basic core skills relevant to a real estate career. Your school's career counseling office may also be of assistance.

From your self-assessment, you may decide that you have strong sales skills, or strong analytical and financial skills, or strong management skills. The question then is: Where can you put your skills to best use?

Developer, Owner, Financial Organization, or Real Estate Services Provider?

Think about what aspects of real estate are of most interest to you. Do you think you might be interested in working for a developer? a property owner? an organization that provides real estate financing? an organization that provides a particular kind of service to real estate companies? These different real estate segments were described in chapters 2 and 3. You can gauge your interest by responding to the following questions.

Developer. Think you might be interested in working for a developer? Would you enjoy helping a developer . . .

- find markets for development?
- find land to develop?
- negotiate to buy land from owners?
- conduct market feasibility studies to determine what to build on a site?
- take a project through the entitlement process?
- work with communities to address issues, resolve conflicts, and win support for projects?
- conduct financial feasibility studies of proposed projects?
- analyze the cash flow of projects?
- structure complex joint ventures and partnerships?

- create and manage project budgets?
- work with architects and contractors to design and build projects?
- sell or lease completed projects?

The operative word here is "helping." In an entry-level position with a development company, you would be helping more experienced people in their jobs. What's important is whether working for a developer interests you. Perhaps only one of these different functions within a development company is of most interest to you, in which case you could look for a specific job within a development organization or for a job with a real estate consultant that provides specific services to development organizations, such as marketing or community relations planning or sales and leasing. If, on the other hand, most of these development functions interest you, you could look for an entry-level job with a developer involving work on many different activities. Such a job would give you broad exposure to the development business and help you to direct your career path into the avenues of most interest to you.

Owner. Think you might be interested in working for an owner? Would you enjoy helping a property owner . . .

- develop property investment strategies?
- research markets for property investment?
- identify prospective investment properties?
- appraise and value properties?
- develop financial feasibility and other studies of prospective investments?
- develop property cash flow models?
- find investment partners?
- structure partnerships to acquire properties?
- negotiate with owners and with their agents to acquire properties?
- develop property operating budgets?
- hire and work with property managers?
- hire and work with leasing brokers?
- structure tenant leases?

- plan future property acquisitions?
- plan future sales of properties in the investment portfolio?

Again, in an entry-level position, you usually will be working with more experienced people on these activities. The question is whether working for an owner is what you want to do.

Financial Organization. Think you might be interested in working for a commercial bank, an investment bank, or some other organization that provides capital—the lifeblood of the real estate business (see chapter 3). Would you enjoy helping a financial company . . .

- market financing services to prospective borrowers?
- qualify prospective borrowers?
- provide construction financing?
- provide financing on income-producing properties?
- structure the financing of large portfolios of real estate loans?
- structure, package, and sell complex securities, such as commercial mortgage–backed securities or government-insured loans?
- restructure problem loans?

Real Estate Services Provider. Think you are interested in working for an architect? a broker? a law firm? You will have to devise your own set of interest-gauging questions for such organizations. The services segment of the real estate industry is so diverse (see chapter 3) that no single set of questions would fit every category. If your interest tends toward accounting, appraisal, architecture, brokerage, consulting, and so forth, you can find books, articles, and other resources pertaining to your area of interest in appendix A.

Q&A: **Heidi Brandl**

A vice president in the deal origination group of IHP Capital Partners (IHP) based in Irvine, California, one of the largest U.S. investment firms dedicated primarily to providing equity financing for residential development. Performs market research and capital underwriting for new single-family developments. A graduate of USC's Master of Real Estate Development (MRED) program

"Go to grad school after working only a few years. You'll have more opportunity to work where you want."

Why did you choose real estate as a career?

I was somewhat influenced by my father's working in construction. I was particularly interested in single-family homebuilding, and I initially studied architecture as an undergraduate at USC. I later switched to accounting to get a general business background and subsequently worked for a Big 4 accounting firm. After a few years I realized that accounting was not for me, and I returned to USC for graduate school.

What was your job-hunting strategy?

Real estate people enjoy talking about their careers and helping students with career planning. I took advantage of this by scheduling informational interviews with senior executives at homebuilding companies throughout southern California, from which I learned more about the industry and about IHP, the company I ended up targeting. I also used my professors as a resource. Most of them are well connected in the real estate industry and could make introductions to prospective employers. I had a fantastic mentor as well, with whom I was able to talk candidly about my career aspirations and concerns.

How did you decide you wanted to work for IHP?

I thought about where I wanted to be in 20 years and what job I could take now to accomplish my goal. From my public accounting experience, I knew that I enjoyed working with multiple companies and clients and being in an advisory role. After researching IHP, I decided to pursue a job there with the goal of advancing within the organization.

How did you get the job?

Even though the company wasn't "officially" hiring at the time, I was aggressive in approaching it about working there. I succeeded in securing an internship following graduation. Four months later, I was offered full-time employment.

What persuaded the company to hire you?

Perhaps the one-page list of my real estate–related qualifications that I gave them. It was a short but effective statement of my qualifications specifically tailored to the company and position for which I was applying. I included relevant coursework, prior real estate work experience, and conferences I attended, as well as detailed references in the industry. My purpose was to demonstrate that while I was fresh out of grad school and making a career change, I was qualified for the job. I was very focused.

What's the value of a graduate degree?

Increasingly, it's a requirement for significant career advancement. Not only do most of the executives at IHP hold advanced degrees but most new hires do as well. In large part this is because the real estate industry has become more technical and complex.

What's the best time to go to grad school?

There's a paradox in company hiring practices. The greater your work experience and expertise in real estate, the more likely companies are to fit you into a specific position. This is particularly challenging if you want to work elsewhere in a company or switch careers within real estate. So I would recommend that you go to grad school after working only a few years. You'll have more opportunity to work where you want.

How should someone job-search?

Start with a function (such as finance or asset management) or a product (such as single-family or commercial development) that interests you. Then narrow your job search to companies that offer opportunities in these areas.

What should a jobseeker consider in targeting an employer?

Decide if the company's characteristics match your requirements. Would you and a prospective employer be a good fit? For example, I wanted a work/life balance that would allow me to manage a career and a family, and it was important to me to find out whether the culture of the targeted company would support this without negative consequences to my career.

What are you doing now to advance your career?

Real estate is notably a network-based industry, and it is critical to maintain relationships with people who may become your clients, customers, or employers, and who can provide advice, support, and assistance in your current endeavors. I stay active by attending the events of industry organizations such as ULI and participating in alumni activities at the USC Lusk Center. I have many friends in the industry, including people I went to school with. We share information about new markets or trends, and just keep in touch.

Narrowing the Field

How do you identify companies in your area(s) of interest? Chapters 2 and 3 provided lists of selected companies by development sector—office, retail, and so forth—or by business—REITs, opportunity funds, brokerage firms, asset managers, and so forth. The Web addresses of those companies are listed in appendix A.

A number of real estate company directories and lists, including those discussed below, are listed in appendix A, along with their URLs. For example:

- *Commercial Property News*, an industry magazine and online publisher, provides 15 classified lists of U.S. companies—for example, top apartment property owners, leading office investors and developers, top property managers—on its Web site.
- The NMHC 50 is a list of the top U.S. apartment owners and managers that can be found on the National Multi Housing Council's Web site.
- *Pension & Investments*, a financial newspaper, publishes online an annual real estate directory listing the top real estate investment managers in the United States.
- The National Association of Real Estate Investment Trusts lists all the REITs in its index, organized by property sector. On NAREIT's home page, click on "Newsroom," "Charts and Tables," and "Company Names, Ticker Symbols."

- ReBuz, an online real estate jobs and job resources search engine contains various directories—for example, retail real estate Web sites or real estate services providers.

Smaller real estate companies will not be included on "top" and "leading" lists. National and local business directories can help you locate smaller companies, or companies in particular geographic areas. Three examples:

- Business.com, an online collection of directories, includes a real estate and construction companies directory.
- The Yahoo! online business directory includes real estate company listings.
- BigBook, a Verizon Information Services SuperPages yellow pages directory site is a national yellow pages that lists real estate businesses under a number of categories, by state and city; it includes addresses, phone numbers, and Web addresses.

You can find local real estate companies with cross-referenced searches on Google. Key words include company, directory, association, list, members, and city—for example, homebuilder + name of city or real estate company + name of city.

Subscription services like Hoover's, offering a database of 12 million companies, allow limited free online searches of their databases, but you must subscribe to obtain full lists or detailed information on companies.

A number of publishers offer local directories of real estate businesses. Two examples:

■ The for-sale print, CD, or online "Book of Lists" series from bizjournals provides contact information and key company facts for more than 60 metro markets, such as Dallas or San Jose; bizjournals has also started putting together industry-specific lists covering the United States, including one on homebuilders and one on general contractors.

■ Local business publications often publish business lists. *Crain's New York Business*, for example, compiles ranked lists of the top companies by business—including property managers, architects, construction firms—in the New York area. The lists include addresses, contacts, and company information and are for sale in print, on CD, or in download.

Trade associations and professional organizations are another source of information on companies. Members can access ULI's membership directory, for example, which lists individual members and their companies. State and local building industry associations usually include company names on their list of the association's officers and committee members.

Local business associations, including chambers of commerce, and other local groups and public agencies put together guides and business lists that cover real estate companies. See for example the online San Diego North County Guide for the names of homebuilders in the area.

Compile a Manageable List

Start with the following five criteria (and any others that are important to you) to reduce the number of prospective employers from thousands to a manageable number:

Location. All real estate is local. In what city or metropolitan area do you want to work?

Business line. In what line of the real estate business—commercial or residential? development or finance? (see chart on page 54 for a list of real estate business lines)—are you most interested?

Company ownership. Do you want to work for a public company owned by shareholders or a private company owned by a few partners and investors. The pros and cons of public versus private are discussed in chapter 4.

Company size. Do you want to work for a large company or a small company? Some pros and cons of either choice are discussed in chapter 4.

Product line. Is a particular development product line—retail, hotel, office, resort, single-family residential (see chart on page 23 for a list of development product lines)—of most interest to you?

Let's say you think that you want to work in the Chicago metro area for a large developer of single-family houses and condominiums. Using a directory of local companies, you identify 25 companies that fit the criteria. You could further narrow the field by, for example, focusing only on the ten public companies on the list. But let's say you start with all 25 as potential employers.

Before approaching these companies, learn as much about them as is possible, looking at each both in terms of its business and in terms of what it can offer you as a place to work and start your career.

Business questions to ask include:

■ What are the company's goals?
■ How are its performance numbers—volume of construction, sales, and so forth—trending?
■ What challenges does it face?
■ How does it plan to grow?
■ What are its strengths?
■ Its weak points?

The company-as-a-place-to-work questions to ask include:

■ What is the company's reputation in the industry, with its customers, among its employees, among its competitors, and with the public?
■ How can its culture be characterized? Is it one in which you would find satisfying work, and could perform up to your expectations—and the company's?
■ What is its management style? Would management provide the right level of supervision and support?
■ Do its employees enjoy working there? Would you?

- Would you have a life besides work?
- Does the company provide training?
- What are the opportunities for advancement? Where could you expect to be in the company in a year or two? Or in five years?

Choose Target Companies

In doing your research on your list of 25 companies, everyone is a resource. Talk to classmates, teachers, alumni of your school, family members, friends who work in real estate, people who attend the meetings of industry groups and professional societies, chance acquaintances. As you begin to learn more about each company, you may decide to drop some, for whatever reason, from consideration. After you have narrowed your possibilities list to, for example, ten to 15 companies, you can start to prioritize. List your prospect companies in order of importance as potential employers and begin to focus on, say, the top five companies. Ask the people you know and meet if they know executives inside your target companies, and, if they do, ask them if they will provide referrals. If they agree, you can call these executives and schedule information interviews.

Obtain Information Interviews

Your goals in an information interview are to learn more about the company and build relationships. Most executives welcome the opportunity to be helpful and will make time in their busy schedules to talk with you. But respect their time. Figure on a 30-minute session, unless you are asked to go on.

Start by mentioning who referred you. Thank your host for taking time for the interview, and perhaps indulge briefly in some small talk about sports, the weather, or whatever. But bring the focus quickly to the company. The information interview provides you an opportunity to show your knowledge of the company's work and your desire to learn more. A cardinal rule of the information interview is to never ask for a job. You are there to gather information.

Among the questions that you might ask:

- What are your company's business goals?
- How is the company structured?
- What are its top priorities?
- How does the company make important real estate decisions, such as whether to start a project?
- Can you describe the process for developing a project, from finding land through completion?
- How does the company finance projects?
- What are the key skills the company looks for in employees?
- What jobs are considered professional entry-level positions?
- What are typical career paths within the company?
- What training opportunities do you offer?
- How would you characterize the company's culture?
- How are employees evaluated and promoted?
- What have I missed? Is there anything else you would like to tell me about the company?

Follow up with a thank-you letter within a week, and maintain your relationship with the company. While it may not have an opening now, one might crop up in the future. If you make a good impression, the company might even create a position for you. Meanwhile, you can continue to conduct information interviews with your other target companies.

Applying for a Job

Picture this: Your diligent networking and information interviewing have paid off. One of your target companies has asked you to come in for a job interview for a job that has opened up—or for a new position. The job title is land acquisition specialist. This person will be expected to help the company define its land needs and identify and qualify vacant land based on these needs. He/she will use county Web sites, Internet searches, aerial photos, and property databases to locate and document available land; create and maintain a land search database; visit sites to confirm the physical status of property that is of interest; and contact property owners and initiate discussions for the eventual purchase of selected properties. The position requires a high level of comfort with search and database technologies and with learning new computer applications and software. Excellent verbal and writing skills are essential.

Résumé

You decide that this is the job you want, and that you have the necessary skills. You need to send a résumé to the company in advance of the interview.

Advice on résumé writing is readily available online. Google "how to write a résumé," for example. And there are any number of books and articles on the subject (some of which are listed in appendix A). Here are just a few dos and don'ts on preparing a résumé:

State up front why you are the right person for the job. What makes you stand out? Tell them. What are the skills, experiences, and characteristics that qualify you for this job? List them.

Say what you've accomplished, not what you've done. Don't merely say you were the membership chair of a student organization. Say you helped to increase the organization's membership by 40 percent.

Don't overlook what you've accomplished. If you were a member of a team that beat five other schools in a real estate case study competition, say so.

Don't claim as accomplishments run-of-the-mill skills. Proficiency in Excel is a baseline expectation for employers, not an accomplishment.

Try to stand out from others who will be competing for the job. If your school gave you an award for your outstanding case study of a development project, note it on your résumé.

Include nonwork experience. As a student or recent graduate, you may have had little or no job experience. Hiring managers want to hear about other relevant experience that can help them measure you for the job. List volunteer work, extracurricular activities, club leadership positions, special classes, and the like in your résumé.

Job Interview

Advice on preparing for a job interview is readily available online. And there are any number of books and articles on the subject (some of which are listed in appendix A). You can also get assistance from your school.

You must spend time planning for a job interview. While you cannot anticipate every question the interviewer will ask, you should be well prepared. You will probably have to field general questions about your abilities, strengths, and weaknesses and specific questions about your interest in real estate and your real estate skills. You will also have opportunities during the interview to ask your own questions to learn more about the company and the position.

Among the general questions that you might be called upon to answer are the following:

- Tell me about yourself.
- Why should we hire you?
- What are your best traits and talents?
- Why did you choose to attend ABC University?
- How has your education prepared you for real estate work?
- What extracurricular activities did you pursue while in school?
- Tell me about a job you had—what you liked and didn't like about it.
- Where do you want to be in ten years?
- Tell me about a significant problem you faced and how you solved it.
- Describe a project that you enjoyed working on.
- What are your strengths?
- Tell me about a time when you went above and beyond the call of duty.
- What are your weaknesses?
- Tell me about a time when your work was criticized.
- Give me an example of work you did as part of a team.
- Tell me about your having taken the initiative to get others going on an important issue—and having achieved the results you wanted.
- What would your teachers say about you?
- Do you have any questions about our company?

Q&A: Allyson S. Watkins

Vice president of The Shoptaw Group (TSG), an affiliated group of real estate investment companies headquartered in Atlanta. Sources and underwrites investment activities for TSG's sponsored funds, conducts property due diligence, prepares financial projections, and coordinates TSG's capital markets activities. Formerly a project director for Gellerstedt Development, an office leasing broker with Cushman & Wakefield, and a relationship underwriter/real estate investments for Bank of America. Graduated from the University of Georgia and received a master's of real estate development (MRED) degree from USC.

"Network! Network! Network! You never know how people you meet might help you—now or in the future."

Why did you choose real estate as a career?

Real estate has always been a part of my life. I got an early education in real estate from my father, Bill Shoptaw, who founded TSG. He was always taking me out to look at properties and projects.

What was your first job after graduate school?

I joined Gellerstedt, a startup development company that buys land and develops condominiums in intown Atlanta. I actually started work the same day the company opened for business. As project director, I was responsible for the financial analysis of potential projects and was in charge of the due-diligence process. I met frequently with design architects and reviewed the feasibility of potential projects.

How did your MRED degree prepare you for working at Gellerstedt?

My education in finance was particularly important, because the company was looking for a numbers person. The degree also gave me the knowledge, skill sets, and confidence to work with architects and other professionals in the industry.

Looking back, are there any grad school classes or programs you wish you had taken or emphasized more?

When I was in the MRED program, I hated taking the architecture classes. But I realized their value after I started working. I wish I had learned more about construction so I could better understand the process.

What advice do you have for students planning to go into real estate?

Network! Network! Network! Look at networking as an opportunity to meet people in the industry, to learn from them, and to build long-term relationships. You never know how people you meet might help you—now or in the future. And remember to write thank-you notes to people who take the time to talk to you, meet with you, or offer you advice and assistance. Don't send an e-mail, which is too impersonal. Write a note. It's a small gesture, but you'll be remembered for it. And continue to network throughout your career. You can never network enough.

What are your long-term career aspirations?

I want to start my own business. My plan is to raise capital to acquire and renovate townhouses and small apartment buildings in Atlanta. I will start by doing two or three projects a year. Once I've established a track record, I'll raise more capital, do more projects, and build my business.

Average Compensation for Selected Positions in Real Estate Companies, 2004–2005

Position	Description	Average Compensation	
		Base Salary	**Total Compensation**
Financial Analyst	Provides financial analysis, development budgets, and accounting reports to management	$61,300	$67,000
Asset Manager	Acts as owner's representative in formulating and implementing business plan and approving budgets for each property in the asset manager's portfolio	$98,400	$126,700
Construction Project Manager	Responsible for overall direction of assigned construction projects, including review of planning and design, contract negotiations, and daily on-site activities	$86,300	$100,400
Tenant Construction Coordinator	Responsible for coordinating construction of tenant space within one or more facilities	$62,200	$67,300
Property Manager (less than 500,000 square feet)	Responsible for one or more properties, including collecting rents, maintaining grounds, interfacing with tenants, and preparing annual budgets	$64,200	$69,600
Assistant Property Manager	Assists the property managers with day-to-day operations of the properties	$44,100	$47,000
Lease Administrator	Responsible for providing analysis and support for property management, facility planning, lease administration, and financial reporting	$51,700	$58,500
Facility Manager	Operates specific properties on a day-to-day basis; directs contract work force in maintenance and operation of physical plant in such areas as janitorial work and electrical and mechanical systems; maintains working relationship with tenants	$58,800	$62,000
Leasing Representative	Responsible for identifying and contacting prospective tenants; participates in lease negotiations for space in existing or new projects	$54,800	$91,000

Source: National Association of Industrial and Office Properties, *2004–2005 Compensation Report*.

Among the specific real estate interest and skills questions that you might be called upon to answer are the following:

- Why are you interested in real estate?
- How did you get interested in real estate?
- What other careers did you consider?
- What have you done to learn about real estate outside the classroom?
- What are some of the key trends in real estate?
- Why are you interested in our company's product line?
- What interests you about our company's operations?
- How skilled are you in using ARGUS?
- How do you value a property? What information would you need?
- What is IRR? Give me an example of how it would be used.
- What is NPV? Give me an example.

Among the questions that you might ask to gauge your interest in the company and the specific job are the following:

- What are the major responsibilities of the job?
- What qualities will be key to success in this position?
- Describe a typical day in this position.
- How would you measure my success in this position?
- What are some of the more difficult problems I would face in this position?
- Tell me about the people with whom I would be working most closely.
- What is the management style of the person who would supervise me?
- Describe the common characteristics of successful employees at this firm.
- What are the usual working hours?
- What are the opportunities for advancement?

Salary Negotiation

During the interview, you may be asked what compensation you have in mind. Until you have a job offer, however, don't discuss salary. Be sure first that you're the candidate the company absolutely has to have. If the company presses you on a salary range, provide a polite but vague answer, such as wanting to discuss the position further.

When the company does make an offer, ask for time to think about it. If the offer is less than you expected, you can come back with a counteroffer. It's part of the negotiating process. But don't get so absorbed in salary issues that you lose sight of the larger picture. You are making a career decision, not a job decision. Your overriding question should be: Am I prepared to invest my career in this company?

Before you get to the point of talking money, it's important to do your homework. You can begin by researching compensation generally in the industry. Some online services such as Salary.com and SalaryExpert.com offer basic salary information and, for a fee, customized salary information on specific kinds of jobs.

CEL & Associates, a firm providing consulting services to real estate companies in many areas including compensation, conducts an annual compensation survey, a summary of which can be found on its Web site (see URL in appendix A). The full survey sells for $795. The National Association of Industrial and Office Properties (NAIOP) publishes a biennial compensation report. The 2004–2005 report was based on a survey of close to 200 companies and businesses and sells for $160 member price or $225 non-member price. These and similar surveys usually provide more information about compensation for senior- and middle-management jobs than for entry-level positions. But they are useful for putting compensation in the industry in perspective. The chart on the preceding page reports average compensation for some of the least senior positions covered in NAIOP's latest compensation report.

For many positions and in many companies, you can expect your base salary to constitute most of your compensation. In NAIOP's average compensation list, for example, the spread between the average base salary and total compensation for a lease administrator, a facility manager, an assistant property manager, and a tenant construction coordinator ranges between $3,000 and $7,000. In brokerage firms, by contrast, you could be paid mainly on a commission basis based on volume of sales closed or leases negotiated; your base pay would be a smaller part of your total compensation.

The existence of annual performance bonuses, profit sharing, and other forms of compensation could widen the spread between total compensation and base pay. Is there a performance bonus program? Find out if it is based on individual performance or company performance (or some combination) and how performance is measured. Is there a profit-sharing plan? Find out if the payments are made in cash or company stock (or some combination). Finally, does the compensation package include a stock purchase plan, stock options, or equity participation in the company. Are company-paid perquisites—such as car allowances, financial and estate planning, tax return preparation, life insurance, annual physicals—offered. You may not qualify for many of these benefits at the start, but it behooves you to get up to speed on salary and compensation trends in the industry and your market, and to use them as a benchmark in evaluating your target companies.

Now the job hunt is coming to an end. You have been offered the position of land acquisition specialist, and it's time to get down to specifics. How will you decide what salary to ask for? Try to ascertain the going rate for that position in your market. Talk to the contacts you've developed in the course of your research: Do they know—or know someone who knows—what residential developers are paying their land acquisition specialists? In deciding on your salary requirements, think in terms of a salary range rather than a specific salary. This will give you flexibility in salary negotiations.

On the Job

Once you've taken the job, start planning your next career step. Learn not only your job, but the job just above you, so you'll be prepared to move up if the opportunity arises. Put all your energy into excelling at your job and building your reputation inside and outside the company. Continue to network and build relationships. Stay attuned to career opportunities. Look for opportunities to help others with their career planning and job searches. Continue with your education. Take executive training courses, night classes, online courses, and certificate programs that will help you to improve your knowledge and skills. If you have a bachelor's degree, think about eventually going back to school to earn an MBA or a real estate master's degree. It's your career. Make the most of it.

Appendix A
Resources on Real Estate and Careers in Real Estate

This appendix provides further resources on the two main subjects of this book—1) real estate and 2) careers and education—organized by the following categories of information and presented in this order:

Real Estate Development, Trends, and People
- Development
- Trends
- Real Estate People
- Periodicals Covering Real Estate

Real Estate Professional and Trade Organizations

Real Estate Companies
- Lists and Directories
- Web Addresses of Companies Mentioned in *Inside Track*

Career Planning, Careers, and Job Hunting
- General Career Planning
- Careers in Real Estate
- Careers in Finance and Law
- Entrepreneurship
- Job Search (Résumés, Interviews)

Real Estate Education
- Programs
- Web Addresses of Real Estate Education Programs Discussed in Chapter 7

Job Listings and Recruiters

Salaries and Compensation

Real Estate

Real Estate Development, Trends, and People

Development

Beyard, Michael, and W. Paul O'Mara. *Shopping Center Development Handbook*. Washington, D.C.: ULI–the Urban Land Institute, 1999.

Frej, Anne B., and others. *Business Park and Industrial Development Handbook*. Washington, D.C.: ULI–the Urban Land Institute, 2001.

Gause, Jo Allen, and W. Paul O'Mara. *Office Development Handbook*. Washington, D.C.: ULI–the Urban Land Institute, 1998.

Peiser, Richard, and Anne B. Frej. *Professional Real Estate Development: The ULI Guide to the Business*. Washington, D.C.: ULI–the Urban Land Institute, 2003.

Schmitz, Adrienne, and others. *Residential Development Handbook*. Washington, D.C.: ULI–the Urban Land Institute, 2004.

Schmitz, Adrienne, and others. *Multifamily Development Handbook*. Washington, D.C.: ULI–the Urban Land Institute, 2000.

Schwanke, Dean, and others. *Mixed-Use Development Handbook*. Washington, D.C.: ULI–the Urban Land Institute, 2003.

Trends

Miles, Mike E., Gayle Berens, and Marc A. Weiss. "The History of Real Estate Development in the United States." In *Real Estate Development: Principles and Process.* 3rd ed. Washington, D.C.: ULI–the Urban Land Institute, 2000.

ULI–the Urban Land Institute and PricewaterhouseCoopers. *Emerging Trends in Real Estate 2006.* Washington, D.C.: ULI–the Urban Land Institute, 2005.

ULI–the Urban Land Institute and PricewaterhouseCoopers. *Emerging Trends in Real Estate Europe 2005.* Washington, D.C.: ULI–the Urban Land Institute, 2005.

Viewpoint Real Estate Value Trends 2005. New York: Integra Realty Resources Inc., 2005.

Weiss, Marc A. *The Rise of the Community Builders: The American Real Estate Industry and Urban Land Planning.* New York: Columbia University Press, 1987.

Real Estate People

Bergsman, Steve. *Maverick Real Estate Investing: The Art of Buying and Selling Properties like Trump, Zell, Simon, and the World's Greatest Land Owners.* Hoboken, New Jersey: John Wiley & Sons, 2004.

Clark, Lindie. Finding a Common Interest: *The Story of Dick Dusseldorp and Lend Lease.* Cambridge, United Kingdom: Cambridge University Press, 2002.

DeLisle, James R., and Elaine Worzala, eds. *Essays in Honor of James A. Graaskamp: Ten Years After.* Research Issues in Real Estate, v. 6. Norwell, Massachusetts: Kluwer Academic Publishers, 2000.

Ewald, William Bragg. *Trammell Crow: A Legacy of Real Estate Innovation.* Washington, D.C.: ULI–the Urban Land Institute, 2005.

Foster, Peter. *The Master Builders: How the Reichmanns Reached for an Empire.* Toronto: Key Porter Books, 1986.

———. *Towers of Debt: The Rise and Fall of the Reichmanns.* London: Hodder & Stoughton, 1993.

French, Desiree. "A Passion for Learning: The ULI/Charles Fraser Senior Resident Fellow for Sustainable Development Is Endowed in Remembrance of an Unconventional Man." *Urban Land,* November/December 2004, 144–146.

French, Desiree, and Mike Sheridan. *Leadership Legacies: Lessons Learned from Ten Real Estate Legends.* Washington, D.C.: ULI–the Urban Land Institute, 2004.

Graaskamp, James A., and Stephen P. Jarchow. *Graaskamp on Real Estate.* Washington, D.C.: ULI–the Urban Land Institute, 1991.

Keane, James Thomas. *Fritz B. Burns and the Development of Los Angeles: The Biography of a Community Developer and Philanthropist.* Los Angeles: Historical Society of Southern California, 2001.

Lassar, Terry J., and Douglas R. Porter. *The Power of Ideas: Five People Who Changed the Urban Landscape.* Washington, D.C.: ULI–the Urban Land Institute, 2004.

Moscow, Alvin. *Building a Business: The Jim Walter Story.* Sarasota, Florida: Pineapple Press, 1995.

Olsen, Josh. *Better Places, Better Lives: A Biography of James Rouse.* Washington, D.C.: ULI–the Urban Land Institute, 2003.

Riggs, Trisha. "Retaining Value: A Look at the Visionary Who Raised the Bar for Commercial Real Estate Development in the Last Half of the 20th Century (Gerald D. Hines)." *Urban Land,* October 2002, 156–161.

———. " Urban Pioneer: Richard D. Baron, This Year's Winner of the ULI J.C. Nichols Prize for Visionaries in Urban Development, Takes a Holistic Approach to Community Building." *Urban Land,* October 2004, 170–175.

Shachtman, Tom. *Skyscraper Dreams: The Great Real Estate Dynasties of New York.* Boston: Little, Brown, 1991.

Shaw, Charles H. *The Shaw Company: Creative and Responsible Development.* New York: Newcomen Society of the United States, 2002.

Sobel, Robert. *Trammell Crow, Master Builder: The Story of America's Largest Real Estate Empire.* New York: Wiley, 1989.

Trump, Donald J., with Kate Bohner. *Trump: The Art of the Comeback*. New York: Times Books, 1997.

Trump, Donald J., with Tony Schwartz. *Trump: The Art of the Deal*. New York: Random House, 1987.

Worley, William S. *J.C. Nichols and the Shaping of Kansas City: Innovation in Planned Residential Communities*. Columbia, Missouri: University of Missouri Press, 1990.

Zeckendorf, William, with Edward McCreary. *Zeckendorf: The Autobiography of William Zeckendorf*. New York: Holt, Rinehart and Winston, 1970; Chicago: Plaza Press, 1987.

Ziewitz, Kathryn, and June M. Wiaz. *Green Empire: The St. Joe Company and the Remaking of Florida's Panhandle*. Gainesville: University Press of Florida, 2004.

Periodicals Covering Real Estate

Affordable Housing Finance
www.housingfinance.com/ahf

Apartment Finance Today
www.housingfinance.com/aft

Architectural Record
www.archrecord.com

Architecture
www.architecturemag.com

Banker & Tradesman
www.bankerandtradesman.com

Builder
www.builderonline.com

Building Design & Construction
www.bdcmag.com

Buildings
www.buildingsmag.com

Chain Store Age
www.chainstoreage.com

Commercial Investment Real Estate Journal
www.ccim.com/magazine

CPN (Commercial Property News)
www.cpnonline.com

DCD (Design Cost Data)
www.dcd.com

ENR (Engineering News-Record)
www.enr.com

Estates Gazette
www.egi.co.uk

Expansion Management
www.expansionmanagement.com

Global Real Estate Now
www.pwcglobal.com

Globe St.com
www.globest.com
Online real estate news.

Inman News
www.inman.com
Online real estate news.

Institutional Real Estate Inc.
www.irei.com
Publisher of real estate periodicals.

JAPA (Journal of the American Planning Association)
www.planning.org

Journal of Real Estate Finance and Economics
www.jrefe.org

Journal of Real Estate Literature
http://cbeweb-1.fullerton.edu/finance/jrel/

Journal of Real Estate Portfolio Management
http://cbeweb-1.fullerton.edu/finance/jrepm/

Journal of Real Estate Research
http://137.151.62.168/finance/journal/

Hotel Business
www.hotelbusiness.com

Hotels
www.hotelsmag.com

Journal of Property Management
www.irem.org

Lodging Hospitality
www.lhonline.com

Midwest Real Estate News
www.mwrenonline.com

Mortgage Banking
www.mortgagebankingmagazine.com

Mortgage Daily
www.mortgagedaily.com

Multifamily Executive Magazine
www.multifamilyexecutive.com

Multifamily Trends
www.uli.org

Multi-Housing Forum
www.remnewsletters.com/globenews_multihousing

Multi-Housing News
www.multi-housingnews.com

National Mortgage News
www.nationalmortgagenews.com

National Real Estate Investor
www.nreionline.com

New Urban News
www.newurbannews.com

Pensions and Investment Age
www.pionline.com

Planning
www.planning.org

Practical Real Estate Lawyer
www.ali-aba.org/aliaba/prel.htm

Professional Builder
www.housingzone.com

Property Week
www.property-week.co.uk

Real Estate Finance
www.aspenpublishers.com

Real Estate Finance Journal
http://west.thomson.com/product/14938747/product.asp

Real Estate Review
http://west.thomson.com/product/14938755/product.asp

Real Estate Forum
www.reforum.com

Real Estate Journal.com
www.realestatejournal.com
A *Wall Street Journal* Web site.

Real Estate Weekly
www.rew-online.com

Realty Stock Review
http://www.realtystockreview.com

Realty Times
www.realtytimes.com

Retail Traffic
www.retailtrafficmag.com

Shopping Center Business
www.shoppingcenterbusiness.com

Shopping Centers Today
www.icsc.org

Site Selection
www.siteselection.com

The Slatin Report
www.theslatinreport.com

Tierra Grande
http://recenter.tamu.edu/tgrande

Units
(National Apartment Association)
www.naahq.org

Urban Land
www.uli.org

Real Estate Professional and Trade Organizations

Note that many of the following organizations publish books, reports, and periodicals on real estate subjects.

American Bankers Association
www.aba.com

American College of Real Estate Lawyers
www.acrel.org

American Hotel & Motel Association
www.ahma.com

American Industrial Real Estate Association (AIREA)
www.airea.com

American Institute of Architects (AIA)
www.aiaonline.com

American Institute of Certified Public Accountants (AICPA)
www.aicpa.org

American Planning Association
www.planning.org

American Real Estate and Urban Economics Association (AREUEA)
www.areuea.org

American Real Estate Society (ARES)
www.aresnet.org

American Resort Development Association
www.arda.org

American Seniors Housing Association
www.nmhc.org
   Affiliated with National Multi Housing Council.

American Society of Appraisers
www.appraisers.org

American Society of Civil Engineers
www.acse.org

American Society of Landscape Architects
www.asla.org

Appraisal Institute
www.appraisalinstitute.org

Architecture for Humanity
www.architectureforhumanity.org

Associated General Contractors of America
www.agc.org

Association of Foreign Investors in Real Estate
www.afire.org

Association of Real Estate Women
www.arew.org

Building Industry Exchange
www.building.org

Building Owners and Managers Association (BOMA)
www.boma.org

Commercial Investment Real Estate Institute
www.ccim.com

Commercial Mortgage Securities Association
www.cmbs.org

Commercial Real Estate Women Network
www.crewnetwork.org/

Common Ground Community
www.commonground.org

Congress for the New Urbanism
www.cnu.org

Construction Financial Management Association
www.cfma.org

CoreNet Global
www.corenetglobal.com

Counselors of Real Estate (CRE)
www.cre.org

CREW Foundation
www.crewfoundation.org

CREW Network. *See* Commercial Real Estate Women Network

CREW Philadelphia Chapter
www.crewphiladelphia.org/default.html

Design-Build Institute of America
www.dbia.org

Enterprise Community Partners
www.enterprisecommunity.org

Institute of Real Estate Management (IREM)
www.irem.org

International Council of Shopping Centers (ICSC)
www.icsc.org

International Downtown Association (IDA)
www.ida_downtown.org

International Real Estate Federation, USA
www.fiabci_usa.com

Lincoln Institute of Land Policy
www.lincolninst.edu

Local Initiatives Support Corporation
www.lisc.org

Manufactured Housing Institute
www.mfghome.org

Mortgage Bankers Association of America
www.mbaa.org

National Apartment Association
www.naahq.org

National Association of Home Builders (NAHB)
www.nahb.com

National Association of Industrial and Office Properties (NAIOP)
www.naiop.org

National Association of Real Estate Consultants
www.narec.com

National Association of Real Estate Editors
www.naree.org

National Association of Real Estate Investment Managers
www.nareim.org

National Association of Real Estate Investment Trusts (NAREIT)
www.nareit.com

National Association of Realtors (NAR)
www.nar.org

National Association of Women in Construction
www.nawic.org

National Council of Real Estate Investment Fiduciaries (NCREIF)
www.ncreif.com

National Multi Housing Council
www.nmhc.org

National Society of Real Estate Appraisers
www.iami.org/narea.cfm

National Trust for Historic Preservation
www.nationaltrust.org

NeighborWorks America
www.nw.org

Pension Real Estate Association (PREA)
www.prea.org

Real Estate Board of New York
www.rebny.com

Real Estate Educators Association
www.reea.org

Real Estate Research Institute
www.reri.org

Real Estate Roundtable
www.rer.org

Royal Institution of Chartered Surveyors
www.rics.org

Society of Industrial and Office Realtors
www.sior.com

Urban Land Institute
www.uli.org

West Angeles Community Housing Development
www.westa.org/ministry_cdc.html

Women in Real Estate (WIRE)
www.womeninrealestate.org

Women in Transportation
www.wtsinternational.org

Real Estate Companies

Lists and Directories
Architecture Week
www.architectureweek.com/directory.html
   A professional online directory that is searchable by keyword and by firm or person name.

Associated General Contractors of America

www.agc.org

The "Find a Contractor" button on this URL leads to a searchable database.

BigBook

www.bigbook.com

The BigBook yellow pages of businesses and organizations are searchable by category (for example, real estate) and location.

Book of Lists

www.bizjournals.com

Bizjournal's Book of Lists series provide contact information and facts for businesses and employers in leading U.S. regional markets; some industry-specific nationwide lists, including a list of general contractors and a list of home-builders, are also available. Titles in the Book of Lists series are available in print, CD, or download versions.

Builder

www.builderonline.com

Builder magazine's "Builder 100 Listing" and "Next 100 Listing" provide company information on the top U.S. homebuilders.

Building Industry Exchange

www.building.org

The Building Industry Exchange, an information exchange center for the building industry, provides a members-only online directory of construction employers; it also provides job and career information.

Business.com

www.business.com

Business.com is a general business search engine and directory.

Commercial Property News

www.commercialpropertynews.com/cpn/index.jsp

CPN publishes various print and online company lists, including:
- apartment property owners
- real estate developers
- hotel companies
- industrial investors and developers
- buyers of commercial real estate
- brokerage firms
- direct lenders
- mortgage bankers and brokers
- multifamily finance companies
- most powerful brokerage firms
- leading players in net lease
- leading office investors and developers
- top property owners
- top property managers
- leading retail investors and developers

Crain's New York Business

www.newyorkbusiness.com

Crain's publishes its rankings of top New York area businesses in a variety of fields.

Engineering News Record

www.enr.com

ENR publishes lists of top-ranked companies in various categories, such as contractors, design firms, or international contractors; it also compiles three sourcebooks each year Sourcebook—The Top 500 Design Firms Sourcebook, The Top 400 Contractors Sourcebook, and the Global Construction Sourcebook—in which firms are ranked by market sector.

Lawyers.com

www.lawyers.com

Lawyers.com has a find-a-lawyer search capability in which one can select the type of lawyer sought, such as zoning and land use.

Martindale

www.martindale.com

Martindale.com offers a lawyer locator in which one can browse for law firms with a real estate practice.

National Association of Real Estate Investment Trusts

www.nareit.org

NAREIT publishes an online directory of REITs by property sector; from its homepage, click "newsrooms" then "charts and tables" then "company names."

National Real Estate Investor

www.nreionline.com.

NREI's Sourcebook is a listing of commercial real estate companies by categories, such as financial services companies, property managers, or real estate software/technology companies.

National Multi Housing Council

www.nmhc.org.

NMHC's "NMHC 50" is an annual ranking of the top 50 apartment owners and the top 50 apartment managers.

Pension & Investments

www.pionline.com

P&I's annual "Real Estate Investment Manager Directory" provides information on top firms; from its homepage, click on "directories."

Professional Builder

www.housingzone.com

PB's annual "400 Giants" lists the top 400 housing companies by total housing revenue.

San Diego North County Guide

www.sandiegoncguide.com

This is an example of a listing of local homebuilding companies.

Yahoo! Business and Economy

http://dir.yahoo.com/Business_and_Economy

Web Addresses of Companies Mentioned in *Inside Track*

Accor North America
www.accor-na.com

AEW Capital Management
www.aew.com

AMB Property Corporation
www.amb.com

AMCAL
www.amcalhousing.com

American Property Management Corporation
www.americanpropertymanagementcorp.com

Apartment Investment & Management
www.aimco.com

Apollo Real Estate Advisors
www.apollorealestate.com

Archstone-Smith Trust
www.archstonesmith.com

The Athena Group
www.theathenagroup.com

AvalonBay Communities
www.avalonbay.com

Bank of America Commercial Real Estate Banking
www.bankofamerica.com (from homepage, click "corporate & institutional" then "real estate")

Bank of America
www.bofasecurities.com

Baymont Inns
www.baymontinns.com

Bear, Stearns & Co.
www.bearstearns.com

Beazer Homes USA
www.beazer.com/Corpinfo

Bedford Property Investors
www.bedfordproperty.com

Blackrock
www.blackrock.com

Blackstone Real Estate Advisors
www.blackstone.com/real_estate

Bluestone Communities
www.bluestone communities.com

Boeing Realty
boeing.com/special/realty

Boston Capital
www.bostoncapital.com

Boston Properties
www.bostonproperties.com

Boykin Lodging Company
www.boykinlodging.com

BRE Properties
www.breproperties.com

Brookfield Properties
www.brookfieldproperties.com

BRT Realty Trust
www.brtrealty.com

Cabot Properties
www.cabotprop.com

Camden Property Trust
www.camdenliving.com

Capital Hotel Management LLC
www.capitalhotelmgt.com/chmwebsite

Capital One
www.capitalone.com

CapitalSource Mortgage
www.capitalsourcemortgage.com

Caruso Affiliated
www.carusoaffiliated.com

CBL & Associates Properties
www.cblproperties.com

CB Richard Ellis
www.cbre.com

CB Richard Ellis Investors
http://www.cbreinvestors.com/

CenterPoint Properties Trust
www.centerpoint-prop.com

Centex Corporation
www.centex.com

Chaffin/Light Associates
www.chaffinlight.com

China Real Estate Investment Company
home.chinarei.com

CIGNA Realty Investors
http://cri.invest.cigna.com

Clarett Group
www.clarett.com

CNL Hospitality Corp
www.cnlonline.com/hospitality

Coldwell Banker Commercial
www.coldwellbankercommercial.com

Colliers International
www.colliers.com

Colonial Properties Trust
www.colonialprop.com

Colony Capital
www.colonyinc.com

Cooper Companies
www.cooperhotels.com

Cousins Properties Incorporated
www.cousinsproperties.com

Credit Suisse First Boston
www.csfb.com

Crescent Real Estate Equities Company
www.crescent.com

CRESA Partners
www.cresapartners.com

CRIIMI Mae Inc.
www.criimimaeinc.com

Cushman & Wakefield
www.cushmanwakefield.com

Daum Commercial Real Estate/TCN Worldwide
www.gvadaum.com

DeBeikes Investment Company
www.debeikes.com/main.htm

Deloitte & Touche USA LLP
www.deloitte.com

Deutsche Bank.
www.db.com

Developers Diversified Realty
www.ddr.com

Divco West Properties
divco.com

D.R. Horton
www.drhorton.com

Duke Realty
www.dukereit.com

The Durst Organization
www.durst.org

Eastdil Realty
www.eastdil.com

Eastern Consolidated Properties
www.easternconsolidated.com

EastGroup Properties
www.eastgroup.net

Equity Inns
www.equityinns.com

Equity Office Properties Trust
www.equityoffice.com

Equity Residential
www.equityapartments.com

Ernst & Young
www.ey.com

Essex Property Trust
www.essexproperties.com

Fairfield Residential
www.fairfield-properties.com

Fannie Mae
http://www.fanniemae.com

Federal Realty Investment Trust
www.federalrealty.com

FelCor Lodging Trust
www.felcor.com

First Industrial Realty Trust
www.firstindustrial.com

First Union Real Estate Investments
www.firstunion-reit.net

Forest City Enterprises
www.forestcity.net

Four Seasons
www.fourseasons.com

Freddie Mac
www.freddiemac.com

Fritz Duda Company
www.fritzduda.com

Gables Residential
www.gables.com

The Gale Company
www.thegalecompany.com

GE Commercial Finance Real Estate
www.gerealestate.com

General Growth Properties
www.generalgrowth.com

George Smith Partners Inc.
www.gspartners.com

GMAC Commercial Mortgage Corporation
www.gmaccm.com

Goldman Sachs
www.gs.com

Goldrich & Kest Industries
www.gkind.com

Greenwich Capital Markets
www.gcm.com

Grubb & Ellis
www.grubb-ellis.com

Hammer Ventures
www.hammerventures.com

Heitman
www.heitman.com

Henry S. Miller Commercial/TCN Worldwide
www.henrysmiller.com

Hersha Group
www.hershahotels.com

Highwoods Properties
www.highwoods.com/home

Hillwood
www.hillwood.com

Hilton Hotels Corporation
www.hilton.com

Hines
www.hines.com

Holiday Fenoglio Fowler LP
www.hfflp.com

Hollywood Community Housing Corporation
http://www.hollywoodhousing.org

Host Marriott Corporation
www.hostmarriott.com

Hovnanian Enterprises
www.khov.com

HyperBina
www.hyperbina.com

IHP Capital Partners
www.ihpinc.com

Innkeepers USA Trust
www.innkeepersusa.com

InterContinental Hotels Group
www.ichotelsgroup.com

INVESCO Real Estate
www.invescorealestate.com

IPC US REIT
www.ipcus.com

Irvine Company
www.irvinecompany.com

Jameson Inns
www.jamesoninns.com

J. E. Robert Companies
www.jer.com

J. F. Shea Co.
www.jfshea.com

John Laing Homes
www.johnlainghomes.com

John Portman & Associates
www.portmanusa.com

Johnson Development Corporation
www.johnsondevelopmentcorp.com

Jones Lang LaSalle
www.joneslanglasalle.com

JP Morgan Asset Management
www.jpmorgan.com (from homepage, click "asset
management")

JP Morgan
www.jpmorgan.com (search on "Real Estate")

KB Home
www.kbhome.com

Kennedy Wilson
www.kennedywilson.com

Kilroy Realty Corporation
www.kilroyrealty.com

KeyBank Real Estate Capital
www.key.com/html/J-6.html

Kimco Realty Corporation
www.kimcorealty.com

Klingbeil Capital Management
www.kcmgt.com

Koll Development Company
www.kolldevelopment.com

KPMG
www.kpmg.com

LaSalle Hotel Properties
www.lasallehotels.com

LaSalle Investment Management
www.lasalle.com

Lazard LLC
www.lazard.com

LCOR Inc.
www.lcor.com

The Lefrak Organization
www.lefrak.com

Legacy Partners
www.legacypartners.com

Legg Mason Real Estate Services
www.lmres.com

Lehman Brothers
www.lehman.com

Lend Lease
www.lendlease.com

Lennar Corporation
www.lennar.com

Lincoln Property Company
www.lincolnproperty.com

Linneman Associates
www.linnemanassociates.com

L. J. Melody & Company
www.ljmelody.com

Lodgian
www.lodgian.com

Loews Hotels
www.loewshotels.com

Lowe Enterprises
www.loweenterprises.com

Lubert-Adler
www.lubertadler.com

Lyon Homes
www.lyonhomes.com

The Macerich Company
www.macerich.com

Mack-Cali Realty Corporation
www.mack-cali.com

Maguire Properties
www.maguireproperties.com

Majestic Realty
www.majesticrealty.com

Marcus & Millichap
www.marcusmillichap.com

McGladrey & Pullen
www.mcgladrey.com

MeriStar Hospitality Corporation
www.meristar.com

Merrill Lynch
www.ml.com

MetLife Real Estate Investments
www.metlife.com (from homepage click "commercial investors" then "real estate investments".)

Mills Corporation
www.millscorp.com

Morgan Stanley Real Estate
www.morganstanley.com/realestate/

Morley Builders
www.morleybuilders.com

National Partnership Investments Corporation (NAPICO)
www.napico.com

New Plan Excel Realty Trust
www.newplan.com

Newmark Knight Frank
www.newmarkre.com

Northstar Capital
www.northstarcapital.com

NVR Inc.
www.nvrinc.com

The Olson Company
www.theolsonco.com

Peabody Hotel Group
www.peabodyhotelgroup.com

Pennsylvania Real Estate Investment Trust
www.preit.com

Phoenix Realty Group
www.phoenixrg.com

Post Properties
www.postproperties.com

PM Realty Group
www.pmrealtygroup.com

PricewaterhouseCoopers
www.pwcglobal.com

Primestor Development
www.primestor.com

Principal Real Estate
www.principal.com

ProLogis
www.prologis.com

Property and Portfolio Research
www.ppr-research.com

Prudential Real Estate Investors (PREI)
www.prudential.com/prei

Public Storage
www.publicstorage.com

Pulte Homes
www.pulte.com

Related Capital Company
www.relatedcapital.com

Rockefeller Development Corporation
www.rockgroupdevelopment.com

Rockwood Capital Corporation
www.rockwoodcap.com

Roseland Property Company
www.roselandproperty.com

RREEF North America
www.rreef.com

The Ryland Group
www.ryland.com

Secured Capital Corp
www.securedcapital.com

Sedway Group
www.sedway.com

Sentinel Real Estate Corporation
www.sentinelcorp.com

Shamrock Holdings
www.shamrock.com

Shamrock Real Estate Group
www.shamrock.com/pages/genesis/genesis.asp

Shea Homes
www.sheahomes.com

The Shoptaw Group (TSG)
www.sgatl.com

Shorenstein
www.shorenstein.com

Silverstein Properties
www.silversteinproperties.com

Simon Property Group
www.simon.com

Sonnenblick-Goldman
www.sonngold.com

Southern California Edison Co.
www.sce.com

Sperry Van Ness
www.svn.com

Starwood Capital Group
www.starwoodcapital.com

Starwood Hotels and Resorts
www.starwoodhotels.com

Staubach
www.staubach.com

Studley
www.studley.com

Suburban Franchise Systems
www.suburbanhotels.com

SunAmerica Affordable Housing Partners
www.sunamericahousing.com

Sunny Hills Palladium
www.sunnyhills-paladium.com

Taubman Centers
www.taubman.com

Tharaldson Lodging
www.tharaldson.com

TIAA-CREF
www.tiaa-cref.org

Tishman Hotel Corporation
www.tishmanhotel.com

Tishman Speyer Properties
www.tishmanspeyer.com

TMG Partners
www.tmgpartners.com

Toll Brothers
www.tollbrothers.com

Trammell Crow
www.trammellcrow.com

Trammell Crow Residential
www.tcresidential.com

Trammell Crow University
www.tramellcrow.com/careers/tcu.asp
The Trammell Crow company's on-the-job career training program.

Transwestern Commercial Services
www.transwestern.net

Trizec Properties
www.trz.com

Trump Organization
www.trump.com/main.htm

UBS
www.ubs.com

United Dominion Realty Trust
www.udrt.com

Vail Resorts Development Company
www.vrdc.com

Vornado Realty Trust
www.vno.com

Wachovia
www.wachovia.com

Walton Street Investment Company
www.waltonst.com

Washington Mutual
www.wamu.com

Watson Land
www.watsonlandcompany.com

Watt Communities
www.wattcommunities.com

Weingarten Realty Investors
www.weingarten.com

Wells Fargo Real Estate Merchant Banking
www.wellsfargo.com/com/realestate_fin/aboutremb

Westcore Properties
www.westcore.net

Westfield America
www.westfield.com

White Lodging Services Corporation
www.whitelodging.com

William Lyon Homes
www.lyonhomes.com

Winegardner & Hammons
www.whihotels.com

York Properties
www.yorkproperties.com

Careers and Education

Career Planning, Careers, and Job Hunting

General Career Planning

Bolles, Richard Nelson. *Mapping Your Career: The Book That Can Help You Find the Job You Want.* Menlo Park, California: Crisp Publications, 2002.

———. *What Color is Your Parachute?* Berkeley, California: Ten Speed Press, 2004.

Camenson, Blythe. *Careers for Born Leaders and Other Decisive Types.* New York: McGraw Hill, 2005.

CareerJournal.com
www.careerjournal.com
    A *Wall Street Journal* Web site.

Center for International Career Development
www.cicdgo.com

CollegeBoard.com
search.collegeboard.com/servlet/sitesearch
    This is a search engine for the College Board site. Type "real estate" in keyword box and check "careers and majors" box to obtain information on various real estate careers.

Hunt, Christopher W., and Scott A. Scanlon. *The Career Navigation Handbook.* Hoboken, New Jersey: John Wiley & Sons, 2004.

O'Rourke, James S. *Beginning Your Career Search: A Hands-on Approach to Building Your Career Portfolio.* Upper Saddle River, New Jersey: Pearson Prentice Hall, 2004.

Schein, Edgar H. *The Corporate Culture Survival Guide: Sense and Nonsense about Culture Change.* Hoboken, New Jersey: John Wiley & Sons, 1999.

U.S. Bureau of Labor Statistics. *Occupational Outlook Handbook.* 2006–2007 ed. Web publication: www.bls.gov/oco.

    This book provides detailed descriptions of professional jobs in fields such as architecture, accounting, and law—including training and qualifications required and the job outlook; and an overview of professions/occupations in the United States, covering, for example, the number of firms, number of employees, and earnings by specific types of firms.

Vault Editors. *College Career Bible.* New York: Vault, 2006. Download version: www.vault.com/store/store_home.jsp.

———. *MBA Career Bible.* New York: Vault, 2006. Download version: www.vault.com/store/store_home.jsp.

Careers in Real Estate

Brophy, Paul C., and Alice Shabecoff. *A Guide to Careers in Community Development.* Washington, D.C.: Island Press, 2001.

Clark, Betty L. *Choosing a Career in Real Estate.* New York: Rosen Publishing Group, 2001.

Evans, Blanche. *The Hottest E-Careers in Real Estate.* Chicago: Real Estate Education Company, 2000.

Evans, Mariwyn. *Opportunities in Property Management Careers.* Rev. ed. Lincolnwood, Illinois: VGM Career Horizons, 2000.

———. *Opportunities in Real Estate Careers.* Chicago: VGM Career Books, 2002.

Institute for Career Research. *Careers in Today's Dynamic Real Estate Business: Developers, Appraisers, Rehabbers, Property Managers, Agents.* Careers Research Monograph. Chicago: Institute for Career Research, 2002.

Lofton, Lynn. "Real Estate Careers Provide Unlimited Opportunities for Young People." *Mississippi Business Journal,* February 14, 2005, p. 30.

Masi, Mary, and Lauren B. Starkey. *Real Estate Career Starter.* 2nd ed. New York: Learning Express, 2001.

Piper, Robert J. *Opportunities in Architecture Careers.* New York: McGraw-Hill, 2006.

Rowh, Mark. *Careers in Real Estate.* VGM Professional Careers series. New York: McGraw-Hill, 2003.

Saavedra, Raul, Jr. *Vault Guide to Real Estate Careers.* New York: Vault, 2003. Download version: www.vault.com/store/store_home.jsp.

Shah, Angela. "As Market Booms, Students Are Taking the Real Estate Career Path." *Dallas Morning News,* January 27, 2005.

Walker Management Library, Owen Graduate School of Management at Vanderbilt University. *Guide to Careers in Real Estate Development.* Web publication: www2.owen.vanderbilt.edu/walker/resourceguides/realestate.pdf.

WetFeet. *Careers in Real Estate.* WetFeet Insider Guide. San Francisco: WetFeet, 2006. Download version: www.wetfeet.com.

Careers in Finance and Law

Echaore-McDavid, Susan. *Career Opportunities in Law and the Legal Industry.* New York: Facts on File, 2002.

Munneke, Gary A. *Careers in Law.* Chicago: VGM Career Books, 2004.

Ring, Trudy. *Careers in Finance.* New York: VGM Career Books, 2005.

Sumichrast, Michael, and Martin A. Sumichrast. *Opportunities in Financial Careers.* New York: VGM Career Books, 2004.

WetFeet. *Careers in Investment Banking.* WetFeet Insider Guide. San Francisco: WetFeet, 2006. Download version: www.wetfeet.com.

Entrepreneurship

Dietsch, Deborah K. "The New Entrepreneurs: Architect-Developers Call Their Own Shots and Make Money While They're at It." *Architecture,* September 2004, pp. 29–31.

Hyatt, Joshua. "The Real Secrets of Entrepreneurs: What Sets the Great Ones Apart Isn't How They Start Businesses. It's How They Keep Them Growing," Innovation Special Report: Entrepreneurs. *Fortune,* November 15, 2004, 189192.

Judson, Bruce. *Go It Alone: The Secret to Building a Successful Business on Your Own.* New York: Harper Business, 2004.

Norman, Jan. *What No One Ever Tells You about Starting Your Own Business: Real Life Startup Advice from 101 Successful Entrepreneurs.* Chicago: Dearborn Trade Publications, 2004.

Timmons, Jeffry A., and Stephen Spinelli. *New Venture Creation: Entrepreneurship for the 21st Century.* 6th ed. Boston: McGraw-Hill/Irwin.

Job Search (Résumés, Interviews)

Greene, Brenda. *Get the Interview Every Time: Fortune 500 Hiring Professionals' Tips for Writing Winning Résumés and Cover Letters.* Chicago: Dearborn Trade Publishing, 2004.

Hayden, C. J. and Frank Traditi. *Get Hired Now! A 28-Day Program for Landing the Job You Want.* Berkeley, California: Bay Tree Publishing, 2005.

Hirsch, Arlene S. *Job Search and Career Checklists: 101 Proven Time-saving Checklists to Organize and Plan Your Career Search.* Indianapolis: JIST Works, 2005.

Hornby, Malcolm. *Get That Job! Easy Steps to the Job You Want.* New York: Prentice Hall/Business, 2005.

Kador, John. *201 Best Questions to Ask on Your Interview.* New York: McGraw-Hill, 2002.

McKinney, Anne, ed. *Real-Résumés for Real Estate & Property Management.* Fayetteville, North Carolina: PREP Publishing, 2005.

VGM Career Books. *Résumés for Architecture and Related Careers.* New York: McGraw-Hill, 2004.

Real Estate Education
Programs

National Association of Industrial and Office Properties
www.naiop.org/careers/universities.cfm

Links to universities offering real estate programs.

Real Estate Associate Program
www.projectreap.org

REAP is an industry-backed, market-driven program that recruits minority people for professional careers in commercial real estate and provides training through education, networking, and professional training with leading firms.

ULI–the Urban Land Institute. *Directory of Real Estate Development and Related Education Programs.* 10th ed. Washington D.C.: ULI–the Urban Land Institute, 2005.

ULI provides links to real estate development and related education programs at www.uli.org/Content/NavigationMenu/MeetingsEducation/ContinuingEducation/DirectoryofRealEstatePrograms/Directory_of_Real_Estate_Programs.htm

Web Addresses of Real Estate Education Programs Discussed in Chapter 7

Baruch College, City University of New York
general
http://www.baruch.cuny.edu
BS program
http://www.baruch.cuny.edu/spa/Academics/BachelorofScienceinRealEstateandMetropolitanDevelopment.jsp
Real Estate and Metropolitan Development program
www.baruch.cuny.edu/ugradprograms/rea.htm
Steven L. Newman Real Estate Institute
www.newmaninstitute.org
Zicklin School of Business
www.zicklin.baruch.cuny.edu

Columbia University
Graduate School of Architecture, Planning, and Preservation
www.arch.columbia.edu
Master of Science in Real Estate program
www.arch.columbia.edu/realestate
Center for High Density Development
www.arch.columbia.edu/realestate/chdd.htm
Graduate School of Business
http://www2.gsb.columbia.edu
Paul Milstein Center for Real Estate
http://www2.gsb.columbia.edu/departments/realestate

Cornell University
Master of Professional Studies in Real Estate program
www.realestate.cornell.edu

Harvard University
general
www.harvard.edu
Harvard Business School
www.hbs.edu
Harvard Graduate School of Design
www.gsd.harvard.edu
Master in Design Studies program
www.gsd.harvard.edu/academic/mdes/
Master of Urban Planning program
www.gsd.harvard.edu/academic/upd
Kennedy School of Government
www.ksg.harvard.edu

Massachusetts Institute of Technology
general
http://web.mit.edu
MIT Center for Real Estate
http://web.mit.edu/cre

University of California at Berkeley
general
http://berkeley.edu
Berkeley Program on Housing and Urban Policy
http://urbanpolicy.berkeley.edu/main.htm
Haas School of Business
www.haas.berkeley.edu
Haas Real Estate Group
http://groups.haas.berkeley.edu/realestate
Fisher Center for Real Estate and Urban Economics
http://groups.haas.berkeley.edu/realestate/Fisher/fisherinfo.asp

University of North Carolina at Chapel Hill
general
www.unc.edu
Kenan Flagler School of Business
www.kenan-flagler.unc.edu
Center for Real Estate Development
www.kenan-flagler.unc.edu/KI/realestate/index.cfm

University of Pennsylvania
general
www.upenn.edu
Wharton School
www.wharton.upenn.edu
Real Estate Department
1) www.wharton.upenn.edu/faculty/acad_depts/realdept.cfm
2) http://rider.wharton.upenn.edu/~wred
Samuel Zell and Robert Lurie Real Estate Center
http://realestate.wharton.upenn.edu/

University of Southern California
general
www.usc.edu
Lusk Center for Real Estate
www.usc.edu/schools/sppd/lusk
Marshall School of Business
www.marshall.usc.edu
Ross Minority Program in Real Estate
www.usc.edu/org/spire
School of Policy, Planning, and Development
www.usc.edu/sppd
Master of Real Estate Development program
www.usc.edu/sppd/mred

University of Texas at Austin
general
www.utexas.edu
McCombs School of Business
www.mccombs.utexas.edu
Real Estate Finance and Investment Center
cref.mccombs.utexas.edu

University of Wisconsin at Madison
general
www.wisc.edu
School of Business
www.bus.wisc.edu
Department of Real Estate and Urban Economics
www.bus.wisc.edu/realestate
Center for Real Estate
www.bus.wisc.edu/wcre

Job Listings and Recruiters

Business.com
www.business.com

CareerBuilder.com
www.careerbuilder.com

Career Journal
http://www.careerjournal.com

Equinox Partners
www.equinoxsearch.com
Recruiter.

Ferguson Partners
www.fplassociates.com
Recruiter.

GlobeSt.com
www.globest.com

Heidrick & Struggles
www.heidrick.com
Recruiter.

iHireRealEstate
www.ihirerealestate.com

indeed.com
www.indeed.com

Korn/Ferry International
www.kornferry.com
Recruiter.

Monster
www.monster.com

Quintessential Careers
www.quintcareers.colm

RealEstateJobs.com
www.realestatejobs.com

RealEstateJobStore.com
www.realestatejobstore.com

Real-Jobs
www.real-jobs.com

RE Buz
www.rebuz.com
Real estate jobs and job resources.

Russell Reynolds Associates
www.russellreynolds.com
Recruiter.

Salary.com
www.salary.com

SelectLeaders
www.selectleaders.com

Spencer Stuart
www.spencerstuart.com
Recruiter.

wetfeet.com
www.wetfeet.com

Yahoo! HotJobs
www.hotjobs.yahoo.com

Salaries and Compensation

CEL & Associates. *2004 Real Estate Compensation and Benefits Survey*. Los Angeles: CEL & Associates, 2004.
This is an annual survey. An online summary of the 2005 survey is available at www.celassociates.com/CompCurrentSummary.cfm.

National Association of Industrial and Office Properties. *2004–2005 Compensation Report*. Washington, D.C.: National Association of Industrial and Office Properties, 2005.

Specialty Consultants. "Construction & Real Estate Executive Compensation Report." *Construction & Real Estate Leaders*, v. 4, no. 1, 2005. Web publication: www.specon.com.

Appendix B
Glossary of Selected Real Estate Terms

This glossary of selected real estate terms is provided to introduce readers to a small sample of the breadth of terminology used in the industry.

Absorption

Filling of space, such as the rental of office space or apartment rentals.

Absorption rate

Rate at which space—such as new office building or condominium units—is occupied or sold annually.

Acre

Measure of land equal to approximately 43,560 square feet (4,840 square yards).

Amenities

Those things that enhance the enjoyment—and therefore the value—of real estate, but are not necessary for its intended use (for example, a scenic view or a swimming pool).

Amortization

Payment of a debt in equal periodic installments of principal and interest.

Appreciation

An increase in the value of real property resulting from positive changes or the elimination of negative elements in the surrounding area. Although the use of the word to describe an increase in value for any reason, including inflation, is incorrect, it is so common as to be acceptable.

Assessed value

Value placed upon property for property tax purposes by the tax assessor.

Assignment

A transfer from one person to another of any property, real or personal, or of any rights or estates in said property. Leases, mortgages, and deeds of trust are commonly assigned, but the term encompasses all transfers of title.

Balloon note

A note calling for periodic payments that are insufficient to fully amortize the face amount of the note prior to maturity, so that a principal sum known as a "balloon" is due at maturity.

Balloon payment

The final payment (balance due) of a balloon note.

Capitalization Rate

Determining the present value of income property by discounting the annual net income (either known or estimated) by use of a rate of return commonly acceptable by buyers of similar properties. For example, if the net income of a property is $10,000 per year, it would be worth $100,000 at a capitalization rate of 10 percent.

Carrying charges

The costs involved in keeping a property that is intended to produce income (by sale or rent), but has not yet done so.

Cash-on-cash return

The amount of cash received compared with the amount of cash invested (also called "equity dividend rule," "cash flow rate," or "equity capitalization rate").

Commercial acres

The portion of a site that may be used for building of structures. For example, if a ten-acre residential development site requires three acres for streets, sidewalks, and other improvements, the remaining seven acres are the commercial acres of the site (also called "net acres").

Common area

In residential condominium or planned unit development projects, the area owned in common by unit owners. In rental commercial projects, the space used in common by all tenants.

Comparables

Properties used as comparisons to determine the value of a specific property.

Construction cost

The total cost of constructing a project, including overhead and profits as well as land, labor, and materials.

Cost-plus contract

A contract adding a fixed profit factor to actual costs; in the case of a builder the profit would be a set percentage of the cost of labor and materials.

Debt service

1) The required interest and principal payments on a debt—on a mortgage or deed of trust on a specific property—over the term of the loan; 2) the interest payments required on a mortgage or deed of trust; or 3) loosely defined, the total amount owing on a mortgage or deed of trust.

Deed of trust

An instrument used in many states in place of a mortgage, in which the borrower transfers property to a trustee in favor of the lender (beneficiary) and the property is reconveyed upon payment in full of the deed of trust.

Default

An omission or failure to perform a legal duty.

Depreciation

1) Decrease in value to real property improvements caused by deterioration or obsolescence; or 2) a loss in value as an accounting procedure to use as a deduction for income tax purposes.

Earnest money

Money given by the buyer with an offer to purchase to show good faith (also called "deposit").

Easement

A right held by one party in the land of another party; an easement is created by grant, reservation, agreement, prescription, or necessary implication.

Equity

1) A legal doctrine based on fairness, rather than strict interpretation of the letter of the law; 2) the market value of real property, less the amount of existing liens; 3) any ownership investment (stocks, real estate, and so forth) as opposed to lender investment (bonds, mortgages, and so forth).

Escrow

Documents, real estate, money, deeds, or securities deposited with a neutral third party (the escrow agent) to be delivered upon fulfillment of certain conditions, as established in a written agreement

Fair market value

Price that probably would be negotiated between a willing seller and a willing buyer in a reasonable time; usually estimated by comparable sales in the area.

Grant deed

One of the many types of deeds used to transfer real property; contains warranties against prior conveyances or encumbrances. When title insurance is purchased, warranties in a deed are of little practical significance.

Gross rent multiplier

The sale price of a property divided by the gross rent; generally, for a single-family property the gross rent divisor is the monthly gross rent and for multifamily units and commercial properties it is the yearly gross rent.

Ground lease

A lease on land exclusive of any building on it; usually a net lease.

Improved land

Land with on-site improvements and/or off-site improvements.

Junior lien

A lien that is subordinate to a prior lien.

Limited partnership

A partnership consisting of one or more general partners who conduct the business and are responsible (liable) for losses, and one or more special (limited) partners who contribute capital and are liable only up to the amount contributed; limited partnerships are used in many real estate syndications.

Master plan

A comprehensive plan for an entire governmental subdivision, such as a city, that allows the city to grown in an orderly and sound manner, both economically and ecologically.

Mortgage-backed securities

Securities based on a pool of mortgages or deeds of trust that usually are insured by the government; the rate of return depends on the interest rate of the mortgages plus early payoffs, which increase the value of any discounts; the price of the securities depends on the rise and fall of comparative (current) interest rates.

Net lease

A lease requiring the tenant to pay a fixed rent plus specified expenses, such as taxes, insurance, or maintenance; in some states, the number of times "net" is used—"net," "net net," or "net net net" (a.k.a. triple net)—indicates how many standard expense items are included in the tenant's rent.

Open listing

A written authorization to a real estate agent by a property owner stating that a commission will be paid to the agent upon presentation of an offer which meets a specified price and terms; however, the agent has no exclusive right to sell and must bring in the offer before any other offer is presented or accepted.

Percentage lease

A lease, generally on a retail business property, using a percentage of the gross or net sales to determine the rent. There is usually a minimum or "base" rental, in the event of poor sales.

Point(s)

A borrower may have to pay fees to the institution that arranged a loan. Such fees are frequently expressed as points, with one point being 1 percent of the amount of the loan.

Prepayment penalty

The penalty under a note, mortgage, or deed of trust that is imposed when the loan is paid before it is due.

Primary Financing

The loan on a property that is secured by a first mortgage or deed of trust.

Raw land

Land that has not been subdivided into lots and that lacks the improvements—water, sewers, streets, utilities, and so forth—that are needed before a structure or structures can be built.

REIT (real estate investment trust)

A corporation or trust that uses the pooled capital of many investors to purchase and manage income property (equity REIT) and/or mortgage loans (mortgage REIT). REITs must meet strict requirements regarding their organization, assets, dividend distributions, and income in order to avoid double taxation. They are traded on major exchanges just like stocks.

Rental concessions

Incentives—such as a month of free rent—that an owner offers rental prospects in order to get them to sign a lease.

Sale-leaseback

A sale of property to a buyer and its subsequent leaseback to the seller. The lease follows the sale, but is agreed to at the time of the sale transaction.

Secondary financing

A loan secured by a mortgage or deed of trust that is junior (secondary) to another mortgage or deed of trust.

Seed money

The initial funds used to begin a project; usually not the major source or amount of the funds necessary to complete the project.

Setback ordinance

Law regulating the distance from the lot line to the point where improvements may be constructed.

Subordinate

To make subject to or junior to.

Title

A legal document establishing evidence of ownership.

Title insurance

Insurance against loss resulting from defects of title (involving the chain of title or encumbrances) to a real property.

Triple net

See net lease.

Vacancy rate

The estimated percentage of vacancies in a rental project; estimate may be based on past records of the property or, for a new project, on a professional guess; similar buildings in the project area may be used for comparison.

Zoning

The division of a city or county by legislative regulations into areas (zones) in which allowable land uses are specified.

Appendix C
Is Real Estate for You? A Questionnaire That Can Help You Decide

Throughout this book, you have heard real estate professionals—people just starting out as well as leaders in the industry—talk about why they went into real estate. The questionnaire that follows can provide guidance for you in deciding whether real estate is for you.

For each question, rate your level of interest/ability on a scale of one to ten, with ten being the highest level of interest and ability and one being the lowest.

1. Do you have a passion for building or owning things?   **1–10:**

2. Are you interested in architecture and design?   **1–10:**

3. Are you interested in the construction process?   **1–10:**

4. Are you interested in helping to create better cities and neighborhoods?   **1–10:**

5. Do you want to contribute to the public good?   **1–10:**

6. Do you want to engage in public issues?   **1–10:**

7. Do you like to solve complex business problems?   **1–10:**

8. Do you have strong analytical skills?   **1–10:**

9. Do you like working with numbers?   **1–10:**

10. Can you tolerate risk?   **1–10:**

11. Can you learn from adversity?   **1–10:**

12. Can you adapt to change?   **1–10:**

13. Do you communicate effectively?   **1–10:**

14. Can you relate to people of diverse backgrounds, experiences, and attitudes?   **1–10:**

15. Do you like working with others?   **1–10:**

16. Are you a team player?   **1–10:** _____

17. Are you a team leader?   **1–10:** _____

18. Are you a self-starter?   **1–10:** _____

19. Can you see the big picture?   **1–10:** _____

20. Do you pay attention to details?   **1–10:** _____

21. Do you finish what you started?   **1–10:** _____

22. Can you multitask?   **1–10:** _____

23. Do you work well under pressure?   **1–10:** _____

24. Are you accountable?   **1–10:** _____

25. Would you defer earning some money now to earn more later on?   **1–10:** _____

The highest possible score is 250. What was your score? If you were realistic in your self-appraisal (if, for example, you asked someone who knows you well to review your self-evaluation) and scored well (above 175 points), you may have a future in real estate. But if you scored low, don't give up on the idea of real estate.

Use this simple questionnaire for guidance, but not for deciding. It is merely intended to help you focus your thinking. Use it with other career planning resources, including those listed in appendix A. And talk to people in real estate and other professions, attend the meetings of real estate trade groups and professional organizations, take classes in finance and other subjects related to real estate, and seek a part-time job or an internship with a real estate company. To make a well-informed decision about whether to go into real estate, you need to invest time and effort in the decision-making process, so use these resources to full value.